LITERATURE
AND POLITICS IN THE
NINETEENTH CENTURY

LITERATURE
AND POLITICS IN THE
NINETEENTH CENTURY

Essays

EDITED WITH AN INTRODUCTION BY
JOHN LUCAS

METHUEN & CO LTD
LONDON

First published in 1971 by
Methuen & Co Ltd
11 New Fetter Lane London EC4
First published as a University Paperback 1975
© *1971 Methuen & Co Ltd*

Printed in Great Britain by
William Clowes & Sons, Limited
London, Beccles and Colchester

ISBN 0 416 44930 1 (hardback edition)
0 416 82690 3 (paperback edition)

Distributed in the USA by
HARPER & ROW PUBLISHERS, INC.
BARNES & NOBLE IMPORT DIVISION

CONTENTS

I

INTRODUCTION

JOHN LUCAS

Politics and Literature. The subject is a daunting one, the relationship between the two so problematic, elusive, uncertain. Yet it is these difficulties which make the subject fascinating and deserving of attention. The most severe problem is perhaps one of form, as the following essays make clear. Indeed, it might well be possible to write a book whose aim was to establish, or argue for, the nature of literary genres that are – or seem – specifically political. We have chosen a different approach, however: from particular works rather than from general assumptions. The only assumption we have permitted ourselves is the very obvious one, that nearly all the great nineteenth-century writers, and many of the minor ones, at one time or another in their careers chose to confront political issues in their work. And we have tried to enquire into how the fact of this confrontation makes formal demands on the poetry and fiction in which it strives for utterance.

The first essay demonstrates that for Tennyson and for Browning the problem was beyond solution. Neither poet could fashion good political verse. But I argue that the concept of inspiration which they inherit from the great Romantics has interesting consequences at least in Browning's work, and is in large part responsible for his development of the dramatic poem that had bulked so vastly in Shelley's work. Shelley stands behind much of *Pauline*, *Paracelsus*, and *Sordello*, just as he stands behind Richard Horne's *Orion* and James Bailey's *Festus*. In the second essay John Goode shows how Clough succeeded in discovering and writing a kind of poem that would allow him to engage with the nature of sexual relationships when they are viewed from the standpoint of an optimistic revolutionary conscious-

I

ness. William Myers argues for the brilliance of the plotting of *Little Dorrit*, and its implications for what might be called the Radical effrontery of Dickens's relationship with his audience, and in his second essay he pursues the question of how far George Eliot's thoroughly worked-out and firmly held political ideas shaped and sometimes distorted her fiction. In two closely related essays David Howard investigates the nature of Meredith's fictional achievement as a novelist of politics and he makes an important distinction between two formal modes: the 'delicate' and the 'epical'. In my second essay I suggest that the particular nature of Conservative thought and fears of revolution in the 1880s are closely connected with a body of related and unsatisfactory novels. Finally, John Goode attempts a major reassessment of the creative work of William Morris during the years of his most vital socialist thinking. And he proposes the literature of 'dream' as a viable medium for Morris's effort to assess and vindicate revolutionary possibilities.

Formal problems take much emphasis in our book. At the same time, we have tried to assess the ways in which the works we consider are not merely a shaping of political ideas into art, but constitute attempts to interpret and render the actual political process. Inevitably, the degree, intensity, scope and success of the attempt varies from writer to writer and within one writer from work to work. What is good art does not necessarily make good politics, and vice versa. On the other hand, much bad art does unquestionably grow from bad political thinking and much of the greatest literature of the nineteenth century is produced by writers whose long, difficult and profound contemplation of political ideas finds proper expression in their work. It may be objected here that 'greatest' has polemical overtones. Certainly, some of the writers and works which we study may seem unfamiliar, and claims for their worth tendentious. Richard Horne's *Orion*, Clough's *Bothie of Tober-Na-Vuolich*, Meredith's *Sandra Belloni* and *Beauchamp's Career*, Morris's *Sigurd the Volsung* – all receive extensive treatment, most are praised. Not, however, because we wish to argue special cases. The truth is simply that we believe that in their different ways such works demonstrate political and literary intelligences working in harness to produce fine political literature.

Introduction

There is no point here in setting out how and why we try to judge the success and failure of political literature or, if the term itself seems unduly provocative, literature which is essentially dictated by a political vision. The discriminations come in the body of the book, in, for example, William Myers's careful establishing of the triumphs and limitations of George Eliot's political ideas and their consequences for her fiction, or in David Howard's argument about why *Vittoria* should be so bad when *Sandra Belloni* is so good. There is, however, some point in saying a little about the book's actual shape and its omissions. It begins with Shelley and it ends in the 1890s, and it can therefore properly be read as a sequence of essays. It has moreover a coherence that derives from the contributors sharing similar political viewpoints. But very obviously our book is not intended to provide anything like an exhaustive account of all that might be called political literature in the nineteenth century, nor does it attempt to engage with all the large political issues that are treated in the literature of that age. For although it is true that there is an extraordinarily close connection between much nineteenth-century literature and many of its major political issues and debates and ideas, it is nevertheless not difficult to think of some issues which, if they are not entirely ignored by writers, can hardly be said to have produced memorable art. *Why* they didn't is, of course, a fascinating subject. But it is also a vast and teasing one and it could hardly have been adequately treated in a book of this length or intention. For *Literature and Politics in the Nineteenth Century* is not so much speculative as concerned with particulars and the issues that they raise. But in that case, it may be asked, where is Disraeli, where are the Chartist poets, where is early Swinburne? I might explain their absence on grounds of lack of space. But more importantly, it does not seem to me that the writers just mentioned – and the list could of course be greatly extended – have produced important political literature. I do not regret not having had the space to include them. I do, however, regret that it was not possible to include an essay on the historical novel. The heritage of Scott, the work of Ainsworth, Dickens, G. P. R. James, Lytton: it is a subject of great interest and, I think, importance. Unfortunately, it also seems to me intractable given the scope of our book and the essay form we chose. And against the omissions we can set the inclusions. For nearly all the great names are here: Tennyson, Browning, Arnold and Clough; Dickens, George Eliot, Meredith and Henry James; Carlyle, Mill, Ruskin and Morris. And we have found room for many of the more minor writers: for Horne, Bailey and Thomas Hood; for Trollope, Mallock and Gissing; for Bagehot, R. H. Hutton and Thorold Rogers.

When all is said, I do not think that our book can justly be accused of having missed out many writers or works of importance in the political literature of the nineteenth century. But it may have to meet another charge, of naivety, ignorance or ineptitude in the handling of political ideas and of political history. Beneath the charge is a really crucial problem. Who, it may be asked, is best fitted to write a book such as we have undertaken, the student of politics or of literature? There is something recalcitrant about literature, Christopher Ricks has said:

> Whereas combining philosophy and history, or sociology and art-history, seems feasible enough, there seem in practice to be great difficulties about combining literary criticism with any of the other disciplines. What too often happens is that only lip-service is paid to those literary demonstrations without which the literary claims are vacuous.[1]

I am reasonably certain that we have paid more than lip-service to literary demonstration. But the problem of reconciling this demonstration with claims about the political sophistication or otherwise of the literature may remain. The matter perhaps resolves itself into one of emphasis, of a tactful withdrawing from too assertive a role, both on the writer's and critic's part. David Howard praises the fictional tact of *Beauchamp's Career*, which deals in the politics of the postponed moment, whereas in the essay which opens the book I suggest that the tactlessness implicit in an inherited metaphysic of inspiration is responsible for the badness of most early Victorian poetry which attempts to confront political issues. It does not entirely solve the problem; political ideas may be well or badly handled but there remains the question of whether they are good or bad ideas, and the further question of whether such ideas, whatever their worth, have a bearing on what I have called the actual political process, or have the sort of bearing on it that the writer ascribes to them. Inevitably, such questions are raised time and again in (and no doubt by) the following essays. And it will almost certainly be true that further questions come up for consideration. But this is as it should be. A book such as the present one cannot hope to be definitive. It can however hope to be a valid contribution to a vast, problematic and vital subject. And it was out of such a hope that *Literature and Politics in the Nineteenth Century* was written.

When this book first appeared it became the subject of some decidedly odd reviews. They ranged in tone from sorrowful incomprehension through irritation that we should have dared to stray beyond the conventional boundaries of lit. crit. (wherever they may be) to downright fury. One reviewer – an economic historian who presumably read the book in a gathering mist of apoplectic rage – got our names wrong, our subjects muddled, and accused us of, above all, inaccuracy. Another tut-tutted at our use of history (it wasn't altogether clear whether he thought we had misunderstood facts or simply got hold of the wrong ones), and an amiably lunatic American explained at great length that we were incapable of valid argument because we either ignored or knew nothing about the deep structures of nineteenth-century novels and minds (all of them).

In their various ways, these responses weren't entirely disheartening. They suggested that at the very least we had been provocative. And I do think that *Literature and Politics in the Nineteenth Century* has its merits. It also has its faults, and I am even more aware of them now than I was in 1970. But to have made major alterations at this stage would in all probability have meant wrecking such coherence as the book has. Misprints have been corrected. The rest is as it was.

NOTES

1. Christopher Ricks, *Victorian Studies*, vol. XI, no. 4, p. 541.

II

POLITICS
AND THE POET'S ROLE

JOHN LUCAS

I

In 1831 W. M. Praed wrote some verses about the clever young poet, Tully St. Paul, whose head 'is stuffed full of knowledge/Of every conceivable thing', including science and logic, and who is magnificently vain.[1] *A Talented Man* is an amusing parody of poetic fashion, but it rather neglects one feature that strikes us about the young poets of the time. For the young Tully St. Paul does not appear to be in any doubt about his poetic gifts. Yet if we so much as glance at the early work of Tennyson and Browning and other lesser men, we are bound to notice how much of it is devoted to statements, analyses and questionings of what it is to be a poet, and how best to use your talent. No doubt the fact that the great Romantic poets had brooded long and arduously over such matters did much to create in their successors a sense that intimate self-questioning was *de rigueur*, but I think that the self-consciousness among those poets with whom I am concerned has much to do with a more general opinion which they encountered, that a poet is the central man of his age and that his responsibilities are therefore enormous.

As we might expect, it was Carlyle who put the case most forcibly:

> He is neither noble nor plebeian, neither liberal nor servile, nor infidel nor devotee; but the best excellence of all these, joined in pure union; 'a clear and universal *Man*'. [His] poetry is no separate faculty, no mental handicraft; but the voice of the whole harmonious manhood: nay it is the very harmony, the living and life-giving harmony of that rich manhood which forms his poetry.[2]

7

Carlyle is talking about Goethe, but his praise acts as a formidable challenge to other poets. It may also be an earnest rebuke to the Peacockian view that

> A poet in our times is a semi-barbarian in a civilized community . . . The highest inspirations of poetry are resolvable into three ingredients: the rant of unregulated passion, the whining of exaggerated feeling, and the cant of factitious sentiment. . . . It can never make a philosopher, nor a statesman, nor in any class of life an useful or rational man.[3]

Intendedly or not, what Carlyle has to say of Goethe directly opposes Peacock's witty assessment of the poet's role (nobody at that time knew how Shelley had also opposed it). Goethe, Carlyle insists, felt the discontent which everyone in his age felt, but 'he alone gave it voice' and so became 'the spokesman of his generation'. Above all else, Goethe is a hero because of the nobility of his life:

> If asked what was the grand characteristic of his writings, we should not say knowledge, but wisdom. A mind that has seen, and suffered, and done, speaks to us of what it has tried and conquered.[4]

In this respect Goethe is the superior of Burns, who too often slipped from the ideal. 'For the words of Milton are true at all times, and were never truer than in this: "He who would write heroic poems, must make his whole life a heroic poem." '[5]

Carlyle's utterances about poetry and the poet are perhaps the most clamorous of the age, but Shelley's influence was greater. We know, for example, that Browning took him as his great model, we know of Richard Horne's ecstatic admiration,[6] and we can hardly avoid the intensity of hero-worship in Ebenezer Jones's letter to his friend M. Considerat:

> Who wrote the *Revolt of Islam*? Not Shelley! 'Tis the mighty utterance of a society whose eyes have just been opened to the glory of truth, and she made him her priest. He was but the lute; she was the God.[7]

Shelley would have agreed with Jones. All artists are companions and prophets of social change, he said in the preface to *Prometheus Unbound*, and they are therefore 'in one sense, the creators, in another, the creations of their age. From this subjection the loftiest do not escape.'[8]

But Shelley left an ambiguous heritage to his disciples. For if he saw the poet as priest and prophet, preaching the word to his people, he also, or so it was claimed, fathered the notion of poetry as mad inspiration, whereby the word became unapproachably vague. 'Mr Shelley', Henry Taylor wrote in 1834,

> was a person of more powerful and expansive imagination than Lord Byron, but he was inferior to him in those practical abilities which (unacceptable as such an opinion may be to those who believe themselves to be writing under the guidance of inspiration) are essential to the production of consummate poetry ... A poet is, in his estimation (if I may venture to infer his principles from his practice), purely and pre-eminently a visionary.... Mr Shelley and his disciples ... – the followers (if I may so call them) of the phantastic school – ... would transfer the domicile of poetry to regions where reason, far from having any supremacy or rule, is all but unknown ... to seats of anarchy and abstraction, where imagination exercises the shadow of an authority, over a people of phantoms, in a land of dreams.[9]

It is unfair to Shelley, but my concern is with his reputation and what was taken to be his example, and there is no doubt that Taylor directs our attention towards a view of poetry that by the mid 1830s had assumed almost a tyranny of acceptance. For J. S. Mill, poetry was 'feeling confessing itself to itself, in moments of solitude,'[10] and he claimed that in the best poets

> the capacity of feeling being so great, feeling, when excited and not voluntarily resisted, seizes the helm of their thoughts, and the succession of ideas and images becomes the mere utterance of an emotion; not, as in other natures, the emotion a mere ornamental colouring of the thought.[11]

Not surprisingly, perhaps, Mill thought a poet better for being ignorant: 'it is not always clear that the poet of acquired ideas has the advantage over him whose feeling has been his sole teacher.'[12]

How typical Mill's position was may be indicated by our noting Hallam's praise of Shelley and Keats, since they were poets 'of sensation rather than reflection'. They were, however, bound to be unpopular, for

> how should they be popular, whose senses told them a richer and ampler tale than most men could understand, and who constantly expressed,

9

because they constantly felt, sentiments of exquisite pleasure or pain, which most men were not permitted to experience.[13]

If this is reminiscent of Wordsworth's claim that a poet is possessed of more than usual organic sensibility, Hallam's next words recall the famous remark in the Preface to the *Lyrical Ballads*, that the poet is nonetheless a man speaking to men:

> Undoubtedly the true poet addresses himself, in all his conceptions, to the common nature of us all. Art is a lofty tree, and may shoot up far beyond our grasp, but its roots are in daily life and experience. Every bosom contains the elements of those complex emotions which the artist feels, and every head can, to a certain extent, go over in itself the process of their combination, so as to understand his expressions and sympathise with his state.[14]

Hallam's chief concern is to reconcile a Shelleyan insistence that artists are partly created by their age with the obvious fact that their age may well reject them. Like Mill, he places the main stress on the poet's unusual intensity and range of feeling; it is that which keeps him apart. But Shelley himself had pointed to a different reason. Shelley had thought that the artist's loneliness sprang from the fact that his *ideas* were misunderstood, even though it was his necessary role to give expression to them. We come here to a crucial issue. The ideas that Shelley had most in mind were political ones, and as G. M. Matthews has pointed out in his brilliant essay 'A Volcano's Voice in Shelley', much of Shelley's poetry bears testimony to his 'perception of revolutionary activity in the external world and in the human mind – of irrepressible collective energy contained by repressive power.'[15] For Shelley was politically a revolutionary poet – 'He believed that a clash between the two classes of society was inevitable, and he eagerly ranged himself on the people's side.'[16] Yet it is not this aspect of Shelley that Hallam takes up. And in his exchange of ideas for feeling as the mark of the poet's isolation we begin to see something of that transformation which came to the discussion of the poet's role during the period with which I am concerned.

But here I must introduce a qualification. Hallam is not speaking of *the* poet so much as claiming attention for one poet in particular –

Tennyson. And Hallam argues that Tennyson has the advantage over Shelley, since 'he comes before the public, unconnected with any political party, or peculiar system of opinions.' [17] On the other hand, Tennyson has enough of Shelley's 'characteristic excellencies' to make him every bit as unpopular. The question is, why should Hallam think Tennyson liable to unpopularity, and this can be answered only if we look at Tennyson's early poetry and note the ways in which it tries to cope with problems of the poet's nature and his role.

II

'Tennyson, we cannot live in art.' Trench's famous rebuke was one that the poet took seriously, and the results are well known. The 'eternal pleasure' of an art that is secluded from the world gives way to an effort at involvement that produces, among its more striking consequences, the suppression of *Hesperides*, the rewriting of the *Lotos-Eaters*, and the attempted dialectic of the *Palace of Art*.[18] Lionel Stevenson thinks that Shelley may well have had an important part to play in the shaping of Tennyson's resolve. He quotes Queen Mab's lines to the spirit Ianthe, after she has shown her a gorgeous dome in her palace:

> were it virtue's only need to dwell
> In a celestial palace, all resigned
> To pleasurable impulses, immured
> Within the prison of itself, the will
> Of changeless nature would be unfulfilled.
> Learn to make others happy.[19]

The selfish, Queen Mab says, lead merely 'valueless and miserable lives.' And if the Lady of Shallott represents the artist's dream of seclusion which the importunities of life threaten and finally destroy, Lady Clara Vere de Vere may well represent the dream gone sour: 'In glowing health, with boundless wealth, / But sickening of a vague disease.'

> Clara, Clara Vere de Vere,
> If Time be heavy on your hands,
> Are there no beggars at your gate,
> Nor any poor about your lands?

Oh! teach the orphan-boy to read,
Or teach the orphan-girl to sew . . .[20]

We know that Tennyson increasingly settled for this 'mask of conformity', to use E. D. H. Johnson's phrase, although the very ambiguous praise given to Telemachus suggests that the poet did not always find it a comfortable fit:

Most blameless is he, centred in the sphere
Of common duties, decent not to fail
In offices of tenderness, and pay
Meet adoration to my household gods,
When I am gone. He works his work, I mine. (p. 564)

One is reminded of Turveydrop: 'Your qualities are not shining, my dear child, but they are steady and useful.'[21] The difference is that we know how to respond to Turveydrop's praise whereas we cannot with any such certainty place Ulysses. And that there should be such ambiguity of tone about the poem and its hero indicates well enough Tennyson's own mixed feelings about the propriety of claims for a life beyond art (Ulysses's heroism may well reside in the fact that he is escaping from the life that Telemachus is tied to). Yet as Johnson has said, 'with the collection of poems published in 1842 Tennyson begins to assume his familiar guise as Victorian prophet.'[22] And for all the ambiguities of *Ulysses*, the certainties of *Locksley Hall* are much more representative of the volume:

Men, my brothers, men the workers, ever reaping something new:
That which they have done but earnest of the things that they shall do:

For I dipt into the future, far as human eye could see,
Saw the Vision of the world, and all the wonder that would be;
. . .
Till the war-drum throbbed no longer, and the battle-flags were furled
In the Parliament of man, the Federation of the world.
. . .
Not in vain the distance beacons. Forward, forward let us range,
Let the great world spin for ever down the ringing grooves of change.
   (pp. 695–9)

As Johnson has pointed out, and as these verses remind us, the 1842 volume testifies to 'that dream of progress towards an Utopian social order, which was so deeply ingrained in the age.'[23] But the dream is a political vision and it is hopelessly inadequate, both as vision and as poetry. Why?

Robert Stange puts what is more or less the official case:

> As a young man, Tennyson had assumed a position of artistic detachment and poetic independence, but as his reputation increased he became more strongly influenced by the public's demand for a *vates*. In his middle years we find him making a conscious effort to transmit to the people the ethos of his age, and to use his poetry as a didactic weapon.[24]

But the explanation is barely adequate. After all, a *vates* isn't supposed to give the public what it wants; Tiresias didn't, nor did Shelley, and neither thought he should. And although, as we have seen, Shelley thought of the poet as *partly* the creation of his age, he was far from assuming that that made him helplessly passive, a mere reflector of what was past or passing or to come. On the contrary, Shelley insists the true poet has to be a critic of his age, and as a prophet he can neither look for nor expect popular honour and approval. Why then should Tennyson be so ready to confuse the poet as *vates* with the poet as popular didact? The answer, I think, is that he had little interest in politics but wanted to be a poet-prophet, since to be that guaranteed the authenticity of his inspiration. And in view of the unfavourable reception of his early work, it is at least conceivable that his belief in his inspiration was badly dented. How better to restore it than to produce work which would bring him popular assent? The argument may seem highly contentious and some may wish to point to what seems on the face of it Tennyson's genuine involvement with such political issues as the abortive Spanish Revolutionary movement of 1830. Yet Sir Charles Tennyson's account of that episode seems to me to prove only that Tennyson saw it as a game of politics.[25] And although Hallam links Tennyson and Shelley as true poets and *therefore* unpopular, the truth is that they represent virtual antitypes, at least as far as their political poetry is concerned. Hallam begs the question when he says that Tennyson has the advantage over Shelley in not belonging to a political party. It is not parties but ideas that count, and Tennyson simply has no political ideas, not in verse anyway. Hence the comfortable clichés of the Victorian prophet.

13

But Tennyson comes much closer to Shelley in his belief in the fact and nature of inspiration, and I need to say some thing about the matter for it has much to do with why Tennyson *qua* poet chose to be engaged in political issues. To start with, I think we have to take seriously Tennyson's trance-like fits, if for no other reason than that he did. They helped convince him of the inviolable fact of inspiration:

> I felt my soul grow mighty, and my Spirit
> With supernatural excitation bound
> Within me, and my mental eye grew large
> With such a vast circumference of thought,
> That in my vanity I seemed to stand
> Upon the outward verge and bound alone
> Of full beatitude. (pp. 175–6).

Those lines from *Timbuctoo* lay claim to inspiration as an infallible power, and this is insisted on elsewhere in the early verse. In the suppressed poem, *The Mystic* occur these lines:

> Angels have talked with him, and showed him thrones:
> Ye knew him not: he was not one of ye,
> Ye scorned him with an undiscerning scorn:
> Ye could not read the marvel in his eye,
> The still serene abstraction . . . (pp. 229–30)

And in *The Poet* we find the stanzas,

> He saw through life and death, through good and ill,
> He saw through his own soul.
> · · ·
> So many minds did gird their orbs with beams,
> Though one did fling the fire.
> Heaven flowed upon the soul in many dreams
> Of high desire.
> · · ·
> And Freedom reared in that august sunrise
> Her beautiful bold brow,
> When rites and forms before his burning eyes
> Melted like snow.
> · · ·

14

> And in her raiment's hem was traced in flame
>   WISDOM, a name to shake
> All evil dreams of power – a sacred name.
>   And when she spake,
>
> Her words did gather thunder as they ran,
>   And as the lightning to the thunder
> Which follows it, riving the spirit of man,
>   Making earth wonder,
>
> So was their meaning to her words. No sword
>   Of wrath her right arm whirled,
> But one poor poet's scroll, and with *his* word
>   She shook the world. (pp. 222–4)

This is very Shelleyan in the way in which the poet is aligned with
Freedom's cause, and equally Shelleyan in the insistence on the
God-given nature of inspiration. We have only to remind ourselves
of the following lines from *Alastor* to see the sort of ancestry which
Tennyson's poem could call on:

>   Every sight
> And sound from the vast earth and ambient air,
> Sent to his heart its choicest impulses.
> The fountains of divine philosophy
> Fled not his thirsting lips, and all of great,
> Or good, or lovely, which the sacred past
> In truth or fable consecrates, he felt
> And knew.[29]

Of course, the theory of inspiration that Tennyson took over, part
psychological and part metaphysical, has its roots in the eighteenth
century; the possible literalness of 'divine' inspiration goes at least
as far back as Akenside and Young, and behind them to Milton.
And it becomes one of the great and problematic themes of English
Romanticism. But Tennyson, presumably convinced or needing
to be convinced of the powers given to his own 'mental eye', contents
himself with accepting a theory that had been elaborately and confusedly evolved and fiercely tested by Wordsworth and Coleridge.
What they had agonized over he simply assumes to be an undeniable
commonplace; when he calls the poet's mind 'holy ground' I think
we have to accept that he uses the phrase in good faith.[27]

Yet once Tennyson has committed himself to such a phrase he finds himself in difficulties. For if the poet is truly inspired in the way that Tennyson thinks he is, it must follow that he can never go wrong. In short, Tennyson's belief in inspiration drives him into accepting the position of *vates*; but as far as politics are concerned once he has become a *vates* he can do no more than mouth the available clichés about ringing grooves of change. To risk saying more would simply be to open himself to the possible charge of telling untruths. And that would mean that he wasn't inspired. The particular way in which inspiration became a doctrine in early Victorian England has much to answer for when we consider the political poetry of the period. And interestingly enough, a late poem reveals that Tennyson himself saw how he had allowed himself to become trapped into a stance whereby he stood revealed as a victim of the cliché notion of the poet as seer. In *Politics* he warned,

> you that drive, and know your Craft,
> Will firmly hold the rein,
> Nor lend an ear to random cries,
> Or you may drive in vain,
> For some cry 'Quick' and some cry 'Slow'. (p. 1343)

But *Politics* takes us a long way beyond the volume of 1842, which is the most convenient stopping place in time for this essay.

III

The fact of Browning's debt to Shelley in *Pauline* (1833) is not in doubt. Its nature is. The Shelley of *Pauline* is the great sun-treader for whom the poem's protagonist feels an awed reverence. He was one

> whom praise of mine shall not offend,
> Who was as calm as beauty, being such
> Unto mankind as thou to me, Pauline, –
> Believing in them and devoting all
> His soul's strength to their winning back to peace;
> Who sent forth hopes and longings for their sake,
> Clothed in all passion's melodies: such first
> Caught me and set me, slave of a sweet task

To disentangle, gather sense from song:
Since, song-inwoven, lurked there words which seemed
A key to a new world, the muttering
Of angels, something yet unguessed by man.[28]

But what is the key? Certainly it has something to do with the inspired truths that poets know and utter. Johnson suggests that like *Paracelsus* and *Sordello*, *Pauline* is about 'the evolution of the creative impulse in artists beset by uncertainty as to the genuineness of their inspiration and the best uses that can be made of their talents.'[29] This is a good deal more sensible than Hillis Miller's claim that the three poems 'are Browning's version of a central adventure of Romanticism – the attempt to identify oneself with God.'[30] Browning's God is Shelley, whom Hillis Miller never mentions; and although I recognize that the Romantic poet's attempt to identify himself with God has much to do with his effort to find an authoritative basis for his concerns and the nature of his inspiration, this is not what Hillis Miller means. Yet it is of the utmost importance. To show how I must quote at greater length from the passage describing the speaker's involvement with Shelley. The poet senses that the 'key' will open a world of truths to him. It will be noted that the truths are political:

How my heart leapt as still I sought and found
Much there, I felt my own soul had conceived,
But there living and burning! Soon the orb
Of his conceptions dawned on me; its praise
Lives in the tongues of men, men's brows are high
When his name means a triumph and a pride,
So, my weak voice may well forbear to shame
What seemed decreed my fate; I threw myself
To meet it, I was vowed to liberty,
Men were to be as gods and earth as heaven,
And I – ah, what a life was mine to prove!
My whole soul rose to meet it. Now, Pauline,
I shall go mad, if I recall that time! (p. 6)

The last lines surely suggest that the speaker has failed his own earlier dreams, has not been able to sustain the meaningful vision of purpose which he had previously enjoyed. But then it turns out rather differently. We are asked to see the vision *not* as authentic, but perhaps as a mere adolescent delusion. And yet I think it will be agreed that the tone of these following lines shifts so considerably that it is practically impossible to locate a point of view which may be said to preside over them. I shall have to quote at some length:

> 'Twas in my plan to look on real life,
> The life all new to me; my theories
> Were firm, so them I left, to look and learn
> Mankind, its cares, hopes, fears, its woes and joys;
> And, as I pondered on their ways, I sought
> How best life's end might be attained – an end
> Comprising every joy. I deeply mused.
>
> And suddenly without heart-wreck I awoke
> As from a dream: I said ''Twas beautiful,
> 'Yet but a dream, and so adieu to it!'
> As some world-wanderer sees in a far meadow
> Strange towers and high-walled gardens thick with trees,
> Where song takes shelter and delicious mirth
> From laughing fairy creatures peeping over,
> And on the morrow when he comes to lie
> For ever 'neath those garden-trees fruit-flushed
> Sung round by fairies, all his search is vain.
> First went my hopes of perfecting mankind,
> Next – faith in them, and then in freedom's self
> And virtue's self, then my own motives, ends
> And aims and loves, and human love went last.
> I felt this no decay, because new powers
> Rose as old feelings left – wit, mockery,
> Light-heartedness; for I had oft been sad,
> Mistrusting my resolves, but now I cast
> Hope joyously away: I laughed and said
> 'No more of this!' I must not think. (p. 6)

What strikes me as very odd about this passage is the way in which the speaker's political vision is given the terms of sensual indulgence. It is as though he is reversing the oppositions of Keats's *Sleep and Poetry*. There, Keats had abandoned the realm of Flora and old Pan for 'a nobler life, / Where I may find the agonies, the strife / Of human hearts.' But for the protagonist of *Pauline* the agonies and strife of human hearts *is* a dream of the realm of Flora and old Pan. Certainly, we have come a long way from those visions which animate the political attitudes of *Queen Mab*.

But we cannot be sure that the protagonist is not himself fully aware of the oddity of his vision. The last lines of the passage suggest that the failure of the dream is very like a failure of his own moral worth. He casts 'Hope joyously away' and settles for a mood of cynical humour. Were this later Browning we would know that such a mood could be read as an admission of human failing. What forbids our being certain about offering a similar interpretation of the lines in *Pauline* is that the political vision itself seems to be of no value. The 'key' does not reveal anything specific, it merely unlocks a view into a private and literary garden. There is nothing, for example, of the 'mean and miserable huts, / And yet more wretched palaces,' that Shelley had seen in *Queen Mab*.[31] Browning's debt to Shelley turns out to be peculiarly difficult to assess, and it is my own feeling that the hesitancies and odd shifting of points of view in *Pauline* may owe much to the poet's struggle to honour the 'fact' of inspiration while acknowledging that it unlocks very few doors on to the truths about 'Mankind, its cares, hopes, fears, its woes and joys.'

On the other hand, the poem's certainties have to do with the power that poets exercise over men.

> And when all's done, how vain seems e'en success –
> The vaunted influence poets have o'er men!
> 'Tis a fine thing that one weak as myself
> Should sit in his lone room, knowing the words
> He utters in his solitude shall move
> Men like a swift wind. (p. 7)

And though the morning may bring a sense that the great poet sings an 'unhonoured song', this gloomy note is played down. For what takes the major stress is the fact that the poet has an *active* role to play, that as an inspired *vates* he is a leader of men (and if it should be thought that I am wrong to identify the speaker of *Pauline* with Browning himself, I can point to the fact that it was Browning *in propria persona* who wrote about Wordsworth as the lost leader). The point is that like Tennyson, Browning is beginning to conceive of the poet's role as that of self-consciously appointed leader of men; and since that means he must be possessed of infallible political insights he is necessarily prohibited from entertaining critical ones. The following lines come very near the end of *Pauline*.

> And one dream came to a pale poet's sleep,
> And he said, 'I am singled out by God,
> No sin must touch me.' (p. 12)

Once the matter is put that way, the sin of being wrong weighs more heavily, and the idea leads to the agonized doubts and vaguenesses that characterize *Paracelsus* (1835) and *Sordello* (1840). Better vague than wrong. But since Browning employs a dramatic form he can cut deeper than Tennyson – I think – dared to, or at all events achieved. For Browning can pretend to discuss the poet in a more objective fashion than Tennyson customarily manages.

It is the aim of Paracelsus to discover the key which the protagonist of *Pauline* thought he had been given. Festus tells Paracelsus that he knows 'you prepared to task to the uttermost / Your strength, in furtherance of a certain aim', which is to find 'the secret of the world, / Of man, and man's true purpose, path and fate.' *Paracelsus* is less specific than *Pauline*. The search for political wisdom is now part of a general desire 'to KNOW'. Festus, it is true, thinks Paracelsus wrong to seek his knowledge 'in strange and untried paths', and enquires whether it wouldn't be better for Paracelsus to learn from men. But the men Festus has in mind turn out to be the great dead, who may be found 'in a fast retreat, / Some one of Learning's many palaces.' Paracelsus is not given the opportunity to reply to Festus's suggestion, he merely says that he is convinced that he has been singled out to save mankind. From childhood, he remarks, he has been possessed 'by a fire'; and once 'life grew plain, and I first viewed the thronged, / The everlasting concourse of mankind,' he knew

> that I must henceforth die,
> Or elevate myself far, far above
> The gorgeous spectacle. I seemed to long
> At once to trample on, yet save mankind,
> To make some unexampled sacrifice
> In their behalf, to wring some wondrous good

From heaven or earth from them, to perish, winning
Eternal weal in the act. (p. 19)

Some unexampled sacrifice, *some* wondrous good. Browning takes a
properly ironic view of the unspecific nature of Paracelsus's ambitions.
They are at once cloudy and arrogant. He says that he goes to gather
'the sacred knowledge, here and there dispersed / About the world,
long lost or never found,' and he adds that 'life / Shall yet be crowned:
twine amarynth: I am priest.' But he finds that matters are not so
simple as he thinks and that he cannot so decidedly assume the
mantle of priest and prophet.

In Book Two Paracelsus learns that in being without love he is too
withdrawn from the ordinary processes of life to possess an authoritative or communicable vision. But in Book Three we find Paracelsus
in Basil insisting that he KNOWS:

> I possess
> Two sorts of knowledge; one, – vast, shadowy,
> Hints of the unbounded aim I once pursued:
> The other consists of many secrets, caught
> While bent on nobler prize, – perhaps a few
> Prime principles which may conduct to much. (p. 42)

Yet he admits that the truth 'is just as far from me as ever'. The point
seems to be that he is improperly chasing chimeras, searching for a
'key' and so mistaking the nature of 'truth', which lies in the lives of
men whom he ignores. So in Book Four Festus tells him that

> I do believe, what you call trust
> Was self-delusion at the best: for, see!
> So long as God would kindly pioneer
> A path for you, and screen you from the world,
> Procure you full exemption from man's lot,
> Man's common hopes and fears, on the mere pretext
> Of your engagement in his service – yield you
> A limitless licence, make you God, in fact,
> And turn your slave – you were content to say
> Most courtly praises! (p. 50)

It ends weakly. We expect Festus to show Paracelsus's aims as
decisively improper, reveal that the assumed nature of inspiration

does not make him God, insist that truth is not found this way. If Festus shies away from that would seem to be the inevitable conclusion it is, I think, because Browning himself is in a considerable dilemma. He may suspect that 'inspiration' does not explain enough, but to abandon it would be to undermine the poet's ability to utter truths, including political ones. I do not think we need to exercise much caution about seeing Paracelsus himself as a poet-figure; but we do need to notice how Browning's adoption of a quasi-dramatic form for his poem allows him to tackle some of the most persistent and troubling of Romantic questionings (the echoes of stanza 6 of *Resolution and Independence* in the lines just quoted is obvious) without having to try and settle them.

Yet the evasiveness of *Paracelsus* reveals how closely Browning was involved in his own creation. In Book Five Paracelsus defends the 'path' which Festus had attacked.

> You may be sure I was not all exempt
> From human trouble; just so much of doubt
> As bade me plant a surer foot upon
> The sun-road, kept my eye unruined 'mid
> The fierce and flashing splendour, set my heart
> Trembling so much as warned me I stood there
> On sufferance – not to idly gaze, but cast
> Light on a darkling race; save for that doubt,
> I stood at first where all aspire at last
> To stand: the secret of the world was mine.
> I knew, I felt, (perception unexpressed,
> Uncomprehended by our narrow thought,
> But somehow felt and known in every shift
> And change in the spirit, – nay, in every pore
> Of the body, even,) – what God is, what we are,
> What life is . . . (pp. 59–60).

Paracelsus is laying claim to the sort of mystical insight which Tennyson had also felt in himself, and which is a common enough feature of Romantic poetry. But the expansiveness of Paracelsus's claim goes beyond what we expect to find, and it would therefore be pleasant to be told what the secret of the world actually is. Unfortunately, of course, it cannot be expressed, But in that case, one may ask, what use is it, especially to a poet who is supposed to be spreading the word among his people? Still, we are given a clue as to the source of the secret. That 'sun-road', after all, reminds us of the description of Shelley as the great 'sun-treader' in *Pauline*. Not that Paracelsus is Shelley, but there is some reason to believe that Browning sees him as the sort of prophet–priest figure with which his great hero was identified. Yet it has to be added that if this is so, Browning is hardly seeing Shelley plain. At all events, Paracelsus has much more to do with the Shelley of *Alastor* than with the Shelley of *Prometheus Unbound*, or *The Triumph of Life*. Paracelsus is the poet of incommunicable secrets dwelling apart from the world rather than the political poet, even though it is at least partly as a political poet – or one possessed of political truths – that he presents himself or is presented.

I say 'presents or is presented' in order to note Browning's ability and readiness to hedge his bets. But it has also be be remarked that at the end of the poem Paracelsus does reveal something of his sacred knowledge. Nature, he tells Festus, fills us with regard for man:

> With apprehension of his passing worth,
> Desire to work his proper nature out,
> And ascertain his rank and final place,
> For these things tend still upward, progress is
> The law of life, man is not Man as yet.
> Nor shall I deem his object served, his end
> Attained, his genuine strength put fairly forth,
> While only here and there a star dispels
> The darkness, here and there a towering mind
> O'erlooks its prostrate fellows: when the host
> Is out at once to the despair of night,
> When all mankind alike is perfected,
> Equal in full-blown powers – then, not till then,
> I say, begins man's general infancy (p. 61).

Browning may not be endorsing Paracelsus's vision, but whatever the truth about that may be – and I see no way of decisively separating author from hero, especially when we think of Browning's customary attitude towards aspiration – the vision is surely vaguely pietistic at best. The essential point is that Browning sees political or social poetry as *vision*, and the sort of vision open to him once he has accepted the notion of 'inspiration' is bound to be vague. Inspiration was supposed to free a poet from being merely the creation of his age; yet nothing is clearer than that Tennyson's and Browning's way of viewing inspiration tied them down. In varying degrees they are the unwilling victims of their own and others' theories.

Browning returned to the problem once more. *Sordello* is by far the finest of all the Victorian poems that deal with the nature of the poet, his art, inspiration and responsibilities; and it seems to me essential to any study of the post-Romantic development of the idea of poetry and its relationship to life. Indeed, with the exception of Clough's brilliant *Amours de Voyage*, it is the only Victorian poem that deals at length and intelligently with the poet's stance towards the world, the nature of his confrontation with it. It is, of course, a poem about poets for poets. Sordello is an obscure forerunner of Dante, the eternal poet, and one of the poem's themes is the way in which one poet may prepare the ground for another. I do not think this theme very important to the poem, however. There is no real suggestion that Dante is the shaper of men's lives which Sordello fails to be. *Sordello* may look as though it is an investigation of why some poets fail to be central forces of their age, but on closer inspection the poem is clearly suggesting that there is little reason to suppose they will *ever* be influential. And although Browning goes some way towards locating the failure of Sordello's ambitions in the poet himself, it is also apparent that he will have nothing to do with the Carlylean notion that poets create their age.

They are, however, created by it. Browning pays a great deal of attention to the setting of his poem, in the interest of thickening the actual context in which the poem's action takes place. *Sordello* may not have the specificity and density of a Victorian novel, but Browning was a little disingenuous when he told Milsand that the setting was intended merely to serve as background.[32] For the background to *Sordello* is one of violence and uncertainty, and the significance of that should not be lost sight of. *Sordello* is neither costume-history nor simplified allegory, but a spirited and, at its best, rich effort of enquiry into the poet as shaped and shaper; and it takes up the problem of how the poet is a communicator and whether communication can ever be socially meaningful.

I have already suggested that Wordsworth stands behind one line of enquiry in *Paracelsus*, about whether it may not be an absurd presumption for the poet to dream of dwelling apart. In *Sordello*, Eglamor, the poet whom Sordello ousts, is defeated precisely because he sees his calling as one

> making him a man apart
> From men – one not to care, take counsel for
> Cold hearts, comfortless faces – (Eglamor
> Was neediest of his tribe) – since verse, the gift,
> Was his, and men, the whole of them, must shift
> Without it, e'en content themselves with wealth
> And pomp and power, snatching a life by stealth. (Book Two,
> p. 111)

But it may be that Sordello falls into the opposite error. For he aims to please men, to 'perform their bidding and no more, / At their own satiating-point give o'er.' He contents himself with 'songs, not deeds,' songs, moreover, that find no room for a troubling wisdom. Sordello is very like a versifying pet-lamb. But he soon jettisons so mean an ambition for the more arduous one of becoming a great poet, and in a fascinating passage we are told how he tries and fails to fashion a language that shall be adequate to his vision. Language, for Sordello, must somehow give him unity of being; he want to be one as poet and as man, to make his whole life an heroic poem. But with the failure to discover a language equal to his ambitious needs, his dream of being

> Man and Bard,
> John's cloud-girt angel, this foot on the land,
> That in the sea, with open in his hand
> A bitter-sweeting of a book – was gone. (p. 116).

As a result he sees 'less and less to strive / About.'

Sordello settles for mediocrity, and in this he is eagerly supported by Naddo, a marvellously comic figure and prototype of Mr Nixon, who urges the poet to give up verse. Norton Crowell takes Naddo's remarks as carrying Browning's approval, which is certainly wrong

25

even if it unintendedly pays tribute to the plausibility of Naddo's case.[33]

> 'Build on the human heart! – why, to be sure
> Yours is one sort of heart – but I mean theirs,
> Ours, every one's, the healthy heart one cares
> To build on! . . .
>
>   And is it true,
> Fire rankles at the heart of every globe?
> Perhaps. But these are matters one may probe
> Too deeply for poetic purposes:
> Rather select a theory that . . . yes,
> Laugh! what does that prove? – stations you midway
> And saves some little o'er-refining.' (p. 117)

Naddo represents the willingness to 'come to terms' which Tennyson was soon to accept and which Browning was later to fall into, but which in *Sordello* is rejected. Sordello again withdraws from public life. The dream of being the complete man revives within him, but only in solitude. 'Heart and brain / Swelled; he expanded to himself again.'

And here we come to what is really the crux of *Sordello*. For on one side it seems plain that Browning wishes to condemn Sordello for his readiness to keep apart – it merely repeats Eglamor's error. Yet against that he sets the possibility that only by such contemplative withdrawal can the poet become true to himself and his vision. We come again here on one of the great Romantic dilemmas, and the fineness of *Sordello* stems in large part from Browning's exhaustively honest probing at it. But it would be wrong not to admit that *Sordello* also seeks the possibility of a solution to its vast dilemma. In Book Three, the poet wonders whether he has not in fact hoped for too much from himself. Perhaps he should have recognized that he can never achieve an important let alone total victory for poetry, and should have contented himself with a partial achievement rather than spurning anything short of total success: 'I have laid / The ladder down; I climb not.' He even considers the possibility that men of action may be preferable to the dreaming poet, since they after all can and do influence the world.

> Not so unwisely does the crowd dispense
> On Salinguerras praise in preference
> To the Sordellos: men of action, these!
> Who, seeing just as little as you please,
> Yet turn that little to account, – engage
> With, do not gaze at, – carry on, a stage,
> The work o' the world, not merely make report
> The work existed ere their day! (p. 130)

And it is on the assumption that men of action are preferable that Sordello builds in Book Four. He weighs the possibility of his coping with ordinary human needs and wants:

> he felt
> An error, an exceeding error melt:
> While he was occupied with Mantuan chants,
> Behoved him think of men, and take their wants,
> Such as he now distinguished every side,
> As his own want which might be satisfied, –
> And, after that, think of rare qualities
> Of his own soul demanding exercise (pp. 134–5)

Yet if the poet/dreamer is to do good, he must somehow convert his dream into reality. Sordello feels that there may be 'A Cause, intact.' which is 'ordained, / For me, its true discoverer.' The cause is to build up Rome as the ideal city so that men living in it can begin to realize their vast potentialities. The problem, very obviously, is that Sordello's dream may be a form of over-reaching, and even if it is not, it may leave men indifferent. The dream can neither be communicated nor even, perhaps, expressed. The language that is to body out the dream will fall to pieces. Like *Paracelsus*, *Sordello* does not really move forward, it circles; again and again it returns to its starting-point, that the poetry of engagement or the poetic vision which will transform the world and prove the poet's true inspiration and his right to be accepted as a prophet is, in the end, unrealizable. In Book Five, a voice tells Sordello

> God has conceded two sights to a man –
> One, of men's whole work, time's completed plan,
> The other, of the minute's work, man's first

27

> Step to the plan's completeness: what's dispersed
> Save hope of that supreme step which, descried
> Earliest, was meant still to remain untried
> Only to give you heart to take your own
> Step, and stay there, leaving the rest alone? (p. 144)

Sordello is then criticized for not being content to take the one step, and although he makes a last effort he fails, so that, Book Six says, Dante arrived too late to be able to mend matters. Had Sordello

> embraced
> Their cause then, men had plucked Hesperian fruit
> And, praising that, just thrown him in to boot
> All he was anxious to appear, but scarce
> Solicitous to be. (p. 164)

Instead, the world has received a perhaps irretrievable set-back, because of 'that step Sordello spurned, for the world's sake.' Brilliant though *Sordello* for the most part is, I find this ending decidedly unsatisfactory. It is not merely that the idea of blaming all that has gone wrong on a poet seems a bit rash, no matter how Browning might have been imagining Carlyle to nod in approval as he read the diagnosis; more particularly, there is little indication of what Sordello has done that is wrong, or how – assuming him to have behaved improperly – he could have done any different. Browning at the last falls victim to the kind of muddle of which he is so often convicted, and which for the most part his poem finely resists – of seeing the poet as shaper of human affairs by the power of his life and art, the two somehow (but how?) combined. To say that this is a familiar Romantic dilemma does not help matters, even if it underlines the difficulties that Browning was confronting; for *Sordello* is a great poem because it probes the dilemma, and it fails where it tries to heal it by the recognizably Victorian tactic of judging the poet as somehow responsible to men – not through his dream, but through some more practical form of help it is assumed he has the right to give just because he is a visionary.

Sordello is probably Browning's last and certainly his most considerable effort to grapple with the nature of the poet's inspiration and his responsibilities to his age. The intensity and grandeur of much of its exploration set it quite apart from all other poetry of the time, but in its lapse into vague assertion of the poet's need to offer immediate help – instant salvation – it does at least connect with a body of work that characterizes the practical zeal of the 1830s and 40s and which may conveniently be called militant poetry, or the verse of political propaganda. Browning knows that to abandon the dream is to abandon poetry. The poets I want now to consider have no dream to abandon. They do not have to choose between an Apollonian vision of completeness or an Eglamor-like concern for preservation through withdrawal. For them, poetry is a vehicle for the expression of concrete political sentiments, outrage and recommendation. The actual political content of the visions of Browning's poet-heroes is, in the end, virtually non-existent; he is concerned less with what they see than with whether they can and ought to be politically influential at all. But the climate of concern about the relationship of poetry to politics also created poets and poems of very precise visions.

IV

> Still, all day, the iron wheels go onward,
> Grinding life down from its mark;
> And the children's souls, which God is calling sunward,
> Spin on blindly in the dark.[34]

Elizabeth Barrett's *Cry of the Children* was written shortly after she had read and, in company with most, been appalled by the Commission set up to enquire into conditions of child labour in England. Her poem makes use of facts presented in the Report, and especially of one that, more than any other, seems to have troubled the conscience of the age.

> Two words, indeed, of praying we remember,
> And at midnight's hour of harm,
> 'Our Father,' looking upward in the chamber,
> We say softly for a charm.[35]

Richard 'Orion' Horne's report on conditions in the Iron Trades in South Staffordshire, Worcestershire and Shropshire had made reference to children whose knowledge of the Lord's Prayer was

29

confined to its first two words. The *Cry of the Children* builds on the shock that readers felt when they came on what Horne had to tell them.

But Elizabeth Barrett's decision to let the children speak for themselves in the poem is not merely a calculated appeal to her audience's sense of the pathetic. It is to be seen as an effort – a very inadequate one – to gain authenticity of utterance, so that the poor may state their own case which therefore becomes more believable. The tactic is common enough in literature of the period and had had something of a recommendation in 1832, when Carlyle, in his review of *Corn-Law Rhymes*, had said that

> for a man gifted with a natural vigour, with a man's character to be developed in him, more especially if in the way of literature, as Thinker and Writer, it is actually, in these strange days, no special misfortune to be trained up among the Uneducated classes, and not among the Educated.[36]

Carlyle is not here making the point that Mill had outlined when he argued for the preferability of ignorant over learned poets. For Carlyle, the educated classes are so torpid and vicious that there is little chance of finding a worthwhile poet among their ranks:

> if you take two men of genius, and put the one between the handles of a plough, and mount the other between the painted coronets of a coach-and-four, and bid them both move along, the former shall arrive a Burns, the latter a Byron.[37]

Obviously the children in Elizabeth Barrett's poem are not Thinkers and Writers, but they are in a sense redeemed by work. The best poets, Carlyle said, are they who must work. And in the years following his dictum, work becomes something of a guarantee of worth. It is so with the Elizabeth Barrett's children, and it is so with the working-class seamstress of Hood's *Song of the Shirt*, written in the same year as the *Cry of the Children*.

The Song of the Shirt is one of the age's more successful attempts to use a ballad-measure as the 'true voice of the people'; and on the whole Hood avoids the pastiche element that harms most of the verse written in similar vein. Hood is far from agreeing with Carlyle's Olympian view that no amount of specific remedies will help 'the diseases of a world lying in wickedness, in heart-sickness and atrophy'.[38]

O! Men with Sisters dear!
  O! Men! with Mothers and Wives!
It is not linen you're wearing out,
  But human creatures' lives!
  Stitch – stitch – stitch,
  In poverty, hunger, and dirt,
Sewing at once, with a double thread,
  A Shroud as well as a Shirt.[39]

Hood's seamstress speaks of remedies because hunger and poverty are not appeased by changes of heart. O! God! – that bread should be so dear, / And flesh and blood so cheap!' The iniquities of the Corn Law come into much of this poetry of political protest. As, for example, in Elizabeth Barrett's *Cry of the Human*.

  The curse of gold upon the land
    The lack of bread enforces;
  The rail-cars snort from strand to strand,
    Like more of Death's White Horses:
  The rich preach 'rights' and 'future days,'
    And hear no angel scoffing,
  The poor die mute, with starving gaze
    On corn-ships in the offing.[40]

The Corn Laws are also attacked in Dickens's *Hymn of the Wiltshire Labourers* and the *Fine Old English Gentleman* ('The bright old day now dawns again; the cry runs through the land, / In England there shall be dear bread');[41] and they are the constant focus for the anger of one of the typical minor poets of the period, Ebenezer Jones.

Behind much of the verse of *Studies of Sensation and Event* (1843), one hears the Shelley of *Queen Mab* and the *Mask of Anarchy*. He is there in the *Song of the Gold Getters* – which takes for epigraph 'The essence of trade is to buy cheap and sell dear' – and he sounds very clearly through the *Song of the Kings of Gold*.

  Ours are all marble halls,
  And untrodden groves,
  Where music ever calls,
  Where faintest perfume roves;
  And thousands toiling moan,

That gorgeous robes may fold
The haughty forms alone
Of us – the Kings of Gold.

(Chorus).   We cannot count our slaves,
Nothing bounds our sway,
Our will destroys and saves,
We let, we create, we slay,
Ha! Ha! Who are Gods?[42]

Jones is quite specific about his targets: the Corn-Law, *laissez-faire* economics, the nation's political structures. And *A Coming Cry*, feigned to be spoken by the collective voice of the working-class, is equally specific in its vision of the future.

Will we, at earth's lords' bidding, build ourselves dishonour'd graves?
Will we who've made this England, endure to be its slaves?
Thrones totter before the answer! (p. 146)

Moreover, Jones has a Shelleyan belief in the power of the poet to change things. He is one of the few prepared to say, and very incautiously at that, that poetry makes things happen. An untitled poem tells of the infant poet who

Is, in embryo beauteousness, one of that band,
Who, telling the sameness of far-parted things,
Plants through the universe, with magician hand,
A clue which makes us following universe-kings,

One of the seers and prophets who bid men pause
In their blind rushing, and awake to know
Fraternal essences and beauteous laws
In many a thing from which in scorn they go.

Yea, at his glance, sin's palaces may fall,
Men rise, and all their demon Gods disown;
For knowledge of hidden resemblances is all
Needed to link mankind in happiness round Love's throne.

(p. 181)

Jones rushes in where Browning and Tennyson fear to tread, perhaps because where they were dubious about the efficacy of their visionary 'keys' to truth, he is certain he has the clue. The clue is, I think, the claims of brotherhood, of the sort which Carlyle in *Past and Present* had been insisting on the need to recognize, which various Commission Reports had shown was sadly lacking, and about which Richard Horne had been concerned for some years.

Horne is one of the crucial figures of the period. A passionate admirer of Shelley and Hazlitt, he paid his debts to his masters in his poetry and dramas, and also in the *New Spirit of the Age*, a compilation of essays on leading figures of the day of which he was editor. In his essay on Carlyle he says – in answer to Carlyle's plea that the world should 'get more soul' –

> The world has long had a sphere-full of unused Soul in it, before Christ and since. If Plato and Socrates, and Michael Angelo and Raphael, and Shakespeare and Milton, and Handel and Haydn, and all the great poets, philosophers and music-magicians, that have left their Souls among us, have still rendered us no protection against starvation, or the disease and damage of the senses and brain by reason of want of food, in GOD's name let us now think a little of the Body . . . What should we think of a philosopher who went to one of our manufacturing towns where the operatives work from sixteen to eighteen hours a day, and are nevertheless badly clothed, dirty and without sufficient food – and to whom the philosopher, as a remedial measure, suggested that they should get more soul?[43]

No doubt Horne's work on the Commission was responsible for some of the anger that can be felt flashing through this passage, but the argument is nonetheless perfectly reasonable, and it found ready assent among the 'militant' poets. They would also accept the point made in the essay on 'Henry Taylor and the Author of Festus' that

> The passion of the heart commands the passion of the brain, where the heart is of the right strength as meant by God for a natural, true man; and in those heart-felt emotions doth God's voice speak – the only inspiration of genius, because a revelation from the Infinite Maker to the finite maker who devoutly conceives these things, and aspires to make them manifest to his brothers of the earth.[44]

Heart-felt emotions are most readily expressed in song and the 'natural true man' is most likely to be a working-man, whose 'brothers

33

of the earth' must receive the clue to their being brothers from his songs.

Horne himself had already provided for such song in his play, *Spirit of Peers and People: A National Tragi-Comedy, Allegory, and Satire*, (1834). The theme of this well-received but unperformed play is the oppression of the English people by the crown, nobility and state. And in a final speech, Robert Vision declares

> Gold is God, and Labour is the Ass;
> But now 'tis ridden to the precipice

Since labour is

> the only source, the only germ
> Of wealth, and power, and vast inheritance

and change must therefore occur and quickly, too, if it is to be accomplished 'Without the flow of fratricidal blood, / Ruin, or injury . . .'[45]

But how will peaceful change occur? Horne's answer places him firmly in the context of the discussion I am conducting. For his answer is that it is in the power of the poet-prophet to transform society. And the answer is set out in the one poem by which he is remembered, *Orion* (1843). Horne himself offered an explanation for his famous 'farthing epic'. It was meant, he says,

> to present a type of the struggle of man with himself, i.e. the contest between the intellect and the senses, when powerful energies are equally balanced. Orion is a man standing naked before Heaven and Destiny, resolved to work as a really free agent to the utmost pitch of his powers for the good of his race . . . He is a dreamer of noble dreams . . . He is the type of a Worker and a Builder for his fellow-men.[46]

Horne's statement is clear enough. The poem itself is less clear. In Book One the hero dreams of accomplishing some high deed, and with the appearance of Artemis the dreams begin to take positive shape. He 'felt new roots / Quicken within him,' and 'for immortal fruit [he] prepared'. The immortal longings are, however, a form of over-reaching, for the Book ends with his being spurned by Artemis. In Book Two he falls in love with Merope, an earthly creature. This represents an opposite vice. Merope typifies a life of sensual indulgence:

> he of thought was sick,
> Save that which round his present object played
> Delicious gambols and high phantasies. (p. 45)

But at this point the allegory begins to grow confused. Orion wishes to marry Merope, but her father, Œnopion, refuses to give his consent until Orion has proved his worth by killing all the beasts in the surrounding countryside. Orion accomplishes the task and Œnopion then goes back on his word. In despair, Orion flees to the forest. And we are told

> Vainly shall he with self-deluding pride
> Of weakness, masked with power seek solitude
> And high remoteness from his fellow-men,
> In all their bitter littleness and strife;
> Their noble efforts, suffering, martyrdom. (p. 60)

I do not quite see how we are to take this. On the face of it Orion's relationship with Merope seems to represent a retreat into the world of the lotos-eaters, of Eglamor. Yet the lines just quoted suggest that in fleeing from her Orion has fled from the world he ought to be confronting and aiding. The terms of the debate which Horne has harnessed to his epic are clear enough, but not how he is using them. What is certain is that as soon as Orion recovers from his despair he snatches Merope away and gluts himself sexually, forgetting any nobler purpose:

> his thoughts
> Sank faintly through each other, fused and lost,
> Till his o'er satisfied existence drooped. (p. 76)

And for that he is punished. Œnopion has him blinded. The poet loses those visionary powers by means of which he could have worked for the good of his race.

Book Three opens with an important passage in which Horne declares his faith in the poet's powers. Limited though Orion's achievement must be, it will prepare the way for future perfection. That is, Orion will do what Sordello found too mean an action:

> There is an age of action in the world;
> An age of thought; lastly, an age of both,
> When thought guides action and men know themselves,

What they would have and how to compass it . . .
In every age an emblem and a type,
Premature, single, ending with itself,
Of future greatness in an after-time,
May germinate, develope, radiate,
And like a star go out and leave no mark
Save high memory. One such is our theme.

The wisdom of mankind creeps slowly on,
Subject to every doubt that can retard,
Or fling it back upon an earlier time;
So timid are men's footsteps in the dark,
But blindest they who have no inner light.
One mind, perchance, in every age contains
The sum of all before, and much to come;
Much that's far distant still . . . (p. 81)

Orion's blindness teaches him 'Self-pride's abasement, more extensive truth, / A higher consciousness and efforts new;' and he recognizes that he must sing his song 'amidst the stoning crowd,' rather than 'stand apart, obscure to man, with God.' The poet must suffer – Horne had already written a play about Marlowe in which the poet was shown as 'destroyed by an ignorant and resentful public, victimized for that sensitivity of feeling and unconventionality of vision that is part of the poetic temperament'[47] – but he must willingly accept suffering , because it is an essential part of his divine mission, and the one way by which he can become a worker and a builder for his fellow-men. Orion has therefore to reject the ideas of Akenitos, who is the Naddo of Horne's poem and all for doing nothing or at most doing only what will please everyone. 'My son, why wouldst thou ever work and build,' he asks, since you will gain only 'certain grief, / Mischief, or error, and not seldom death'. But Orion resists the appeal to sloth, partly helped in this by the fact that Merope runs off with another suitor, and partly also by the fact that Eos, the Goddess of Morning, restores his sight. And so

With re-awakened love, and sight enlarged
For all things beautiful, and nobly true,
To the great elements that rule the world,

Orion's mind, left to itself, reviewed
Past knowledge, and of wisdom saw the fruit
Far nearer than before, the path less rough ... (p. 97)

Orion decides to make it his particular cause to end war and waste.
The poet now has a plan of action whereby men may be saved. He
will lock the God of War in a cave, 'while o'er his head / The sea-
wide corn fields, smiled in golden waves'. Unfortunately, Artemis
destroys him before he can put his plan into operation. Akenitos
comments

So fares it ever
With the world's builder. He, from wall to beam,
From pillar to roof, from shade to corporal form,
From the first vague Thought to the Temple vast,
A ceaseless contest with the crowd endures,
For whom he labours. (p. 112)

This again is less than clear. Orion has not been killed by the crowd
but by Artemis; and since he has learnt to aspire humbly and has been
rewarded by having his sight restored it is difficult to see the logic
of his destruction. On the other hand, it is quite clear that had
Orion not died Horne would have been in the rather absurd position
of having said that the poet had got rid of wars, had proved politically
efficacious. And the truth is that Horne hasn't really any idea as to
how the poet's vision can validly issue in political activity. Jack
Lindsay put his finger on the problem when he noted that *Orion*

reveals by its contradictions a mixture of clarities and vaguenesses, a
strong impact of contemporary conflicts and the uncertainty as to the
way in which those conflicts were to be historically resolved.[48]

It is a shrewd point. For Horne, as for Tennyson and Browning,
poetry ought to resist the sort of specific polemics that we find in the
poems by Elizabeth Barrett, Thomas Hood and Ebenezer Jones to
which I have drawn attention (and they, of course, are only a representative few of the many poets engaged with similar subjects during
the 1830s and 40s); yet to travel away from the local means always
moving in the direction of vague images of aspiration, of doing good
and being fully heroic simply because the poet is a prophet and a
divinely inspired truth-teller who can be neither guilty of error nor of

37

being himself misled as to the nature of his gifts. Tennyson, Browning, Horne: they all criticize the poet who denies his public function, yet apart from identifying that function with a readiness to suffer they do not know what it is. To put the matter plainly: the poets I have been talking about believed – or felt they ought to believe – in poetry's unopposable might, truthfulness, and utility. As a result, they dared not be wrong.

V

I have tried to suggest why it is that poets of the 1830s and early 40s found themselves faced with the issue of poetry's involvement with politics. I want to close this survey by mentioning one other poem which extends the logic of contemporary beliefs about the nature of inspiration and the poet's authoritative vision, and finally collapses the whole business. In 1839 James Bailey published his epic poem, *Festus*. It provides the perfect escape-hatch for poets seemingly imprisoned in their inherited image of responsible and heroic truth-tellers. *Festus* is sublimely vatic. Bailey takes over the Romantic attitudes that reach back through Carlyle to Shelley, but in his poem we reach a final reduction of the doctrine of the unchallengeable nature of inspiration. In the first edition of his poem, Bailey sets out a Faustian tale of a gifted youth who longs for greater knowledge and is fatally attractive to women. Shelleyan enough, but the chorus of praise that greeted the poem's appearance encouraged Bailey to turn *Festus* into a much more self-conscious meditation about poetry and the poet. In the second edition of 1845, therefore, he added a 'Proem' and a scene between Festus and a student which is at least partly about poetry, prophecy, and the nature of inspiration.

In the *Proem* Bailey remarks that

> Poetry is itself a thing of God;
> He made his prophets poets: and the more
> We feel of poesie do we become
> Like God in love and power, – under-makers.
> All great lays, equals to the minds of men,
> Deal more or less with the Divine, and have
> For end some good of mind or soul of man.[49]

If in the first edition Festus is a sort of world-hero, there can be no doubt that in later versions he is a poet. Not that poetry is confined to books, as he tells the student, and he tactfully if predictably adds that he himself 'cannot tell thee all I feel,' since his life 'holdeth fruit and proof of deeper feeling / Than the poor pen can utter' (shades of Alastor's 'strange truths', of Tennyson's poet, of Paracelsus). The dialogue with the student now assumes a quite crucial position in the poem as a whole. Festus explains that the true poet will always be despised and misunderstood because of the rare complexity of his vision. The vision, indeed, has to be complex because a true poem 'has a plan, but no plot. Life hath none.' He has, he adds, a particular poem in mind, written by a friend of his, but although he knows it to be a true poem because derived from God, he himself understands it only in part. The parts he relates are allegories, dreams of life, which can be only approximately translated. Bailey is thus able to make the maximum claim for poetry while honouring the minimum specificity. Not surprisingly, he tells the student that the poet knows 'the old hid treasure, truth.' We are back with the 'key'. And in case the student should miss the point, Festus adds that poetry 'is un-derived, except from God.'

In its trivial way this is really rather neat. Bailey can proclaim the poet as a true prophet without having to do any actual prophesying. The only vision we are granted is a cheerful one of the future, perhaps reminiscent of the vision of *Locksley Hall*:

> I can conceive a time when the world shall be
> Much better visibly, and when, as far
> As social life and its relations tend,
> Men, morals, manners shall be lifted up
> To a pure height we know not of nor dream; –
> When all men's rights and duties shall be clear,
> And charitably exercised and borne;
> When education, conscience, and good deeds
> Shall have just equal sway, and civil claims; –
> Great crimes shall be cast out, as were of old
> Devils possessing madmen: – Truth shall reign,
> Nature shall be rethroned, and man sublimed.[50]

39

And if you ask how Festus can see all this, the answer is that he is a poet. Vision alone transforms the world.

In an essay of 1853, 'Thoughts on Shelley and Byron', Charles Kingsley delivered a lengthy attack on Shelley and his influence on a later generation of poets:

> Must we not thank the man who gives us fresh hope that this earth will not be always as it is now? His notion of what it will be may be, as Shelley's was, vague, even in some things wrong and undesirable. Still, we must accept his hope and faith in the spirit, not in the letter. . . . So men have felt Shelley's spell a wondrous one – perhaps, they think, a life-giving regenerative one. And yet what dream at once more shallow and impossible?[51]

As an account of Shelley's political poetry, Kingsley's essay is ridiculously unfair. As an account of what was made of that poetry, it is extremely acute:

> Let the poet speak – what he is to say, being, of course, a matter of utterly secondary import, provided only that he is a poet; and then the millenium will appear of itself, and the devil will be exorcised with a kiss from all hearts.[52]

In the course of this essay I have wanted to show that poets of the 1830s and 40s tried to face up to the troubling question of how to reconcile the notion of inspiration, which they took over in large part from the great Romantic poets, with the fact that their position as *vates* seemed to require of them political poetry. The Spasmodic solution is, I think, the logical conclusion of their difficulties and at the same time makes for a total ban on mature political verse. The poet is simply to be believed and belief is aided by a grand cloudiness. The poet's heroic life is realizable only in and through heroic dream, which validates the life. And the vaster and more grandiose the dream the more unchallengeably heroic is the poet's achievement. Such, at least, is the theory. And the two problems which so troubled Tennyson and Browning, how and whether to engage in politics, and to what degree the engagement should come through 'inspired' political poetry, are dissolved by an appeal to that vaticism which had itself originally been a major cause of the trouble. It is perhaps no wonder that Clough should voice a preference for the modern novel over the modern poem by remarking that 'The novelist does try to build us a real house to be lived in.'[53] Given the nature of the dilemmas I have been discussing, it was hardly possible for poets to build real houses. Not ones that could stand in a political world, anyway.

NOTES

1. *The Poems of W. M. Praed*, 2 vols., London, 1864, vol. 2, pp. 204–6.
2. T. Carlyle, *Critical and Miscellaneous Essays*, 4 vols., London, 1870, vol. 1, p. 214.
3. T. L. Peacock, *The Four Ages of Poetry*, ed. H. Brett-Smith, London, 1921, pp. 16–17.
4. Carlyle, *Critical and Miscellaneous Essays*, op. cit., p. 224.
5. Ibid. The essay on Burns, p. 324.
6. For this see Cyril Pearl, *Always Morning: the Life of Richard Henry 'Orion' Horne*, Melbourne, 1960, esp. pp. 20–31.
7. Ebenezer Jones, *Studies of Sensation and Event*, London, 1883. Edited by R. H. Shepherd, and with Memorial Notes by Sumnor Jones and W. J. Linton. The volume had first appeared in 1843, and the letter from which I quote is printed in part on p. xliv of Sumnor Jones's note. Shepherd prints the dedication which had apparently been intended for the first edition, in which Jones says that he inscribes his work to Shelley, 'Not so much in reverence for his perfection in art as in love of the infinite goodness of his nature.'
8. *Shelley's Prose*, ed. D. L. Clark, Albuquerque, 1954, p. 328.
9. Sir Henry Taylor, *Collected Works*, London, 1883. The sentences come from the Preface to Taylor's play *Philip van Artefelde*, pp. xlii–xv.
10. J. S. Mill, 'What is Poetry', in *The Emergence of Victorian Consciousness*, ed. George Levine, London, 1967, p. 391.
11. 'Two kinds of Poetry', Ibid., p. 396.
12. Ibid., p. 398.
13. Henry Arthur Hallam, 'Modern Poetry', In *The Emergence of Victorian Consciousness*, op. cit. p. 403.
14. Ibid., p. 405.
15. G. M. Matthews, 'A Volcano's Voice in Shelley', *E.L.H.* vol. 24, 1957, p. 222.
16. Mary Shelley's note to Shelley's 1819 volume, quoted by Matthews, ibid., p. 222.
17. Hallam, op. cit., p. 408.
18. 'Hesperides' has been well analysed by Robert Stange in 'Tennyson's Garden of Art: A Study of the Hesperides', reprinted in *Critical Essays on the Poetry of Tennyson*, ed. J. Killham, London, 1960; and Alan Grob has written illuminatingly on the two versions of the 'Lotos-Eaters', in 'Tennyson's

The Lotos-Eaters; Two Versions of Art', *Modern Philology*, vol. LXII, no. 2, 1964, pp. 118–29. E. D. H. Johnson's, *The Alien Vision of Victorian Poetry*, Princeton, 1952, remains the standard account of Tennyson's effort to come to terms with the point of view Trench urged on him.

19. See Stevenson's essay, 'The "High-Born Maiden" Symbol in Tennyson', reprinted in Killham, op. cit.
20. All references to Tennyson's poetry come from *The Poems of Tennyson*, ed. Christopher Ricks, London, 1969. Page references will be given in parentheses after the quotations. The quotation from 'Lady Clara Vere de Vere' comes from p. 638.
21. *Bleak House*, ch. 23.
22. Johnson, *The Alien Vision of Victorian Poetry*, op. cit., p. 12.
23. Ibid., p. 15.
24. See *Critical Essays on Tennyson's Poetry*, op. cit., p. 110.
25. See Sir Charles Tennyson, *Alfred Tennyson*, London, 1949, ch. 10.
26. *Shelley's Poems*, 2 vols., London, 1953, vol. 1, pp. 164–5.
27. In 'The Poet's Mind', *The Poems of Tennyson*, op. cit., p. 224.
28. *The Poetical Works of Robert Browning*, O.U.P. 1949, p. 6. All future references are to this edition. Page references will be given in parentheses after the quotations.
29. Johnson, op. cit., p. 72.
30. J. Hillis Miller, *The Disappearance of God*, New York, 1965, p. 95.
31. *Shelley's Poems*, op. cit., vol. 1, p. 75.
32. In the Preface to the edition of 1863. 'The historical decoration was purposely of no more importance than a background requires'. *Poetical Works*, op. cit., p. 97.
33. See Norton Crowell, *The Convex Glass: The Mind of Robert Browning*, Albuquerque. 1968, Crowell's discussion of *Sordello* seems to me almost totally wrong.
34. *The Poetical Works of Elizabeth Barrett Browning*, London, 1897, p. 248.
35. Ibid., p. 249.
36. Carlyle, *Critical and Miscellaneous Essays*, op. cit., vol. 2, p. 219.
37. Ibid., pp. 213–4.
38. Ibid., p. 230.
39. *The Poetical Works of Thomas Hood*, ed. W. Jerrold, London, 1906, p. 625.
40. *The Poetical Works of Elizabeth Barrett Browning*, op. cit., p. 260. 'The Cry of the Human' appeared in her volume of 1844. It is perhaps worth comparing her image of the train as Death's White Horse with Dickens's description of the railway engine as 'the triumphant Monster, Death' in *Dombey and Son*.
41. *The Poems and Verses of Charles Dickens*, ed. F. G. Kitton, London, 1903, p. 62.
42. *Studies of Sensation and Event*, op. cit., p. 47. All future references are to this edition, and page references will be given in parentheses after the quotation.
43. Quoted in *Always Morning*, op. cit., p. 81.

44. *A New Spirit of the Age*, 2 vols., London, 1844, vol. 2, p. 307. Whether Horne was the author of this particular essay scarcely matters. As editor he saw to it that all contributions were in harmony with his ideas and reflected his attitudes.

45. Quoted in *Always Morning*, op. cit., p. 31.

46. *Orion*. Facsimile of 1st edition, ed., Eric Partridge, London, 1928, p. xxvii. All future references are to this edition and page numbers are given in parentheses after the quotations. Horne added the note for the 9th ed. of his poem, 1872.

47. See Ann Blainey, *The Farthing Poet*, London, 1968, p. 83.

48. Jack Lindsay, *George Meredith, His Life and Work*, London, 1956, p. 44.

49. James Bailey, *Festus*, 1845, p. v.

50. *Festus*, 1845 edn., pp. 107–8.

51. Charles Kingsley, *Literary and General Essays*, London, 1890, p. 49. The essay was originally published in *Fraser's Magazine*.

52. Ibid., p. 50.

53. Quoted in W. E. Houghton, *The Poetry of Clough*, London, 1963, p. 97.

III

1848
AND THE STRANGE DISEASE
OF MODERN LOVE

JOHN GOODE

I

The way in which any major historical event registers itself in the literature of the succeeding epoch is difficult to define. But 1848 has problems of its own. In the first place the Revolutions of that year have very ambiguous results. Both the English Revolution of 1688 and the French Revolution of 1789 are visibly linked, either causally or reflectively, with major changes in the political constitution and reorientations of the social structure. The Revolutions of 1848 don't have this clear historical status: in France, for example, the regime changes in content, but hardly at all in form, and the most obvious social change after 1848 is the re-emergence of the bourgeoisie in newly strengthened force. In actual terms, it is possible to speak, like Jacques Droz,[1] of the failure of the Revolution. Nevertheless, its significance is vast and undeniable, so that even a very conservative historian like Cobban describes the June days as 'a turning point'.[2] It is an event in which socialism first manifests itself as an active ideology, and one which leaves the proletariat ranged against the ruling classes. If it failed, it was because the social factor had become so important that the mere political overthrow of the existing régime was insufficient, and because the social structure remained resilient to the effects of political change. Political history had definitively become the explicit vehicle of social conflict.

The second problem is that as far as England was concerned, 1848 was a pathetic non-event. Even the 1789 Revolution, although it was

45

purely national, constituted more of a threat to the English government than the Chartist Demonstration of 1848.[3] Indeed, Royden Harrison has convincingly argued that 10 April was really a theatrical performance engineered by the Government to give 'a form to the conflict which outstripped its real content'.[4] But this does not allow us to dismiss the event as insignificant. On the one hand, the demise of Chartism demonstrates the power of those forces behind the reform movement which had already been successful in 1846. And on the other, the working class movement underwent a complex but definite transformation after 1848. The Co-operative movement became more capitalist in outlook and in organization;[5] the Trade Union movement became deliberately less radical, and political activity within the working class declined. In this sense, the working class pays tacit tribute to the triumph of the manufacturing classes. But equally, it meant that the various working class movements (particularly the unions) were becoming more skilled in organization and more professional in their encounter with employers.[6] We must link with this the reform movement of the fifties, which, as F. B. Smith has shown, is dominated by the 'incorporation theme':

> The radical manufacturing employers were concerned to extend the functions of the House because they agreed that if the workingmen were kept outside the electorate, they would come to believe that they held an interest independent of their masters, and would resort to strikes and coercion to gain higher wages and shorter hours.[7]

Of course, what Bright meant by incorporation was the assimilation into the *pays légal* of the labour aristocracy which meant leaving four out of five adult males outside (he was to refer to them as 'the residuum'), and so dividing the articulate workers from the masses. It would be ridiculous, naturally, to ascribe all these developments to the failure of the Chartists on 10 April. But what seems undeniable is that after 1848, the relationships between political power and social organization begin to change. The manufacturing sections of the bourgeoisie became more dominant, but at the same time, at least on the continent, an alternative ideology to theirs had manifested itself closely linked to the industrial proletariat, which in England was making its articulate presence felt, and therefore the most far-sighted manufacturers showed themselves responsive both to the need and possibility of transforming working class consciousness to their own. If the repeal of the Corn Laws and the fall of Chartism can together be seen as a sign of the supreme triumph of the manu-facturing class against the landed interest on the one hand and the lower class on the other, the political history of the next twenty years demonstrates the paradoxes of its triumph.

It is undeniable too that the literature of the epoch following 1848 shows a marked change in its social consciousness. It displays no unity, of course, except that negatively there is a decreasing capacity to see historical change and the possibilities for historical change at all clearly. The writers who dominate the literary scene tend either to try to divorce literature from society altogether, or to seize on irrelevant analogies (notably the natural sciences) to mediate their encounter with the social world. The two writers whose work dominates both the forties and the fifties, Carlyle and Dickens, grow increasingly pessimistic. More specifically, there is an anxious acknowledgement of bourgeois virtues (Rouncewell, Doyce, Adam Bede) combined with a vigorous but often unco-ordinated portrayal of the oppressiveness of bourgeois convention. One of the most striking examples here is *Shirley*. When it is dealing with the Luddite disturbances the novel embodies a middle class myth (as Edward Thompson describes it). Yet it is also a painful and moving attempt to rescue sexual relations from the inequalities and dilutions of bourgeois marriage. As a result, *Shirley* remains two novels totally dissevered. Most of these generalizations are commonplace, though that doesn't mean that they are generally accepted, let alone self-evident. There is certainly no definitive way of relating them to 1848, even if we take that as a symbolic event. To link them to each other at all would involve an unwarrantable commitment to the concept of a *Zeitgeist*. What we can do, I think, is to gain a perspective on these themes and problems through the analysis of specific responses to 1848, to show that, in a general way, the despair, hysteria or mystification which appears in so much of the literature of the mid-Victorian period is encapsulated in works which respond to the Revolutions.

47

We can begin to define a framework by looking first at Bagehot's essay on the *coup d'état* of 1851. For this specifically political work displays many of the general features of social consciousness with which mid-Victorian literature has to cope. It is a highly intelligent and deeply cynical defence of the *coup*, and an attack therefore on the aspirations of the Revolution. Bagehot's premiss is that 'the first duty of a Government is to ensure the security of that industry which is the condition of social life and civilized cultivation',[8] which is significantly committed to a capitalist sense of priorities, but which is on the face of it perfectly reasonable. What is striking about Bagehot is that he is under no illusions about the specific nature of industry's value: 'For this is the odd peculiarity of commercial civilization. The life, the welfare, the existence of thousands depend on their being paid for doing what seems nothing when done' (p. 9). Society depends, that is, on production for production's sake, on what Marx was later to define as commodity fetishism. This awareness is accompanied by a despairing mystification of the social process. The social fabric has come into being through a random coagulation of virtue, stupidity and mediocrity, and because of it people 'contrive' to go out to work, that is to keep themselves occupied until evening and to resist starvation. Society becomes therefore basically unalterable by any conscious human action. To change things radically is only to destroy the social fabric. Thus, 'the first duty of society is to preserve society' (p. 9). It is a familiar argument, but it is also unusually honest because it makes no attempt to rationalize man's social activity except in terms of an endless cycle of production and preservation. There is just one point at which the underlying naivety shows through the shrewd empirical exterior. And that is where Bagehot tries to explain the relativity of social institutions by 'national character'. This gives him a chance to justify the oppressions of Louis Napoleon by suggesting that the French need to be repressed because they are so rationally consistent that they are likely to overthrow their society completely in the interests of creating a more just system. Thus, having cited approvingly Burke's view that politics are 'made of time and place' (p. 25) (which Bagehot immediately reduces to 'politics are but a piece of business'), and cannot be judged by 'immutable ethics', he is able to sublimate the historicity of politics by a mystical and immutable concept. Hence, on the one hand, he portrays a social process which is meaningless except in terms of its own preservation, and on the other explains differences between societies by a pseudo-scientific absolute which determines the way in which society must preserve itself. There is a second myth on which Bagehot relies and which is significant for other writers. In spite of praising Louis Napoleon, he acknowledges that he is no Augustus, and goes on 'A feeble parody may suffice for an inferior stage and not too gigantic generation' (p. 20). The degeneration myth, like the national character, is a gesture of rationalization confronted with the opacity and apparently meaninglessness of the process of production.

There is one final point to be made about the world view the *coup d'état* reveals in an acquiescent mind like Bagehot's, and that is the way in which he views personality. He argues that Louis Napoleon is to be admired because he is an 'homme de caractère', but to prove this cites a view of him that describes him as completely dualistic: 'The President is a superior man, but his superiority is the sort that is hidden under a dubious exterior: his life is entirely internal' (p. 13). He is a shrewd operator in other words, the effective representative of a society which has defended successfully its meaningless social fabric. An opacity which reason can only undermine is best served by a man who is himself opaque and contradictory.

Bagehot's sense of the mystification of social relations and the implication that the best man to cope with such relations is a dualistic parody, is not exclusive to his conservative 'empiricism'. Leslie Stephen argued in favour of reform partly because he could see no threat to upper class supremacy by legislation since it depended on 'the occult and unacknowledged forces which are not dependent on legislative machinery'.[9] And in an entirely different context, that of 'liberal' theology, Jowett wrote in 1861:

> An ideal is, by its very nature, far removed from actual life. It is enshrined not in the material things of the external, but in the heart and conscience. Mankind are dissatisfied at this separation: they fancy that they can make the inward kingdom an outward one also. But this is not possible. The frame of civilization, that is to say, institutions and laws, the usages of business, the customs of society, these are for the most part

mechanical, capable only in a certain degree of a higher spiritual life. Christian motives have never existed in such strength, as to make it safe or possible to entrust them with the preservation of society . . . For in religion, as in philosophy, there are two opposite poles; of truth and action, of doctrine and practice, of idea and fact.[10]

Thus the dislocation between truth and society becomes inexorable. There is no continuity between the individual and his world.

We should juxtapose this dualism against the work of the greatest liberal of the age, John Stuart Mill. Mill, of course, defended the Revolution and even showed some limited sympathy with the Socialist ideas it had brought to the fore. What is most interesting about his reply to Brougham is that he contrasts what has happened in France with the dualistic compromise on which the stability of the English social fabric relies: 'The English are fond of boasting that they do not regard the theory, but only the practice of institutions; but their boast stops short of the truth; they actually prefer that their theory should be at variance with their practice'.[11] *On Liberty* is surely a challenge to that variance, a challenge motivated partly by the failure of the triumphant middle classes to give concrete expression to the theories which provided its rationale. For what is most problematic about the essay is not what it says, but what brought it about. After all, it is little more than a restatement of Locke, and although one can see in it a challenge to socialist doctrines, and although, as Packe points out,[12] the atmosphere of ideas in which it was written was full of variations on a collectivist theme, the chief animus in the essay is against the middle class itself:

> Already energetic characters on any large scale are beoming merely traditional. There is now scarcely any outlet for energy in this country except business. (p. 13)

It is important that Mill explicitly separates the principle of liberty from the doctrine of Free Trade (p. 151), for what he is concerned above all to affirm is the organic unity of the individual against the pressures of society to conform to its demands: 'Human nature is not a machine to be built after a model, and set to do exactly the work prescribed for it, but a tree, which requires to grow and develop itself on all sides, according to the tendency of the inward forces which make it a living thing' (p. 117). The affirmative image of personal integrity sharply dissociates itself both from the industrial revolution and the work ethic which was its moral premiss. It is not surprising that, a quarter of a century later, Hardy was to take the opening sentence of the paragraph from which this comes as the major intellectual referent of his novel of protest against middle-class conformism. *On Liberty* turns the bourgeois ideology on the bourgeoisie. Before 1848, Mill had made himself the apologist of the new economic world against feudalism (though admittedly a not uncritical apologist), but once its triumph and its true nature had become clear, he became its consistent accuser. And at the basis of the accusation, is the threat that bourgeois society makes to the whole individual.

But equally, we are struck by the note of desperation in the essay. Underlying the charged affirmations there is a sense of having lost to the collective mediocrity of the middle class, and out of the almost pedestrian diligence of the argument there erupts an almost anarchist note of hysteria: 'In this age, the mere example of non-conformity, the mere refusal to bend the knee to custom, is itself a service' (p. 124). It grows out of a very positive sense that the real threat to individuality comes not so much from the state as from the pressures of public opinion which arise in a class-structured society. The tree image has to be taken in the context of the assertion (in *Utilitarianism*) that man is a social animal, and that his nature is to amend nature (*Nature*). It is not social action that Mill protests against, but social coercion, not collectivism but hegemony. And what the essay registers above all is that the vitality of man has been undermined by the triumph of bourgeois morality. Between Bagehot and Mill, at opposite poles ideologically, we have the acquiescent and protesting responses to a society based on the heroic individualism of industry become isolated from the individuals in it, and threatening to the organicism of consciousness. What I am primarily concerned to show in this essay is how the Revolution of 1848 seemed to offer other possibilities, and how its failure seemed to make for a world in which the individual had no place except as a function of the class he belonged to.

II

Clough is the writer whose work most dramatically responds to the Revolutions of 1848. It is well known that he went to Paris in May, and that he acquired such a radical reputation in Oxford that a mock proclamation of the revolutionary takeover of the university whose signatories were headed by 'Citizen Clough' was published.[14] But it goes much deeper than this. Clough's whole poetic career seems tied to the curve of events on the continent. His first major poem was written in 1848 before the election of Louis Napoleon, and it is his most affirmative work. *Amours de Voyage* is both thematically and tonally bound up with the ironies of the French siege of Rome in 1849, and his most bitter, unfinished work, *Dipsychus* was begun after the abandonment of universal suffrage in May 1850. After the *coup d'état* at the end of 1851, Clough's poetry withers. Naturally, there are purely personal factors here, but Clough himself was never able to think of his private affairs purely hermetically, and the enclosure of the strange eruption of his creative talent within the revolutionary period, and its clear development from affirmation to despair, cannot be dissociated from the political fortunes of the democratic movement.

Moreover, Clough's attitude to political events in the post-revolutionary period is remarkably free of class-based fears and reservations. He was not, for example, sent into fits of hysteria by the June Days. He reported to Tom Arnold that the rumoured atrocities were 'unquestionably exaggerated', and went on to reveal an uncommonly radical attitude to the violence: 'I confess I regard it in the same light as a great battle – with, on the whole, *less* horror, and certainly more meaning than most great battles that one reads of.'[15] His letters of this period also, of course, are full of doubts and uncertainties, but these stem from the fear that the Revolution has not gone far enough because it has not created the basis for a new social structure. And what he specifically fears is the re-emergence of a triumphant bourgeoisie. On 14 May, two weeks after his arrival in Paris, he linked both of these points in a letter to his sister which creates a very clear and prescient perspective:

I don't expect much good will come of this present Assembly. – It is extremely shopkeeperish and merchantish in its feelings, and won't set to work at the organization of labour at all, at all. But will prefer going to war to keep the people amused, rather than open any disagreeable social questions . . . The Socialist people are all in the dumps.

The last sentence suggests how much Clough's point of view was tied to that of the Socialists, and a letter of the same day to Stanley quotes a St. Simonian as saying, as Marx was to do, that the Revolution at that point was 'A Bourgeoisistic triumph'.[17] The famous 'glory is departed' letter of 19 May is motivated by the emergence of 'Well-to-doism' and the driving back of Liberty, Equality and Fraternity into 'dingiest St. Antoine'.[18] Clough grew disillusioned with the Revolution because of its failure, not because of its vision.

Nevertheless, it is true that by February of 1849, Clough seems to have accepted Matthew Arnold's much more sceptical attitude to the Revolutions. His letter to Tom Arnold of 15 February suggests positive as well as negative concurrence: 'The millenium, as Matt says, won't come this bout, I am myself much more inclined to be patient and make allowance for existing necessities than I was'.[19] On the other hand, the incompatibility between the two writers remains one of the most celebrated in literature. We only have Arnold's side of the quarrel, but it is clear enough why Clough was never able to accept Arnold's apparent poise. For even in this letter, Clough's patience has little to do with Arnold's cult of the inner self. Clough goes on to say that he has learnt from the fighting in the Revolution that there are worse things than pain and that therefore the less acute but more chronic miseries of society 'are also stages towards good'. I'm not so much concerned with the attitude here, which is neither logical nor consistently adhered to, as with what it shows us of Clough's bent of mind: it suggests a changed attitude towards social progress, not the recognition that there are more permanent human issues than are evident in the particularities of history. And in the poetry, as we shall see, Clough never relinquishes the sense that individual being can only be defined in its relationship to the social structure it confronts. Arnold's bitter denunciation of *The Bothie of Tober Na Vuolich* in 1848 surely recognizes the incompatibility in more objective terms than the moral browbeating he treated Clough to in later letters and in *Thyrsis*: 'Yes I said to myself something tells me I can, if need be, at last dispense with them all, even with him: better that, than be sucked for an hour into the Time Stream in which they plunge and bellow'.[20] The trouble with Clough, as far as Arnold was concerned, was that he challenged his own attempt to define himself apart from the *Zeitgeist*.

The attempt is riddled with contradictions, and the contradictions are manifest in the two sonnets Arnold wrote in 1848 to answer Clough's revolutionary commitment. The first sonnet seems to pay tribute to the motives of revolutionary sympathy, but the second line, 'and practised by too few'[21] quickly introduces a crucial reservation since it immediately drives a wedge between the sympathy and its object. This obliquely inserted opinion has, by the end of the poem, become an accepted fact as the strong positive verbs of the octet ('but prized, but loved', 'despised') give way to trivializing and passive words such as 'sadness' and 'disquieted'. 'The long heart wasting show' becomes something which the great ones can do little about except feel sad, and the sadness is only a distraction anyway. 'Show' makes the great ones mere spectators of a theatrical illusion. This severing is completed by the clumsy syntax of 'If thoughts not idle, while before me flow / The armies of the homeless and unfed'. The crude assimilation of the great one's vision into his own by the sudden intrusion of the first person without any syntactical justification enables Arnold to evade any confrontation with their attitude as a different one from his, and the self detachment is managed by a purely connotative rhetoric as the implied inner freedom of 'thoughts not idle' is held apart from the undifferentiated necessity of 'flow'. The state of society which is the cause of the Revolution is assigned to a realm of necessity to which Clough, Arnold and the great ones generally are not subject. 'God knows it I am with you' is an empty rhetorical gesture seeking only to undermine rational argument.

The second sonnet is thus superfluous in terms of political debate. But it seems on the face of it to rebuild the link between the armies and the great ones by involving all in the same necessity. However, Arnold's use of the concept of necessity is here, as throughout his work, a rhetorical expedient whose purpose is to release the individual from the determinations of his epoch. For the mountains of necessity are not seen as having anything to do with the heart wasting show created by the coexistence of comfortable moles and hungry armies, but as the static boundaries of the individual landscape, uno'erleaped, it is true, but essentially apart from the life of the mind. Its margin is still there as a clearly defined space. Human history now seems to be 'A network superposed' and its relationship to the mountains is not clear. We only sense that it clutters up the margin which anyway is a dream-world. It is clear enough, I think, that Arnold uses imagery in a completely irresponsible way. Moles, armies, mountains, networks are all granting stern cover to a muddled and sentimental attempt to assert an absolute freedom from history within a mystified absolute determinism. It is also significant that Arnold needs to use two sonnets to make his point. The Petrarchan sonnet, because of its twofold structure, seems fitting for an argument which is based on 'if . . . but', but Arnold can't fit his argument into its unity, for there is no unity in what he is thinking: he merely juxtaposes two levels of argument in order to make one seem irrelevant. He is compelled to acknowledge that Clough's sympathy for the Revolution is a genuine response to an aspect of human experience: he avoids engaging with it by asserting that it is not a response to another aspect. In one sense, Arnold, who usually convinces himself that he is uncontaminated by the conventional wisdom, looks forward to one of the most effective means of rationalization of the *status quo* of the generation that followed the 1848 Revolution: that social action is made irrelevant by biological necessity. It is ironic that in 1848, Arnold should have been attacking the *Times* for precisely the same rationalization.[22]

The continuing importance of the confusions we have noted here in Arnold's work does not require much demonstration. No-one uses the concept of the *Zeitgeist* more than he does, but his attitude towards it is profoundly ambiguous. Both in his letters and in his criticism (for example, the *Preface* of 1853 and 'The Function of Criticism at the Present Time') he takes refuge in the degeneracy myth that we have seen in Bagehot. But the *Zeitgeist* is something to be acknowledged primarily in order that it may be transcended: 'He will not, however, maintain a hostile attitude towards the false pretensions of his age; he will content himself with not being overwhelmed by them' (p. 606). There is no possibility of affecting the spirit of the age, only of proclaiming that one isn't contaminated by it. The noumenal thus becomes both a way of condemning the actual world and all attempts to participate in it by social action as illusory, and an escape from its intractability. The *Zeitgeist* is a totally deterministic concept – an epoch is what it is, and not to recognize this is to be immature – but to recognize its determinism is to be granted special dispensation from it. And because of this separation, the historical world becomes static in Arnold's work. So that, for example, the analysis of the three classes in *Culture and Anarchy* is more of a debased Platonic allegory than it is social criticism. It is not an analysis of class at all, but of something more like 'rank'. There is no essential difference between the classes – they only reduplicate each other's structure with varying specific contents, and they are not defined in any way by their relationship to each other. Arnold could only see the popular demonstrations of 1866 and 1867 as the populace's expression of *laissez-faire*. *Culture and Anarchy* springs from the need, defined in 'Democracy', to assert a national interest against class interest. But Arnold is so incapable of seeing the national spirit in terms of historical possibility that he fails even to consider that unbridled individualism may be specifically the product of one class, the class with supreme power. Yet a social critic with at least as much of an idealizing bent as Arnold, R. H. Hutton, had drawn the obvious conclusion from the overwhelming evidence of co-operatives, unions and so on: if a new loyalty to the state and to the social whole was to be sought, it had to be sought in the working class who were distinguished from other classes by their capacity for organization and their collectivist spirit.[23] Hutton's essay is sentimental and pervaded by a nervous assurance that the former political jealousy of the working class has gone, but it does at least look at the distinctive identity of the class. Arnold can get no further than the recognition that classes exist, and they are no more than agglomerations of that subjectivity which superposes an illusory network on the vale of life.

Paradoxically, the 'objectivity' which Arnold opposes to the network is defined primarily in terms of isolation. For culture is really no different from the buried life. Again, this is a paradox manifest in Arnold's poems to Clough. *Religious Isolation* accuses Clough of being childish in wishing to relate his inner life to the world outside (in this case not merely society but nature itself). What is startling about Arnold's poetry of these years is how complete the affirmation of isolation is. 'Live by thy light and earth will live by hers' is not simply an assertion of individualism, it denies the relevance of human relationship. To seek for continuity at all is a wish 'unworthy of a man full grown' (p. 104). The love poems of this period are really anti-love poems. He rebukes Marguerite for seeking her complement in him. 'Our true affinities of soul' (p. 127) are not in the man-woman relationship but in an identical search for the static, and this consummation is only to be found in death, 'All our unquiet pulses cease' (p. 128). When love is affirmed, as in *The Buried Life* it is because it works as a reminder of the inward knowledge of the buried self – 'The eye sinks inward, and the heart lies plain' (p. 275) – and even then it is not a way of being at all but merely a 'lull in the hot race'. Arnold never goes beyond this sense that the only objectivity is in the assertion of discontinuity with the stream of time. Culture, for all its connotations of wholeness, is a rationale of detachment adumbrating a mystical harmony beyond human history and human relationship. To change the actual world therefore is to tinker with a dream. Education might seem to be the exception. But Arnold's belief in the need for a national educational system is based on the need to provide a check to democratization by the creation of 'leaders' (significantly among the middle class). This is why he focuses not on elementary education (which is a force making for greater equality) but on secondary education. It is thus that the absolute isolation affirmed in the poems immediately after the revolution develops into a commitment to the establishment. For isolation is a resistance to experience, an assertion of the idea against the multitudinousness of life,[24] and this resistance bases itself on a transcendent reality, which is at once a subterranean necessity and a celestial harmony, a reality manifested in the shreds of authority resistant to human change and human desire.

It is precisely in the difference between their attitudes to the world's multitudinousness that the incompatibility between Clough and Matthew Arnold lies. For Clough too the chaotic intrusion of outer experience is problematic and threatening (see especially *Blank Misgivings of A Creature Moving about in Worlds Not Realised*), but for him finally there is no pseudo-Hegelian 'idea' to act as refuge. Multitudinousness, the immediacy of experience is therefore precisely what his poetry seeks to confront. And the confrontation explains the most obvious differences between his poetry and Arnold's, the concern in Clough with the contemporary and the decisive role in his three most important poems of sexual love. Arnold's defence of the use of subjects from the past seems to be just critical good sense. But he uses such subjects in a very ambiguous way. Empedocles is a modern intellectual given authority by his historicization. *Balder Dead* reads very much like an allegory of the class war, but since it is on a mythological plane Arnold can avoid defining the role of the individual in the creation of history, and Balder's new heaven is either a mental attitude (aestheticism) or a utopia for the educated. It doesn't have to be assessed in real terms at all. Love is just as problematic for Clough as for Arnold, but it is also an ineluctable force of continuity rather than at best a comforter of alienation and at worst a distraction. It is problematic for Clough because he accepts its impersonality (*Natura Naturans*), and impersonality is problematic not because it threatens a spurious individualism, but because it challenges the contractual relationship demanded by the social structure between the inner and the outer world. Love changes both – it destroys both the buried self and 'duty'. This recognition is inextricably bound up with Clough's involvement with the Revolution, for that too insists on a new concept of human unity: 'I contemplate with infinite thankfulness the blue blouses, garnished with red, of the garde mobile; and emit a perpetual incense of devout rejoicing for the purified state of the Tuileries'.[25]

We can define the link between sex and politics by looking briefly at Tom Arnold's Equator Letters. Arnold was probably the prototype of Philip Hewson and Clough is reported as having found the letters remarkable.[26] Certainly they have a clear bearing on *The Bothie of Tober Na Vuolich*. Although they were written at the end of 1847, they clearly embody a revolutionary point of view, and it is obvious from Tom Arnold's letters of 1848 that he saw the Revolution as a potential fulfilment of the ideas he expressed in them; and even as late as July, 1849, he was writing to Clough: 'I always said before leaving England that I would return at once if there was a Revolution; and so I would' (p. 124). As a whole, the letters form an apologia for emigration, and what lies at the core is a sense of the total distortion of human relationships caused by the systematization of selfishness manifest above all in 'the class of capitalists' (p. 214). Emigration is the result of feeling 'the futility of all individual efforts to stem the stream'. The positive against which modern society is measured and found to be a systematic betrayer is specifically revolutionary, 'the sacred symbol, "Freedom, Equality, Brotherhood"' (p. 217). Arnold's view is pervaded by religious idealism, but for two reasons this idealism doesn't lead him to acquiescent patience. In the first place, although modern society has as its props the very inversions of the sacred symbol, 'The falsehood, the injustice, the inequality', there is no despair because they are the props of an 'unstable fabric' so that the religious idealism is never used as a substitute for the affirmation of historical change. Secondly, and it is clearly linked, there is no attempt to dissociate the subject perceiving the historical process from the process itself. Thus the sacred symbol is the source of personal emotion, 'inexpressible joy'. At the same time, the mental attitude which is critical of society in no way mitigates an oppressive social action:

> I am one of this rich class. I have *servants* to wait upon me; I am fed and clothed by the labour of the poor, and do nothing for them in return. The life I lead is an outrage and a wrong to humanity. (p. 218)

It is an outrage to humanity because it replaces 'brotherhood' with the social mediants of class relations. Tom Arnold is able to see himself as much a part of history as the armies of the houseless and unfed.

When the Revolution came, Arnold insisted to his sister that it was the penetration of the false social structure by the real basis of human relationships: 'It is not a class triumphing over a class, but a whole people getting rid of a *sham*, trampling under foot a lie' (p. 69). Behind this affirmation, it is true, there is an idealized concept of national unity which depends on a sentimental assertion of brotherhood ('And what allows us to be very hopeful of their success is that they seem to *love each other*'), and this assertion is debased by much post-revolutionary literature to become a rationale of patient reform and a counter to the antagonism provoked by injustice. Arnold even cites Disraeli in this letter. And the claim that class is a sham links with his brother's denial of the reality of class in *Culture and Anarchy*. But although it is a real intellectual limitation in Tom Arnold, the concept of 'ideal unity' and brotherhood is not, for him, a means of avoiding social conflict by arguing that there are buried bonds between men which no division can destroy, and that therefore inequalities do not need to be wiped out immediately. For Tom Arnold, the buried bonds must be manifested in the social actuality. Human solidarity is not a consolation for social oppression, it is a reality whose fulfilment demands the complete overthrow of the social structure, and the creation of a new society. The only means of effecting this is revolution, and if revolution is not available the only hope is to go away completely and start again.

Thus although Tom Arnold is, like his brother, dominated by an Hegelian idealism, it is an idealism which is, in a way totally alien to Matthew, historicistic. His belief in human continuity is critical rather than quiescent because it implies the manifestation of the Idea in time rather than in 'those elementary feelings which subsist permanently in the race and which are independent of time' (Allott, pp. 593–4). It implies it because Tom Arnold's vision of man's consciousness is antidualistic. His return to religious belief is described specifically as a recognition of the unity of spiritual and secular history, and the consequent sense of a continuity between man and nature:

> The history of Man and Nature then appeared like the seamless vesture, whole and undivided, enveloped in eternal beauty. Facts, institutions, characters, which had hitherto seemed to subsist independently of his being, and to draw their life and meaning from sources inaccessible to his thought, and unappreciable by his reason, yielded one after another to the test of the new idea, and from paradoxes and exceptions in Nature, became living realities, fraught with lessons for all time. . . . There were not two orders of things – the natural and the supernatural – according to the Christian system, but one only, infinite and divine, – he saw that

there was no fact, no institution, no doctrine, of which it could truly be said 'This is not governed by the ordinary laws of the world, and therefore the ordinary laws of thought do not apply to it' – but that all things that are, and were, and shall be, grow alike out of the one Soul which in Man has become conscious of itself, and recognizes throughout past history the work of its own hands. (p. 214)

Much of this is Carlylean, but there are significant differences. In the first place it affirms the unbounded potentiality of human reason, so that there is no leap of faith and commitment to 'duty'. Secondly, it recognizes that human consciousness declares itself in the whole of human history and not merely in the mind of the individual, so that history is not reversible, or escapable or marginal, but a total human creation continuous with nature. Because of this, inward development, with which Tom Arnold is as much concerned as his brother, is not a self alienating process of intellection, but a continuing and coalescing encounter between consciousness and experience: 'Reading and reflection had before this convinced him that, for the individual, true knowledge was attainable only by encouraging and consulting the *spontaneous* movements of the mind . . .' (p. 210). Such movements, acknowledging the unity of experience, neither release him to a higher plane, nor commit him blindly to the task at hand, but take him back with critical awareness to the society he inhabits.

Take him back, that is, to seek in history the manifestation of that joy he has found inwardly, for since its essence is continuity it cannot be expressed except in terms of social relationships. And in the end, of course, this process leads to contradiction. For the given social relationships are exact denials of this continuity, and to submit to them is to be contaminated. Significantly, immediately after he has encountered directly the poverty of London, Arnold declares the ineradicable hostility which the progressive mind must feel towards society, and at the same time reveals the thinness of the thread of faith to which it clings:

Take but one step in submission, and all the rest is easy: persuade yourself that your reluctance to subscribe to Articles which you do not believe is a foolish scruple, and then you may take orders and marry,

and be happy; satisfy yourself that you may honestly defend an un-
righteous cause, and then you may go to the Bar, and become distinguished, and perhaps in the end sway the counsels of the State; prove to
yourself, by the soundest arguments which political economy can furnish,
that you may lawfully keep several hundred men, women, and children at
work for twelve hours a day in your unwholesome factory, and then you
may become wealthy and influential, and erect public baths and patronize artists. All this is open to you; while if you refuse to tamper in a single
point with the integrity of your conscience, isolation awaits you, and
unhappy love, and the contempt of men; and amidst the general bustle
and movement of the world you will be stricken with a kind of impotence,
and your arm will seem to be paralysed, and there will be moments
when you will almost doubt whether truth indeed exists, or, at least,
whether it is fitted for man. Yet in your loneliness you will be visited by
consolations which the world knows not of; and you will feel that, if
renunciation has separated you from the men of your own generation,
it has united you to the great company of just men throughout all past
time; nay, that even now, there is a little band of Renunciants scattered
over the world, of whom you are one, whose you are, and who are yours
for ever. (pp. 215–16)

The end of this passage may not seem to be very different from
Matthew Arnold (poems such as *Quiet Work*, *Courage* and
Human Life are making similar points). But in its context it is very
different. In the first place, since what underwrites this is a belief in
continuity, Tom Arnold shows himself to be much more vulnerable
to social experience ('you will be stricken with a kind of impotence').
Secondly, this is not the end, the final position, it is only the starting
point of the decision to take social action by emigrating. And finally,
even the end projects into the future, and we are reminded of his
assertion to return to England if there were a revolution.

Nevertheless, we are confronted with an unresolved contradiction.
The rational basis of integrity is the spontaneous recognition of
human consciousness in human history. In the light of this claim,
the passage is really affirmative: the discovered integrity cannot deny
its basis in continuity by the acceptance of conventions which
divide men from each other, and the enquiring mind from accepted
belief. Yet the little band of renunciants seem to be those who are
'self reliant', who attempt to define themselves apart from their

social being. The major difference between this and the contradictions we have noted in the work of his brother is that it is not an ideological contradiction, but one which grows out of the paradoxes of the specific historical situation – the personal predicament of the revolutionary mind in a non-revolutionary situation. And this too explains why Arnold is incapable of accepting accommodation while protesting his inner freedom. There is no choice for him between becoming an agent of social oppression and opting out altogether. And even then, opting out does not mean death but going to a new world. There is no refuge in your own light. In its starkness, this passage might stand as epigraph to Clough's major poetry.

But there is another, more specific reason for its relevance to Clough. The most surprising phrase in this passage is surely 'unhappy love' which clearly links with the sense of impotence the just man may feel. It is not merely a general philanthropic feeling that it is wrong to have servants which gives Arnold the subjective feeling of alienation and links him with the oppressions of the whole of society. What finally leads him to the realization that there can be for him no mid-point (not even the consolations of the community of just men) between submission and rejection, is his reading of *Jacques*, a novel about the thwarting of love by convention. Love is a mode of continuity, but the social structure imposes itself even on this: 'in the age in which we live, and in the society in which we move, there is a curse on love and marriage for those who will not bow the knee to the world's laws; those who have resolved to put away illusions, and to live for truth, be it at the risk of all that is held precious here below, rest, happiness, nay, of love itself which is the very life of life' (p. 217). Love is the life of life because it is what brings us to the unity of the universe. In a society based on division, love is cursed, distorted into the dualistic laws of the world. Love and revolution are thus brought together – their fates are bound up. If Tom Arnold's decision to emigrate is a collapse into an amalgam of evasion and utopianism, we should not underestimate the radical integrity which made it seem the only personal solution. His brother resolves the impasse of the confrontation between the free intelligence and a a hostile society by ascribing the confrontation itself to a world of dream, so that he can submit in action asserting freedom of the mind as though thought were action. Clough's integrity, like Tom Arnold's, has no such comfort, and sexual love is what denies it, for it demands a wholeness of being that Matthew could do without.

III

The Bothie of Tober Na Vuolich shares the affirmative ambience registered in the Equator Letters, and if its tone is more exuberant it is surely in part because the instability of the social fabric which opposes Tom Arnold's sacred symbol had been revealed in European history. As we should expect in a major work of literature, its concern is not with vague generalities, but with concretely realized experience. It is not a poem about revolution, but a revolutionary poem about love, the personal emotion which existing society most directly challenges, and which, through its insistence on human continuity against social divisiveness, most immediately brings the individual consciousness into conflict with society. The poem celebrates the possibility of love, and defines its relationship to the contemporary social structure. Precisely because it is such an affirmative poem about love, and love cannot merely be seen as a relief or escape from the social structure, it necessarily becomes a radical critique of society and a vision of the possibilities of historical change. But, at the same time, because it is a celebration so concretely realized, its affirmations have themselves to undergo sharp scrutiny.

I am speaking here of *The Bothie* of 1848 which is a different, and, I think, more radical poem than that printed by Lowry, Norrington and Mulhauser, which is based on a posthumous edition of 1863.[27] Clough revised the poem in 1859, cutting out about 200 lines. It is the character of Philip which is most affected by the changes. His contribution to the debate in Canto II, his meditations in Canto IV and his letter to Adam in Canto IX receive the heaviest cuts. In the first edition, he is both more forceful and less callow. An index of this is the variation of Canto II, line 39. 'Never, believe me, revealed itself to me the sexual glory' becomes in 1863, 'Never, believe me, I knew of the feelings between men and women'. Much of the revision is straightforward bowdlerization. At the same time, Adam is less dramatically realized in the later text so that he becomes more of a Socratic commentator and less of an actor in a drama of conflicting values. So, for example, in Canto II, when Adam has spoken with sympathy but detachment of Philip's praise of functional beauty, the 1848 edition has Philip retort that old men can speak with such detachment because they have lost the impulse which their wisdom rationalizes and accommodates to social inequality through 'duty'. Adam does not answer this until he has paused in emotional acknowledgement, and in his reply he admits that his own wisdom means discarding the original instinct that motivates one's continuity with others.

It is not simply that Philip is not allowed, in the later text, to be so damaging a critic of the conventional moral wisdom, it is also that, in this excised interchange, he introduces an image which gives coherence, throughout the poem, to the ideological significance of the love between himself and Elspie, and keeps its meaning completely distinct from Adam's wisdom. Philip has claimed that in the vision of sexual glory released by the peasant girl lies the most meaningful relationship with life:

> So women feel, not dolls; so feel the sap of existence
> Circulate up through their roots from the far away centre of all things,
> Circulate up from the depths of the bud on the twig that is utmost!
>
> (II. 12)

When Adam replies that what he really seeks is the good, and that this has nothing intrinsically to do with Philip's praise of the lower orders, Philip redefines the sense of this life-centrality (the Lawrentian phrase is relevant to the whole poem) in terms of magnetism:

> . . . the grown-up man puts-by the youthful instinct,
> Learns to deal with the good, but what is good discerns not;
> Learns to handle the helm, but breaks the compass to steer by;
>
> (II. 15)

The metaphor defines his relationship with Elspie; throughout the poem she acts as his compass, as he explicitly realizes, and she too, in another excised passage, defines what she feels for him in terms of the same metaphor:

> there in my dreaming,
> There I feel the great key-stone coming in, and through it
> Feel the other part – all the other stones of the archway,
> Joined into mine with a queer happy sense of completeness, tingling

65

All the way up from the other side's basement-stones in the water,
Through the very grains of mine: just like, when the steel, that you
   showed us
Moved to the magnet, it seemed a feeling got hold of them both. (VII. 41)

The omission of everything from 'tingling' has an important effect on the image of the archway, for without the sense of process, the image becomes petrified, as though the completeness were a single unrepeated action. Thus what Elspie and Philip find becomes, in 1863, much more compatible with the ethical structure which Adam stands for. But more importantly, by playing down the magnetic image pattern, Clough takes out of the poem one of its most important affirmations, that of the Goethean concept of the elective affinity. In 1848, the poem grants love an independent coherence and validity: the spontaneous movements of mind discover their own image of continuity which is not merely accommodated by Adam's ethical commitment. Another of Philip's taunts is that in mastering the syllogism Adam has lost sight of the premiss, and it is precisely the premiss that he has to redefine for himself in terms of his own experience: 'Though I should like to be clear what standing in earth means' (II. 17). And the logic he discovers is radically different from Adam's – 'Only let each man seek to be that for which Nature meant him' (IX. 49) cuts completely across the social structure, while Adam's 'We all must do something, and in my judgement do it / In our station' (II. 16) is a rationale of accommodation.

Love is revolutionary because it penetrates the false dichotomies in which the characters are caught. Landscape and erotic joy are made one by Elspie's dream, so that love becomes the spontaneous movement of mind which recognizes the seamfree vesture of man and nature, soul and body, understanding and experience. At the opening of the poem, Clough creates a specious pastoral world in which the feudal community only thinly disguises the divisive capitalist reality, and in which masculinity is reduced to display with the ladies obscenely but harmlessly 'fingering kilt and sporran' (I. 5). Philip is critical of this world, and it is his refusal to participate fully in its pretences that draws David Mackaye towards him, for David, we note, has none of the bogus trappings of the feast – he is dressed as the Saxon. But initially, Philip's response is purely antithetical. He can replace one sham only with an equally false inversion, another false pastoral, the depersonalizing and socially mediated cult of the peasantry. So that it is psychologically apt that his love for Katie, though, in the 1848 text, it participates fragmentarily in the impersonality which he has found lacking in the self-regarding world of 'society',–'Elements fuse and resolve, as affinity draws and repels them' (IV. 27) – should be full of contradictions. Though it is erotic, its physical realization would merely contaminate: it is opposed to the falsity of social marriage, and it thus becomes involved in marriage's social antithesis, sexual defilement. Katie and the Lady Maria stand for escape from and submission to the social convention, but the escape fails because the impersonality of love cannot be disentangled from social depersonalization, so that Philip is hurled to the opposite pole, the extreme and cynical cult of personality in the oppressive beauty of Lady Maria. Elspie is different from these in a quite radical way. Evoking the primacy of physical desire, paying tribute to the unconscious and impersonal forces of love, she makes sexuality mutual rather than acquisitive, and recognizing it as a rhythm (the flood) she is able to disentangle sexual submission from its petrified societal image, inequality. It is no paradox that she acknowledges the impersonality of her desire for Philip, and yet that she chiefly educates him to penetrate the falsities of depersonalization: 'People here too are people, and not as fairy land creatures' (IV. 29). For this is the distortion in the social structure of the biological realities.

The poem as a whole is organized to reveal the continuous reality which is overridden by the fairy land of social forms. It moves primarily from mock heroic to heroic. In the opening cantos, the conventions of highland festivities and academic debate ironically manifest the tensions they gloss over. Knowledge, in particular, is severed from activity, so that the students' day is mathematically divided between study and physical recreation, and the vitality of the landscape is accommodated through mythologization and 'sport'. The debate about women in Canto II is concerned with genuine issues (above all the paradoxical conflict between social feeling and social form), but only inside the permitted convention which verbalizes harmlessly. So that, although Philip and Adam are serious, their respective attitudes are fittingly placed by the reductive parody of their supporters, Hobbes and Lindsay. The poem's development depends on Philip's capacity to break away from this atrophied world where community is servitude and sexuality is abstract ideology. Philip's colleagues, including Adam, serve as an index of his development, as they come to seem and to feel increasingly remote from the experience the poem is realizing. By the time Philip has found Elspie, we have seen them as amused spectators, as bewildered friends and as totally indifferent acquaintances. They recognize at a distance what has happened, but they are part of the old world Philip and Elspie are leaving behind, and if Adam is brought at the end into the relationship, it is only to rationalize a *fait accompli*. Hobbes registers this movement to a new immediacy in the development of his frames of reference. When Philip is opposing the distortions of society in a purely theoretical way, Hobbes is able to scale down his ideas to fit a fashionable intellectual system – Pugin's cult of Gothic architecture. Once Elspie and Philip are together, his analogy is to the elemental story of Rachel and Leah, and it is not a closed analogy, as the allusion to Pugin is; for he sees Philip and Elspie as resolving the conflicts of the story. He pays tribute at once to the depth of significance their love has, and to the millennial possibilities it portends. Rachel and Leah are one – the old conflict between romantic love and marriage is resolved through the new freedom and mutuality of affinity.

The political implications are made explicit in the final Canto. As we have seen, Philip redefines individuality in terms not determined by class. And if, to Adam's view that to follow our own instincts irrespective of the given social order is to be like soldiers in battle who ignore the commands of the Field Marshal, Philip replies with the Thucydidean image Arnold was to use at the end of *Dover Beach*, the implication is diametrically opposed. For it is not a rationale of detachment, but on the contrary an affirmation of the value of spontaneous action in a world motivated not by an opaque *Zeitgeist*, but by affinity. Significantly, Philip later describes the return of the 'old democratic fervour' in terms of the same imagery which Elspie had used to define her sense of his masculinity. Love and democracy are aspects of each other because they are visions of the unity of life beyond the false dichotomies of a class structured society.

Of course, like Tom Arnold's socialism, Philip's final affirmation is utopian, but I think the poem recognizes this. At the end, Philip is still a comically contradictory figure. If the flood of masculinity releases the old democratic fervour, the light of female responsiveness creates affinity with the populous city at dawn. To be sure, the image created is one of human potentiality – 'All its unfinished houses, lots for sale, and railway outworks, – / Seems reaccepted, resumed to Primal Nature and Beauty' (IX. 52) – but the acquiescence is seen as antithetical to the democratic fervour because it is a general faith in humanity, and not a specifically revolutionary faith. At the same time, the accepting light does not finally replace the democratic energy – both are forces in a continuing sexual rhythm. Clough is simply recognizing that the link between the sexual affirmations that the poem makes and the revolutionary fervour that grows from them is problematic in terms of human history. The human forces which make for revolution are realized in personal terms, but their manifestation in the social totality remains implicit. This necessary ambiguity is borne out by the ending of the poem itself. At the end of his letter to Adam, Philip directs his attention towards the bourgeois oppressiveness of marriage for the woman: 'How many are spoilt for wives by the means to become so, / Spoilt for wives and mothers, and anything else moreover' (IX. 51). The relationship between Philip and Elspie, despite its generalized implications, is thus placed as exceptional. Philip and Elspie come together partly because of the remote unpretentiousness of the Bothie itself, and their marriage is necessarily conditional on escaping from the society they transcend. Emigration is seen as a way of perpetuating the Bothie, of per-petuating its remoteness and avoiding contamination. The end of the poem necessarily reminds us of Gigadibs. He too remains mentally resilient to the acquiescent cynicism of Blougram, but the only answer he has in terms of action is to get out of the world in which Blougram's dualistic attitude seems to be necessary. Browning sees his idealist as slightly silly; Clough has too much integrity to be so patronizing. But the ironies are there. Philip has become a more empirically motivated radical, but the experience finally takes him from the roots of society.

I think that in spite of the ambiguities of its ending, *The Bothie* remains affirmative: the actualization of love envisages the potentiality of revolution, even though the potential remains unrealized except in terms of a private escape. It is as Europe appears to manifest again the triumph of well-to-doism, that Clough begins in his poetry to scrutinize the curse on love. One of the most significant poems of 1849, in view of what we have been discussing, is *Jacob's Wives*. Rachel and Leah are not one, and this poem is a bitter quarrel between them, always dominated by the ethically superior and psychologically depersonalizing Leah. She doesn't 'win' because the conflict is endless, but she offers a compromise which is a savage comment on bourgeois marriage:

> And Leah ended, Father of my sons,
> Come, thou shalt dream of Rachel if thou wilt,
> So Leah fold thee in a wife's embrace. (p. 84)

Sexual love is inexorably split between the romantic moment and the social role of procreation – they are resolved only in dream. Jacob himself speaks in another poem of this year, and it is clear that he is a pillar of the community who has reached wisdom only by the sacrifice of personal integrity and aspiration. The closing lines of the poem are a very clear expression of what Lukács has called the 'malédiction tragique'[28] which develops out of the contradiction in the bourgeoisie between class consciousness and class interest:

> The stony hard resolve,
> The chase, the competition, and the craft
> Which seems to be the poison of our life
> And yet is the condition of our life!
> To have done things on which the eye with shame
> Looks back, the closed hand clutching still the prize!
> Alas! what of all these things shall I say?
> Take me away unto thy sleep, O God!
> I thank thee it is over, yet I think
> It was a work appointed me of thee.
> How is it? I have striven all my days
> To do my duty to my house and hearth,
> And to the purpose of my father's race,
> Yet is my heart therewith not satisfied. (p. 87)

In one sense this is more pessimistic than anything in Arnold because there is no retreat into an ideal beyond historical necessity. Jacob's life is full of distortion but it is the will of God. At the same time, the diction establishes this despair as a specifically class based one. The vocabulary is the vocabulary of Protestant self-help: 'chase', 'competition', 'craft', 'prize' are words of individualist enterprise. Yet this individualism is seen as a depersonalizing conformity to the will of God, and we note too the presence of 'resolve', 'work appointed', 'duty' as words that morally rationalize that enterprise and which are taken over as positives even by critics of mammonism, Carlyle and Arnold himself. The will of God prevails, but it is not compatible with the free light of reason. Personal love and work, in these two poems, turn against the individualism of which they are the primary affirmations.

For Clough there is no individuality without continuity, but continuity is manifested on the personal level by relationship and by action. In the world of the present, devoid of the immediate prospect of social change, the modes of continuity become agents of divisiveness both in the sense that they destroy human equality and fraternity in the cause of individualism and in the sense that they destroy liberty by turning that individualism into a conformity. I have already shown elsewhere how the elemental modes of continuity are seen, in *Amours de Voyage*, as factitious – bourgeois love, theatrical nationalism and romantic concepts of growth are only rhetorical gestures which rationalize experience in a way that can be contained by the social structure. In a world which seemed to hold the possibility of a renewal of society on the basis of free community, Clough is able to make concrete the personal experience of continuity. As the moment fades, he has to return again to a closer scrutiny of the treacherous affirmatives of bourgeois society.

Dipsychus is surely the product of this scrutiny, and not, simply, as has often been asserted, the confrontation of a fastidious intellect with an unethical but realistic common sense. Dipsychus is double minded because he has no concept of affinity with which to oppose the specious double morality of Cosmocrator. In Scene 11A for example, the Spirit's attitude to sex is not realistic, it is simply obscene and voyeuristic, but Dipsychus fails to oppose him because he is too urgently concerned to talk away his own terrifying desires with misty romantic clichés, and since the idea of mutuality doesn't enter, he can only offer social arguments which the Spirit can convert because he is social man. Dipsychus can see that prostitution is exploitation, but the only positive he has to offer is an equally reifying cult of virginity, so that the Spirit can counter with the idea that since virginity is unregainable, you aren't making matters worse by having a prostitute. Next, Dipsychus's affirmation against this is a depersonalizing philanthropism – the most degraded may be saved. The Spirit can accommodate this too, both with an Arnoldian assertion of ultimate necessity and with a brilliantly cynical epigram celebrating the Victorian salve of an exploiting conscience:

> As women are and the world goes
> They're not so badly off – who knows?
> They die, as we do in the end;
> They marry; or they – *superintend*:
> And Sidney Herberts sometimes rise,
> And send them out to colonize (p. 536)

And Dipsychus then has to resort to an exaltation of marriage – which the Spirit immediately offers him. The comedy here, and throughout the whole poem, is that Dipsychus can never sustain values that the Spirit can't assimilate. The whole structure of the poem indeed is one in which, as Dipsychus resists one temptation after another, he finds himself with a choice between action and inaction. And the temptations too become more and more morally charged. The opening scenes are invitations to pleasure and self glorification – by the end, the Spirit is calling on him to submit. The only choice is between the abstract dissipation of energy (which anyway is not uncontaminated by the social structure – as the gondolier reminds Dipsychus, and as he himself realizes when he sees intellectual activity as the safety valve of 'the procreant heat and fervour of our youth'), and, on the other hand the sluicing out of the active self into canals. *Dipsychus Continued* merely encapsulates the many ironies of this predicament, for the returning prostitute not only undermines his respectability, she also complains that pleasure has been reduced to guilt. Society demands the total atrophy of the self from its

desires. *Dipsychus* is the despairing protest of a man for whom the
social structure has become the only reality.

And yet even in this poem other possibilities are glimpsed. The
gondola episode affirms a vision of freedom which is only undermined
because in the particular world of which Dipsychus is a product, it can
only be freedom for an élite so that it becomes an oblivious idealism.
And at the Lido too, Dipsychus' plunge into the elemental sea un-
nerves the Spirit completely. What makes such gestures futile is that
there is no way of relating them to the given world without changing
it, and the prospect of the given world being changed has gone.
Clough is finally defeated by the world, and the defeat is deplorable,
but I think also that it is informed by an exceptional integrity. He
put *Dipsychus* aside, and he came to see *The Bothie* as 'childishly
innocent',[29] but at the same time he never convinced himself that in
accepting the social structure he could maintain a world of art
uncontaminated by it. There is a letter of 1851, affirming the English
tendency to moralize against the German genius for psychological
insight, which is in one sense horrifying in its implicit philistinism,
but in another profoundly aware of the intellectual dilemma of
bourgeois consciousness:

> The English fault therefore appears to me to consist, *not* in the pro-
> pensity to apply a moral rule to all character and life, but in making their
> rule so narrow as to taking (sic) only a portion of our nature, and so
> purely external and mechanical as to misjudge the inner soul. The
> German reaction from this fault, – however fascinating as a deliverance
> from a thraldom felt to be oppressive, – seems to me to involve a far
> more dangerous falsehood. It treats all spiritual phenomena, all passions,
> all impulses, as mere developments of irresistible nature, which are to be
> accepted as being there, and among which we are not to demand any
> harmony, any subordination, or to recognize any obligatory ideal of
> perfection. As a kind of revolutionary assertion of the rights of a nature
> cramped by ungenial rigour, this anarchical doctrine may be generously
> borne with in individuals and in an age of transition. But, in itself it is,
> I must think, utterly false in philosophy, and most destructive in social
> tendency. Whenever the German Revolution works itself out into power,
> we shall see the effects of this faith in a divine Lawlessness, in terrible
> contrast to the English Puritan Revolution as an expression of faith in
> divine Law. For purposes of mere *Art*, the contemplation of life as a

necessary growth from the spontaneity of nature, is perhaps the most favourable: but for the healthy action of individual men and the organic existence of the State, it is in my opinion fatal.[30]

Such illiberalism may tempt us to think nostalgically of Arnold's essay on Heine or even of *Culture and Anarchy*, but what is important here is the last sentence. Clough sees the inexorable conflict between the creative mind and accommodated man, and sees it specifically in terms of the implications of the middle class revolution. He found it better to keep silent than to go on pretending to himself that he could acknowledge the multitudinousness of life and still go on living in his own society. The volcanic eruption of his creative talent, and its total obliteration in the struggle for social survival, creates obvious and far reaching perspectives on the literature of the next two decades.

NOTES

1. Jacques Droz, *Europe Between Revolutions*, London 1967, p. 255.
2. Alfred Cobban, *A History of Modern France*, London, 1965, vol. 2, p. 146.
3. E. P. Thompson, *The Making of the English Working Class*, London, 1963, shows how widespread was the revolutionary movement in England in the 1790s.
4. Royden Harrison, *Before the Socialists*, London, 1965, p. 79.
5. Sidney Pollard, 'Nineteenth Century Co-Operation: From Community Building to Shopkeeping', in *Essays in Labour History*, ed. Briggs and Saville, London 1967, pp. 74–112.
6. E. J. Hobsbawm, 'Custom, Wages, and Work-Load in Nineteenth Century Industry', in *Essays in Labour History*, p. 114.
7. F. B. Smith, *The Making of the Second Reform Bill*, London, 1966, pp. 24–5.
8. Walter Bagehot, *Literary Studies*, London, 1898, vol. 3, p. 6. All subsequent references are from this edition and page references are indicated in parentheses. The 'Letters on the French Coup d'Etat of 1851' originally appeared in the *Inquirer* early in 1852.
9. Leslie Stephen, 'On the Choice of Representatives by Popular Constituencies', *Essays on Reform*, London, 1867, p. 106. A number of these essays are concerned to play down the effects of the Reform Bill. Cf. Cracroft, 'The Analysis of the House of Commons, or Indirect Representation', who notes that 'A Concurrence of causes has rendered Democracy in this country impossible', ibid., p. 190.

10. Benjamin Jowett, 'On the Interpretation of Scripture', *Essays and Reviews*, London, 1861, p. 356.

11. J. S. Mill, 'Vindication of the French Revolution of 1848', *Dissertations and Discussions*, London, 1859, vol. 2, p. 355. The essay originally appeared in the *Westminster Review*, April, 1849.

12. Michael St. John Packe, *The Life of John Stuart Mill*, London, 1954, p. 402. Packe undoubtedly exaggerates however. See J. C. Rees, *Mill and his Early Critics*, Leicster, 1956, p. 3.

13. J. S. Mill, *Utilitarianism, Liberty, Representative Government*, London, 1957, p. 127. All subsequent quotations are from this edition, and page references are given in parentheses.

14. Bertram, *The New Zealand Letters of Thomas Arnold the Younger*, Auckland, p. 221, reprints the proclamation. The joke is not without a serious basis. A letter to Stanley of May 28th, 1848, which cannot, in view of Clough's resignation, be taken as merely whimsical, proposes five 'Chartist' reforms of Oxford. See Mulhauser, *The Correspondence of Arthur Hugh Clough*, Oxford, 1957, p. 211. Hereafter referred to as *Mulhauser*.

15. *Mulhauser*, p. 215.

16. Ibid., p. 204.

17. Ibid., p. 206.

18. Ibid., p. 207.

19. Ibid., p. 243, 'Say Not the Struggle Nought Availeth' seems to be the poetic manifestation of this 'patience'. If, however, as two biographers of Clough have asserted, it is a political poem, the patience seems to be a strengthened faith in progress.

20. Lowry, *The Letters of Matthew Arnold to Arthur Hugh Clough*, London, 1932, p. 95. Hereafter referred to as *Lowry*.

21. This and all subsequent quotations from Arnold's poems and prefaces, is taken from Kenneth Allot, the *Poems of Matthew Arnold*, London, 1965. Page references, where necessary, are given in parentheses. This sonnet and its sequel are printed pp. 102–3.

22. *Lowry*, op. cit., p. 68.

23. R. H. Hutton, *Essays on Reform*, London, 1867, pp. 27–44.

24. See his letter to Clough, *Lowry*, op. cit., p. 97.

25. *Mulhauser*, op. cit., p. 206.

26. Bertram, *The New Zealand Letters of Thomas Arnold the Younger*, op. cit., p. 207. All quotations from Arnold are from this source and I give page references in parentheses except where a quotation is from the same page as the preceding quotation. I follow Bertram in calling him Tom Arnold in order to avoid confusion with Thomas Arnold Senr.

27. This is not to criticize their editing, since Clough revised it himself. They print the variants in an appendix. See the *Poems of Arthur Hugh Clough*, ed. Lowry, Norrington and Mulhauser, Oxford, 1951, pp. 496–511. Since it is so important to my argument that I use the first edition, I have taken all

quotations from it (Oxford, 1848). References in parentheses are to Canto (Roman numeral) and page in this edition (Arabic numeral). Quotations from other poems are taken from the 1951 edition, and page references are given in parentheses.

28. Lukács, *Histoire et Conscience de Classe*, Paris, 1965, p. 85. The general framework of this essay owes a great deal to this text of Lukács' and to his literary criticism.
29. *Mulhauser*, op. cit., p. 338.
30. Ibid., pp. 293-3.

IV

THE RADICALISM OF 'LITTLE DORRIT'

WILLIAM MYERS

I

To understand the strategy of *Little Dorrit* – especially in its political and social implications – proper recognition must be given to the plot, which is still too frequently dismissed or undervalued. John Wain maintains that it is 'in essence, a plotless novel. For all the scurry of event on its surface, it never for a moment suggests genuine movement';[1] and even Raymond Williams can write of the action being 'properly one of collision, of chance, of unlooked for connection and involvement . . .'[2] Both of course recognize that coincidence, mystery, and mechanical connections between characters suggest specific and significant views of man and society – but at best they give the impression of an artistic ineptitude (which the plotting of the early novels certainly was) being at last turned to good use. A more positive recognition of Dickens's achievement as a story-teller is needed, and in the case of *Little Dorrit* this involves distinguishing between its 'mystery' element and the rest of the action. There *is*, of course, an important element of chance and unlooked for connection in the novel, but for nine-tenths of the book it remains fixed, a setting for the action, not the action itself. The secrets of Arthur Clennam's birth, of Mrs Clennam's connection with the Dorrits, and of Blandois's association with Flintwich's brother and Miss Wade, have above all the function of reassuring the reader, of promising that some, at least, of the novel's problems can be solved like a puzzle – simply by persistence and ingenuity. They are not, however, the 'story' because they do not make for any real suspense. In contrast, the interest and excitement aroused by Pancks's search for the Dorrit money (the details of which are never mechanically revealed), or the fear which must be felt for Amy at the prospect of her father's marrying Mrs General, do involve the reader not merely on a symbolic level but on the level also of sheer narrative excitement. Exactly the right blend of predictable and unpredictable events in the action (Fanny's marriage, Arthur's fatal speculations) make it impossible to dip into *Little Dorrit* as one might into *Pickwick*. The novel must be read in sequence because, apart from the deliberate mystery element, it unfolds freely and yet with the inevitability of a well-told story – damming up and then releasing the reader's mental energy by turns in a way which Dickens was clearly very conscious of, and which must, if the novel has any value at all, relate centrally to its meaning.

It is important to understand also Dickens's own sense of this freely developing action. His accounts of its development certainly suggest growth rather than mechanical contrivance, and growth especially in the narrative. Decisions about it occur late. He is well into the novel before deciding to make Amy 'very strong' and (tentatively) to overwhelm the Dorrits with wealth;[3] and though his plans for Merdle and the Circumlocution Office develop early, with Mr Merdle's complaint emerging 'as the last drop in the silver cream-jug on Hampstead Heath', it is not until June 1856, when he is working on the ninth number, that he is able to write: 'The story lies before me, I hope, strong and clear. Not to be easily told; but nothing of that sort I S to be easily done that *I* know of.'[4] As Butt and Tillotson point out, however, the cover-design of the first number had already indicated very precisely the main themes of the novel,[5] which suggests that in Dickens's mind there was on the one hand great clarity and confidence about the ideas he wanted to deal with, on the other an exploratory and tentative approach to the action. The book comes alive for him only when action and theme fuse, and the novel *as a story* lies before him strong and clear. He can then see his way to a prolonged and complex manipulation of the vast public which was waiting for each successive number as he wrote it; and it is precisely as a carefully organized assault on the consciousness of a specific readership that *Little Dorrit* is meaningful.

The Radicalism of 'Little Dorrit'

We know that for Dickens the experience of writing *Little Dorrit* was very much tied up with an agonizing sense of political despair, and that, in particular, the maladministration revealed by the Crimean war provided him with one of his main themes. But it is not just a novel about the political problems of the 1850s (though set in the 1820s). Because Dickens and his public, together as it were, and over a long period, experience the complex pressures of a tensely told story with a political theme, *Little Dorrit* is, in a sense, an organized political event in the society which it describes. The descriptions of, and judgements on society which it contains, are only comprehensible in terms of an extensive, intimate and *developing* relationship between book and public. This means, of course, that *Little Dorrit* must reflect and acknowledge the values and experience of its readers – that is, by and large, the English middle-class. But it must also, as a work of art, be *against* the reader in a certain sense; it must disconcert his aesthetic expectations; it must trap, surprise, and frustrate, as well as gratify, the literary appetites of the English bourgeoisie. And because it is, as we have seen, centrally about politics, in intention at least, its success in disconcerting the reader in literary terms will necessarily involve disconcerting him morally and politically as well. The question is how strong these opposing tendencies are. When at last the story of *Little Dorrit* lay before Dickens, strong and clear, some of the effort it called from him was obviously required to strengthen the conventional political and social attitudes he shared with his readers, to intensify their mutual intimacy; but some, equally, would have been involved in challenging those conventions – and though this may have taken a specifically literary rather than narrowly political form, it would still have had to challenge in some way, as a matter of aesthetic necessity, the very social order in which the novel itself operated so intensively. How radical this literary and political challenge was can be seen only through an examination of *Little Dorrit* as a sequence of experiences; and this of course necessarily involves taking it seriously as a narrative.

II

In suggesting that the aesthetic tensions in *Little Dorrit* express tensions between bourgeois and antibourgeois political attitudes, I do not want to give the impression that one or other is the authentic Dickensian point of view. It would certainly be wrong, for instance, to suggest that the humane associate of Angela Burdett-Coutts is Dickens the artist, while the reactionary bourgeois is Dickens the journalist, stage-manager, and public relations man. Because Dickens is within the situation he is describing, the middle-class *paterfamilias* penetrates the novel at every level. The act of writing and publishing serially for a particular public, and the experience of pleasing them, is for Dickens to enact his own involvement in English society. The world he writes about is his world; the world the novel describes is the world in which it is read – which is why, as Orwell rightly points out, it lacks any historical perspective.[6] Dickens never adopted a detached, theoretical point of view; he is quite incapable of thinking of human relations as phenomena; and being a member of the English middle-class, middle-class values are fundamental to his activity as a writer. There are relatively superficial signs of this – the careful use, for instance, of Maggie as chaperone and no chaperone ('So, at last, Clennam's purpose in remaining was attained, and he could speak to Little Dorrit with nobody by. Maggie counted as nobody, and she was by' (i, 31)),[7] or the happy tolerance of Mr Meagles's philistinism. But middle-class commitments and right-wing habits of thought and feeling contribute to the novel at a deeper level also. When the landlady of the Break of Day, for instance, dismisses 'philosophical philanthropy' with the words '... there are people who have no human heart, and who must be crushed like savage beasts and cleared out of the way ...' (i, 11), the themes of frustration, violence and repression which work so intensively in the novel become involved with, and support, a position uncompromisingly hard and anti-intellectual. There is no doubt about the kind of mind this remark will appeal to, nor about Dickens's own pleasure in it. Nor is there any doubt that the imaginative energy deriving from such pleasure is central to the whole experience of the novel.

To say *Little Dorrit* is a middle-class novel, moreover, is not to deny it a thoroughly effective radicalism in the Bright and Chamberlain tradition. There is nothing incompatible with middle-class values in Dickens's anti-Sabbatarianism or his anger at Westminster landlords. And even if this sort of radicalism can become a source of bourgeois self-congratulation (it is the special achievement of our century and our class to think scientifically and act energetically on matters of public health and housing) it gives rise also to Dickensian rhetoric of the most effective and satisfying kind:

> Ten thousand responsible houses surrounded him, frowning as heavily on the streets they composed, as if they were every one inhabited by the ten young men of the Calender's story, who blackened their faces and bemoaned their miseries every night. Fifty thousand lairs surrounded him where people lived so unwholesomely, that fair water put into their rooms on Saturday night, would be corrupt on Sunday morning; albeit my lord, their county member, was amazed that they failed to sleep in company with their butcher's meat. (i, 3)

The anger is accurate, honest, and directed at a real political enemy. Dickens and his readers know that they think and feel differently from both aristocratic members of parliament and tenants of slum property. They know also that their forthright opposition to restrictive legislation is generous, humane, and just.

Hence the energetic confidence in the tone of certain parts of *Little Dorrit*, Dickens's easy masculine conviction that what he says and how he says it will be popular. The attack on the county member, for instance, could easily have gone into *Household Words*, just as the famous 'Nobody, Somebody, and Everybody' article[8] could have found its way into *Little Dorrit*. Whatever he happens to be writing, letter, article, or novel, Dickens has the power to drop all doubts about what he is saying and how it will be received, and to press forward in prose which at times is almost violent in its simplifications. Whether he is writing laudatory letters about the sturdy, no-nonsense rebelliousness of the Swiss,[9] or, ten years later in *Little Dorrit*, describing Merdle as '*simply* the greatest Forger and the greatest Thief that ever cheated the gallows' (ii. 25, italics mine), the effect is the same: he presents a thoroughly articulate and rather more sophisticated version of Mr Meagles's rage in the Circumlocution Office. And though there is a great deal more to be said about his handling of Merdle's death, it remains true that his talent for the simplifications of energetic belief is one of the dominating – and essentially bourgeois – features of *Little Dorrit*.

It combines with a disturbing confidence in the moral values of his class. One of the most disconcerting instances of this occurs in a passage of considerable importance in view of its anticipation of the last paragraph in the whole work – namely Amy's conversation with Arthur about her feeling that Mr Dorrit ought not to have to pay his debts 'in life and money both' (i, 35). Unhesitatingly Dickens calls this moving and justified reaction a 'taint' in Little Dorrit, the first and last speck Clennam ever sees 'of the prison atmosphere upon her'; and he makes this astonishing judgement in spite of his having given us earlier the careful translation 'Forgive us our debts as we forgive our debtors' (i, 5), in order to show up the radical contradictions in Mrs Clennam's religious views. He recognizes of course that forgiveness of debts is a virtue in creditors; he denies that it is ever a matter of substantial human right in debtors. It is thus wrong to think of Arthur's sense of obligation about his debts as having mainly symbolic importance. In writing *Little Dorrit*, Dickens as a moralist and a writer is committed to the view that debts represent inalienable and human obligations. This commitment is inextricably a part of the vision and energy of the whole work.

The confident dogmatism which marks the expression of such opinions in *Little Dorrit* finds further expression in Dickens's readiness to type and classify his characters. This is a habit which many of the characters themselves indulge in; it helps them and the reader to establish a substantial, relatively stable world, in which the problems facing society can be solidly and concretely represented in relatively simple terms. The process is typified in Mr Meagles's remarks about the French:

'. . . They're always at it. As to Marseilles, we know what Marseilles is. It sent the most insurrectionary tune into the world that was ever composed. It couldn't exist without allonging and marshonging to something or other – victory or death, or blazes, or something'. (i, 2)

Mr Meagles makes his world coherent by reducing and simplifying revolution and insurrection to a matter of 'allonging and marshonging'. In exactly the same way the world of the novel is secured by the reduction and simplification of a number of representative characters, from Mr Merdle's Chief Butler, through Bar, Physician, Bishop, and the Barnacles, to the fuller and more detailed studies of Mrs Gowan, Mrs General, Mr Casby, the Plornishes, and Cavalletto. But it would be to underestimate the complexity of Dickens's method to imagine that Mr Meagles's efforts in the same direction show its limits; nor is it to criticize the mode adversely to suggest that it offers the reader (as in Dickens's early novels) fixed, generally reassuring and familiar categories of good and evil, truth and error, right and wrong, neatly and dramatically polarized in figures like John Baptist and Blandois. It is here that Dickens establishes a confident common ground with his readers; and though the judgements implicit in, say, the portrait of Mr Casby may be complex, causing the middle-class reader at least some discomfort, the laughter he is betrayed into, in spite of his own opinions and interests, arises out of an imaginative world in which the basic moral categories (love, patience, duty, debt) and the basic social facts (riches, government, poverty, crime) are as fixed and familiar as the changeless caricatures involved in the action.

The imaginative flexibility of this technique is considerable; it can even stand the strain of self-parody and self-criticism (often with brilliantly funny results) as in the description of the ladies in Mrs Merdle's drawing-room: 'the file of beauty was closed up by the bosom. Treasury said, Juno. Bishop said, Judith' (i, 21). More significant is the splendidly unpleasant 'Patriarch', Mr Casby. His choice, in bad faith, of a fixed simple role for himself suggests the secured smugness such an approach can lead to. But an even greater challenge to this habit of simplifying the human condition into fixed roles and types is suggested by Blandois. Thinking exclusively in such terms is at the heart of his wickedness. In choosing the role of 'cosmopolitan gentleman' for himself and imposing on others roles that suit his convenience, he identifies life with acquisitiveness: '. . . If you try to prejudice me, by making out that I have lived by my wits – how do your lawyers live – your politicians – your intriguers – your men of the Exchange?' (i, 1). His grotesque division of human beings into strong and weak, gentlemen and servants, exposes in an extreme form the inhumanity inherent in reducing men and women into types. And yet this is all he is himself – a crudely typed villain-figure. Nevertheless it is through him that

Dickens states his keen awareness of the moral, if not the aesthetic limitations inherent in this method of presenting character.

The question arises however – is there more than just self-diagnosis here? Did Dickens merely recognize the limitations of his method or did he rise above them? Most modern criticism still sticks to the view that Dickens rarely gives us anything but 'fixed figures, in phrase and appearance, "grossly and sharply told"' (as Raymond Williams puts it); his characters, 'isolated by their fixed public appearance',[10] are thereby limited in their relations with each other to the arbitrary interconnections of chance and coincidence. Williams of course is gratifyingly insistent on keeping Dickens in mind as a writer 'whose view of society is not available for reduction or detachment from his whole view of life, and to whom what others call an "interest" in society or sociology is a directly personal energy and commitment';[11] but he does set a limit, nonetheless, on Dickens's whole approach to the novel and therefore on the vision of man and society which arises out of it. Everything that is hidden or falsified by 'fixed figures, in phrase and appearance' must be hidden and falsified in a Dickens novel. Nor will it do to argue that those obscurities and falsifications are what Dickens wishes to expose; the question put by Henry James in his review of *Our Mutual Friend* has to be met:

> Who represents nature?
> Accepting half of Mr Dickens's persons as intentionally grotesque, where are those exemplars of sound humanity who should afford us the proper measure of their companions' variations?[12]

If Dickens does confine himself to grotesque or fixed characters, if he never brings book and reader into contact with humanity unfixed and free, then his view of people and society is necessarily a limited one. Edmund Wilson would be right to argue that Dickens's 'concrete way of looking at society' makes him 'sometimes actually stupid about politics';[13] and a similar logical link would be established between Orwell's suggestions, that Dickens's characters are 'finished and perfect',[14] and that his view of society is of an unchangeable natural order.[15] In other words the traditional judgement, voiced by James and still accepted by critics as influential as Wilson and Williams, that Dickens gives us only grotesques and no 'exemplars of sound humanity' places Dickens, logically, as being more or less conservative in his social attitudes and judgements. Certainly he can only be considered a truly radical writer if he breaks out of this grotesquerie. Equally, because this grotesquerie is merely what his readers want from him, it is necessary to show that he is ready to risk a really thorough-going radicalism if James's judgement – that he is a *superficial* novelist – is to be resisted.

Mr Meagles and his household suggest very clearly how the problem can be met. Mr Meagles is a good humane man; the failures, therefore, in his approach to life – and as we have seen his approach is precisely the 'safe' one of controlling the world by categorizing it – bring the novel into contact with dangerously unfixed human experiences. His insufficiencies go beyond that middle-class failure of intelligence which makes his estimate of Doyce so grossly inadequate; his failure with Tattycoram points to a complete breakdown, in terms of sympathy, understanding and charity, between the classes. What the well-intentioned, warm-hearted Meagles family cannot admit to themselves is their inability to give Tattycoram equal human status with Pet. The ugly fact is disguised in a funny name, the awkwardness glossed over in a show of eccentricity, informality, and facetiousness, by tricks in fact which are distinctively Dickensian. Tattycoram might almost be the representative of all Dickens's other grotesques rising in violent revolt against their author for giving them silly names and fixing them in phrase and appearance; but it is precisely this revolt – against phrase and appearance – which registers the rage of the servant-class against cosy, middle-class paternalism. Dickens in short recognizes the close relation between his fixed comic world and his fixed bourgeois attitudes – and arranges for both to blow up in the faces of his readers and poor Mr Meagles at the same moment.

The effects of Tattycoram's rebelliousness are thoroughly unsettling. We are not merely faced with irreconcilable claims on our sympathy (which both the Meagleses and Tattycoram certainly have a right to), but with a dangerous loss of all clear moral perspective – especially in relation to Pet:

'Oh, Tatty!' murmured her mistress, 'take your hands away. I feel as if some one else was touching me!'

She said it in a quick involuntary way, but half playfully, and not more petulantly or disagreeably than a favourite child might have done, who laughed next moment. Tattycoram set her full red lips together, and crossed her arms upon her bosom. (i, 16)

Nothing here is certain. Tattycoram's feelings towards Pet are anyway ambiguous ('. . . I hate her! They make a fool of her, they spoil her . . .' (i, 2)) and her resentment has something to do with her own adult intelligence which enables her to see the mistakes the Meagleses are making. But she *touches* Pet, and in view of her developing relations with Miss Wade, this thoroughly unsettles all easy interpretations of the incident. It becomes impossible to decide which reaction (Pet's to Tattycoram's touch, Tattycoram's to Pet's rudeness) is the healthier and more human. What becomes clear, however, is that both are alive in dangerously unfixed ways which cannot be contained in their roles of child–mistress and child–maid. They are something altogether different from the sort of human beings suggested by the silly names a loving, sentimental, and insecure Mr Meagles has given them.

Tattycoram's rebellion leads to Miss Wade. In spite of Dickens's expressed hope that 'The History of a Self-Tormentor' (ii, 21) would integrate smoothly with the rest of the novel,[16] it seems to me an excellent thing that it does not. Its awkwardness challenges the reader. It cannot be explained away as mere background or the tidying up of loose ends (like, for instance, the hurried account of Mrs Clennam's past sins). Instead, in the unfolding of the story, it intrudes as something which is gratuitous and ugly and which therefore cannot be ignored. And because it calls attention to itself like this, it challenges uncompromisingly the domestic security of all the Meagles-type households in which the novel is being read. The autobiography of a lesbian who is first engaged to a pleasant middle-class young man, then runs off with his aristocratic friend, and finally seduces the maid-servant of her own ex-lover's wife – it defies the whole range of literary and domestic decorum which the domestic reading of novels in middle-class families assumed. It is relentlessly ambiguous ('Upon that, the aunt fondled her . . .'); motives are subconsciously sullied ('The mother was young and pretty. From the first, she made a show of behaving to me with great delicacy.' 'I saw directly, that they had taken me in, for the sake of the dead woman . . .'); ordinary habits of mind are bitterly scrutinized ('I have an unhappy temper, I suppose.' – 'I did not say that.' – 'It is an easy way of accounting for anything'). Of course Dickens condemns Miss Wade. He rightly expects the reader to be shocked and angered by her, and not to be misled by false sympathy either for her or for Tattycoram, into rejecting the human good represented by Mr Meagles. But he insists that Miss Wade cannot be ignored and that Mr Meagles has no effective way of coping with such bitterness of heart. Dickens takes his stand firmly in the Victorian sitting-room, but with an adult consciousness of raw, uncontrollable human fact which is incompatible with all Mr Meagles stands for. This recognition is thoroughly 'radical'. It strains the assured manly confidence of his relations with his readers, between his art and their sensibility, between shared laughter in a safe world and shared humanity in an unsafe one.

It is because the novel shifts between secure fixtures, clear judgements, confident assertions, and middle-class values on the one hand, and unfixed dangers and ambiguities on the other, that its development and therefore its narrative structure are so important. The reader must first be made familiar with a solid world in which the broad facts of human life are fixed in controllable categories; only then can the break-up of that world challenge his sense of personal and social security. It must not be thought however that Dickens does not remain, in part, committed to the fixed world. The tensions are as present for him as for his readers; in a sense they are experienced simultaneously. Dickens, Mr Meagles, and the reader are all one, just as the aesthetic, psychological and social contradictions, which the novel deals with, are all one. The effort for Dickens was almost unbearable; it is significant that he should have become obsessed with the idea of setting an entire story 'on the top of the Great St Bernhard', just as, two years earlier, he had longed to break free himself from life, and live 'above the snow-line in Switzerland'.[17] The strain of belonging and not belonging, simultaneously and with equal energy, was too great.

The position of Arthur Clennam in the novel is thus like Dickens's own as author. Throughout the book Arthur is constantly having to revise or withhold judgements about the people he meets – Pancks for instance; he is unable to relax in the certainties implied by fixed phrase and appearance. He is equally tentative and uncertain in his general ideas, at once anxious not to project his own depression on the world at large, and yet constantly finding that the world is reinforcing his private anxieties; he is confident on matters of principle, tense and uncertain in the face of life itself. In other words, both Arthur and Dickens are actively and dangerously *inside* the very situations they observe with detachment; and, like the reader, they need to see the world in the reassuring terms of fixed phrase and appearance as well as to feel the dangers and learn the lessons of finding that it is not so.

Both Flora and John Chivery are relatively simple instances of how these tensions reveal themselves. On the one hand they are comic formulae; Flora, the 'moral mermaid' is a caricature of the middle-aged Maria Beadnell, John 'great of soul, poetical, expansive, faithful' (i, 18), a caricature of the young Dickens who had loved her so extravagantly. But they are not left as puppets whose antics are only a sign of the puppet-master's energy and vision. When John Chivery approaches Amy on the bridge, she backs away from him 'with an expression in her face of fright and something like dislike . . .' (i, 18); and the fact of this understandable but hurtful dislike modifies our sense of John's sensibility as something merely comic. The ground is prepared in fact for his great encounter with Mr Dorrit's feeble snobberies on the latter's last visit to London; his vulnerability makes John's point of view, and not merely Dickens's important. In the same way Flora comes generously alive at the wedding of Amy and Arthur. Without losing their fixed phrases and appearances, John his inventiveness as a composer of epitaphs, Flora her free-associating garrulity, both break out of their comic shells as a challenge to their fellow-characters and the reader alike. As John Holloway has pointed out,[18] this happens to a large number of characters in *Little Dorrit*. It is moreover, a central element in the treatment of class and wealth in the novel.

Throughout *Little Dorrit* the entire class-system is seen in terms of the imposition of roles on other people. Mrs Gowan assimilates the Meagleses by confining them to roles in which she can patronize them. William Dorrit does the same to his 'pensioner', Old Nandy. Fixing the world's appearance hides the uncomfortable facts of social reality. It obscures human truths and human obligations. It is corrupt, evasive, and – in Mr Dorrit – sad:

> The Father of the Marshalsea had never been offered tribute in copper yet. His children often had, and with his perfect acquiescence it had gone into the common purse, to buy meat that he had eaten, and drink that he had drunk; but fustian splashed with white lime, bestowing halfpence on him, front to front, was new.
> 'How dare you!' he said to the man, and feebly burst into tears.
> The Plasterer turned him towards the wall, that his face might not be seen; and the action was so delicate, and the man was so penetrated with repentance, and asked pardon so honestly, that he could make him no less acknowledgement than, 'I know you meant it kindly. Say no more'. (i, 6)

When the fixities of the class-system break down, Dorrit and Plornish have to face their exposed common humanity: they quickly retreat. The whole strategy of *Little Dorrit* is to confront the reader with a similar breakdown and to cut off his retreat, so that he has to face the full implications, social, political, and personal, of being simply human.

These tensions – between fixed and unfixed positions and between defensive and challenging social and political attitudes – explain the ambiguity in the novel's symbolism. Only rarely is a challenging symbol simple: Doyce, for instance, is a fixed figure who survives the clumsier attempts of Mr Meagles and the Circumlocution Office to categorize him in ways that suit themselves; but apart from Amy he is in this unique, a point of firm, confident assertion. Generally in *Little Dorrit* the imaginative categories in which Dickens thinks about human problems are shifting and ambiguous. The great images (prison, river, journey, labyrinth etc.) may seem to have the solidity not of symbols but of phenomena observed; yet at the same time they are very hard to grasp and judge. The accoutrements of the soldiers in Italy hanging on the buildings, for instance (Dickens was clearly thinking of Napoleon III's occupying forces) seem 'like hosts of rats . . . (happily) eating away the props of the edifices that supported them . . .' (ii, 3). Rats here might seem a simple enough image if the first mention of them in the novel had not referred to them as 'other unseen vermin, in addition to the seen vermin, the two men' (i, 1); one of these men, admittedly, is Blandois, but the other is Cavelletto. Even more striking is the description of Covent Garden at night:

> where the miserable children in rags . . ., like young rats, slunk and hid, fed on offal, huddled together for warmth, and were hunted about (look to the rats young and old, all ye Barnacles, for before God they are eating away our foundations, and will bring the roofs on our heads!) . . .
>
> (i, 14)

'Rats' are obviously a complex and distinctively political idea in Dickens's thinking, relating significantly to that larger vision of the poor suggested by the hangers-on round the Marshalsea:

> As they eyed the stranger in passing, they eyed him with borrowing eyes – hungry, sharp, speculative as to his softness if they were accredited to him, and the likelihood of his standing something handsome. Mendicity on commission stooped in their high shoulders, . . . frayed their button-holes, leaked out of their figures in dirty little ends of tape, and issued from their mouths in alcoholic breathings. (i, 9)

Lawrence describing miners could not be more subtle, acute and uncompromising. The phrases and appearance of mendicity – static, sullen, impersonal – discover and identify a social evil. As in the rat images, the reader is faced with *fact*, and simultaneously his own reactions are exposed with disconcerting ruthlessness: anger at injustice mingles disturbingly with distaste for its victims. Dickens, in effect, like Mr Meagles, thinks about society in fixed, solid categories – 'Doyce', 'rats', 'mendicity' – but unlike Mr Meagles (or William Dorrit, or Mrs Gowan) he does not always do so for his own or the reader's comfort.

In contrast, the treatment of the upper-classes, high finance and the civil service in *Little Dorrit* must seem oddly brash and mechanical – in spite of Lionel Trilling's suggestion that the novel's 'finest power of imagination appears in the great general images whose abstractness is their actuality, like Mr Merdle's dinner parties, or the Circumlocution Office itself.'[19] This is another version, of course, of the fixed characters 'grossly and sharply told' praised by Raymond Williams, with institutions in this case replacing characters, and it is certainly true that the cumulative effect of writing of this sort is impressive. Sharpness of telling is as important as grossness. That Dickens should describe Bar, for instance, as 'in reference to KF, a suggested likeness in . . . many touches'[20] indicates how detailed these great abstract images were for him. The overall effect, however, is not of close observation but of an abstract satirical construction, of inflexible imaginative fixity, symbolizing the oppressive inhumanity of a whole social system. Man becomes his function. Bar and Bishop lack even Affery's individuality; mere cardboard figures, they surround stiffly the oozy nothing of Merdle's wealth. It is a brilliant image – and yet, beside the organic complexity of the great images in the novel of journeys, prison, and the family, it seems unsubtle, remote from that passionate, difficult, questioning thinking about society which one finds, for instance, in the descriptions of the Marshalsea, or the frozen figures in the St Bernhard Pass. It is, in short, satire Mr Meagles would easily – too easily – see the point of; but it is also the most overtly political element in the novel. Is it then the case that when it came to attacking the actual political and economic structures of English society the radicalism of Dickens's imagination faltered, and the reader's imagination was left morally and politically unharassed?

In this connection, however, the emergence of Mr Merdle is crucial. To begin with he is just a fixed figure, perpetually taking himself into custody. Then the following exchange takes place between him and Mrs Merdle, and for the first time we sense the man himself, lonely, jaded, detached from life:

'You don't want me to scream, Mrs. Merdle, I suppose,' said Mr. Merdle, taking a chair.

'Indeed I don't know,' reported Mrs. Merdle, 'but that you had better do that, than be so moody and distraught. One would at least know that you were sensible of what was going on around you.'

'A man might scream, and yet not be that, Mrs. Merdle', said Mr. Merdle, heavily. (i, 33)

He reappears in this mood in that singularly oppressive chapter 'The Evening of a Long Day' (ii, 24). The reader, of course, knows why he wants to borrow the tortoise-shell handled penknife, and it is this which makes the lonely emptiness of his exchange with Fanny so terrifying. It is all part of the tremendous build-up before the long-expected crash which follows Merdle's suicide and which overwhelms all the major characters. The desire for Merdle to kill himself and the crash to come, the desire in other words for the relief that must follow of just and vigorous anger at corruption and fraud in high places, intensifies unbearably. And when it does come it is gratifyingly complete. In a great wave of impassioned, angry prose, Dickens, on behalf of small investors everywhere, couples 'the name of Merdle . . . with every form of execration' and declares him to be 'simply the greatest Forger and the greatest Thief that ever cheated the gallows'. On the other hand, the image of Merdle in Fanny's vexed, watery eyes, going to his death and yet appearing 'to leap, and waltz, and gyrate, as if he were possessed by several Devils' (ii, 24), calls the whole simplification into question.

The key to this doubt is provided by Physician. Dickens heightens the tension before the suicide by dawdling, as it were, over this unexpectedly enigmatic figure who is, however, more than a mere narrative trick. He finds his way into life's 'darkest places', 'like the rain, among the just and the unjust', and yet he is also an attractive man: 'Where he was, something real was', and the guests at his dinner table 'came out so surprisingly . . . they were almost natural' (ii, 25). It is in the company of this man that we are led, in the middle of the night, to the dead Merdle:

> There was a bath in that corner, from which the water had been hastily drained off. Lying in it, as in a grave or sarcophagus, with a hurried drapery of sheet and blanket thrown across it, was the body of a heavily-made man, with an obtuse head, and coarse, mean, common features.

Merdle, who had been 'the name of the age', according to Mr Dorrit (ii, 5), is now 'carrion at the bottom of a bath'; but dead flesh under the frock-coat of a financier is precisely the reality, 'the monstrous impropriety' (ii, 25), which Physician knows and faces. The reader has been drawn by narrative excitement and the anticipated pleasures of righteous anger to face something every bit as indecorous as the sins of Miss Wade – the naked grey corpse of a suicide. The novel's great abstract images of power and class, finance and government, with their stiff abstract anonymity, their comfortingly obvious failings, their reassuring fixity in ridiculous postures, collapse; like Tattycoram bursting out of her name, Physician's reality – humanity stripped – breaks out of the fixtures of phrase and appearance which Dickens has lured the reader into accepting; and the full range of human, sensuous activity which Merdle's naked body at once suggests and denies is seen to stand in frightening opposition to the *whole* world of the novel, to the domestic intimacy of Dickens's relations with his readers as well as to the imperturbability of Bar and Bishop. The point comes over more impressively if we think of Mrs Merdle's comically marble bosom, her comically unchucked chin, and her envy of 'Savages in Tropical Seas'. Cold flesh is no longer funny. In both the Merdles it points to areas of dangerous truth which a whole society is bent on suppressing.

Ten years earlier, Dickens had attacked the Malthusian economists with their

> politico-economical principle that a surplus population must and ought to starve . . . There is a sense and humanity in the mass, in the long run, that will not bear them . . . Not all the figures that Babbage's calculating machine could turn up in twenty generations, would stand in the long run against the general heart.[21]

'Physician's reality' is this 'general heart', the humanity which Merdleism and Barnacleism deny. It enforces an astonishingly profound radicalism. In effect, having first of all allied himself with his middle-class public in caricaturing and ridiculing the posturings of the great and powerful, Dickens suddenly presents them with this image of a 'face and figure . . . clammy to the touch' and a white marble bath 'veined with dreadful red', with an image, in short, of humanity denied, which is as shattering to their own peace of mind as it is to the system they have felt comfortably free to criticize. *Little Dorrit* thus breaks out of its own imprisoning ways of thought and feeling; and because those ways of thought and feeling have successfully portrayed the political, economic and social structures of nineteenth-century England to break out of them is to assert that English society is itself an imprisoning structure.

III

If, then, *Little Dorrit* enacts its own liberation, revolution must be one of its main themes. Arthur Clennam's fantasies, for instance, when he is accidentally locked up inside the most inflexible fixture in the novel – the Marshalsea – have precise political as well as psychological significance:

> As to escaping [he wonders], what chances there were of escape? Whether a prisoner could scale the walls . . . alight on a housetop, steal down a staircase, let himself out at a door, and get lost in the crowd? As to Fire in the prison, if one were to break out while he lay there? (i, 8)

Fantasies about an individual's liberation lead naturally to frightened fantasies of the whole prison-structure being destroyed. But terms like 'individual' and 'society' are hardly applicable. For Dickens, social, political, and economic tensions in conflict with human freedom merge into psychological tensions. Writing to Layard while at work on *Little Dorrit* he described the mood of the English poor as 'extremely like the general mind of France before the breaking-out of the first Revolution, and is in danger of being turned . . . into such a devil of a conflagration as never has been beheld since'; he finds the tensions unbearable and longs for the people to 'stir themselves in the vigorous national manner'.[22] In another letter he describes the writing of *Little Dorrit* as a blowing off of steam 'which would otherwise blow me up . . .'[23] *Little Dorrit* was written in other words by a Dickens intensely conscious not only of social imprisonment, but also of the violence implicit in it, and the need for, and yet the dangers of, a decisive conflagration 'breaking out'.

It would be a mistake however to see the violent Dickens as the most revolutionary. The very impatience of his radicalism, his tendency to smash through imprisoning difficulties, is rather like the reactionary fierceness of the landlady at the Break of Day; and quite clearly the novel supports a respectable kind of middle-class violence, like Mr Meagles's in the Circumlocution Office. More disturbing is the figure of Frederick Dorrit, breaking out of his fixed condition of being 'dead without being aware of it' (i, 20), and charging down the footman who, he thinks, has insulted Amy, nearly trampling him to death with his mule (ii, 3). This delight in outbursts of rage in

Little Dorrit cannot be dissociated from Dickens's tendency to assert, 'in the vigorous national manner', strong-armed, simple-minded solutions to human problems, to think, in other words, in the idiom of *A Child's History of England*. This links up with the unsatisfactory collapse of Mrs Clennam's house; on all but the first reading anyway, it is an amusingly and carefully prepared red-herring in the plot, but as a piece of symbolism it is altogether too crude. Certainly if, as T. A. Jackson suggests, it prophesies 'a like fate awaiting the Circumlocution Office . . .',[24] the gesture is too simple to be genuinely radical. Violence of this kind in *Little Dorrit* is part of the indignant, 'Meagles' side of Dickens which seeks arbitrary solutions to particular problems rather than risk calling in question the viability of the whole structure. It is after all just this false sort of approach which Dickens is able (with remarkable honesty and inclusive awareness) to satirize in William Dorrit:

> '. . . I – hum – I caused you to be respected there, Amy. I – ha hum – I gave my family a position there. I deserve a return. I claim a return. I say, sweep it off the face of the earth and begin afresh. Is that much? I ask, is *that* much?' (ii, 5)

There could be no acuter exposure of the deficiencies of a certain kind of radicalism. It is another, and a far more complex radicalism which is at the heart of the novel's political vision.

The problems posed by violence are central to this complexity. After all, the central issue in the nineteenth-century debate about democracy was, precisely, violence; and unlike most of his contemporaries – Arnold, Mill, George Eliot – Dickens recognized both that violence already existed in the very structures of capitalism and possibly in human nature itself also, and that the problems posed by non-violence were every bit as complex as those posed by violence. The former point of view is clearly suggested in the excesses endured by Affery at the hand of Flintwich, and even more significantly in Mr F's Aunt, with her blackly comic paroxysms of formless hatred against Arthur Clennam. It is easy enough to see the violent malice in Blandois, Henry Gowan, Miss Wade, and Tattycoram as an *addition* to their personalities, the product of choice; but the violence

95

in Mr F's Aunt is simply a fact of nature. On the other hand, in Doyce, peacefulness too looks like a fact of nature. Doyce offers a definite norm of steadiness: his 'composed and unobtrusive self-sustainment' is based on 'a calm knowledge that what was true must remain true . . .' (i, 16). Dickens is too complex a writer, however, to rest content with such a simple antithesis. Beside the intellectual repose of Doyce there is the nauseous glow of 'vacant serenity' in Mr Casby, at whose table 'everything . . . promoted quiet digestion . . .' (i, 13). Peace, the absence of the fierce energies which arise out of repressed instinct and feeling, is as ambiguous as the violence it replaces.

It is significant, too, that Doyce and Casby are 'peaceful' precisely in their public functions as inventor and landlord; and in this connection the figure of Mrs General, 'delegated on her mission, as it were by Church and State . . .' (ii, 2), becomes important. Her peace, and that of her Cathedral city rentier class, is secured by a wilful blindness to all that might disturb it, and since the serenity she thereby secures comes so near to injuring Amy, it is perhaps the unloveliest condition the novel describes. It is based on lies: 'Accidents, miseries, and offences' are not to be mentioned before her, and 'Passion . . . [must] go to sleep' in her presence. That 'passion' is the enemy to her way of life, becomes vividly obvious whenever she goes to sleep herself, whether she is just 'safely tucked up for some hours' (ii, 7), or, more elaborately, sent to dream dreams ' – if she had any – ' that 'ought to have been varnished . . . lying asleep in the arms of the good Saint Bernhard, with the feathery snow falling on his house-top' (ii, 2). It is not revolution as such which threatens Mrs General's world, but the insurrections of ordinary human feeling.

The theme of passivity has thus the deepest and most disturbing implications for the whole novel. In the Marshalsea, indeed, it is a disease:

'. . . Elsewhere [says the doctor who delivered Little Dorrit], people are restless, worried, hurried about, anxious respecting one thing, anxious respecting another. Nothing of the kind here, sir. We have done all that – we know the worst of it; we have got to the bottom, we can't fall, and what have we found? Peace. That's the word for it. Peace'. (i, 6)

Dickens is acutely sensitive to the human degeneration involved in surrender to hopeless circumstances, passive submission to social evil. He has also a profound sympathy for those who seek this kind of *ersatz* salvation, debtors in the Marshalsea, blank-faced musicians in cheap theatres, old drunkards stumbling back to the workhouse, even the imprisoned Arthur Clennam. But above all in William Dorrit he confronts us with a humane and moving study of both violent and peaceful impotence. In his worst moods Dorrit turns on Amy with a feeble cruelty which only invented dignities for himself, and promises of like dignity for her, can soothe; only then can he lie down 'with wet eyelashes, serene, in a manner majestic, after bestowing his life of degradation as a sort of portion on the devoted child upon whom its miseries had fallen so heavily . . .' (i, 19). In the Marshalsea there is no question of resorting or not resorting to violence: society has deprived men of any adequate response, passive or enraged, to the conditions in which it has placed them.

This is the context for the two major studies of 'rebellion' in the novel, of Pancks against Casby and of Fanny against Mrs Merdle and Mrs General. Casby's corrupt passivity obviously contrasts with Pancks's explosive restlessness, and yet from the start Arthur Clennam is confusingly doubtful about him. Pancks's manner, unlike that of the other grotesques, makes it very difficult to pass even preliminary judgement on him. He is simultaneously benevolent and sinister, especially in his savage self-satire.

> 'Here am I,' said Pancks . . . 'What else do you suppose I think I am made for? Nothing. Rattle me out of bed early, set me going, give me as short a time as you like to bolt my meals in, and keep me at it. Keep me always at it, and I'll keep you always at it, you keep somebody else always at it. There you are with the Whole Duty of Man in a commercial country.' (i, 13)

This is more than an attack on Samuel Smiles. As in his insistence that in helping the Dorrit family he is only doing 'business', and in his terrible question, 'What business have I in this present world, except to stick to business? No business' (i, 23), Pancks here points to a level of pain only the greatest satire touches. Yet he is himself dangerous: 'a shadow on [Arthur's] papers caused him to look up for the cause. The cause was Mr Pancks.' The word 'cause' is insisted on almost cruelly. Most significantly of all, he is in a sense repudiated (just as he is preparing his triumph in bringing the Dorrits to a fortune) by Amy herself; 'looking musingly down into the dark valley of the prison', she doubts 'if he could tell many people, even their past or present fortunes'; when Maggie asks if he could have told 'the Princess' or 'the tiny woman' theirs, Amy, 'with the sunset very bright upon her', answers firmly 'No' (i, 24).

It is of course Pancks who gives Arthur 'the dangerous infection with which he was laden' (ii, 13) – Merdleism, and in doing so outlines the strongest possible case for co-operating with the Merdle system:

> 'One word more, Mr. Clennam,' retorted Pancks, 'and then enough for to-night. Why should you leave all the gains to the gluttons, knaves, and imposters? Why should you leave all the gains that are to be got, to my proprietor and the like of him? Yet you're always doing it. When I say you, I mean such men as you. You know you are. Why, I see it every day of my life. I see nothing else. It's my business to see it. Therefore, I say, urged Pancks, 'Go in and win!' (ii, 13)

Pancks here is rationalizing. In fact he hates himself for being infatuated with business, and his plea to Arthur is an attempt to get round what his own compulsion illustrates, that business and human feeling are incompatible. Distrusting himself, he looks to Arthur for the right combination of business success and human motivation. The attempt fails, Arthur is imprisoned, and Pancks has to face up to his dilemma on his own: so he turns on his proprietor, the Patriarch, and symbolically castrates him by cutting off his hair. It is a savagely radical gesture, but too quick, too easy, leaving an after-taste of ugliness and futility. Typically and tragically to the very end of the novel, Pancks, who is a good, brave man, can only give the reader a slightly alloyed pleasure.

Fanny offers a similarly paradoxical study in the pains and penalties of rebellion. Generosity and selfishness, pride and self-abasement, integrity and self-betrayal are continually at war in her. Trilling argues that Fanny is among those characters whom the novel condemns for sharing its own 'social bitterness',[25] but this is to miss that fact that in Fanny violent, uncontrolled rage is frequently the outcrop of her integrity. She wins our sympathy, for instance, in her first encounter with Mrs Merdle, though the things she says are clearly 'wrong' and painful to Amy, precisely because of her fierce hatred of patronage. She insists that it is necessary to make Mrs Merdle 'pay for it, you mean little thing. What else can you make her do? Make her pay for it, you stupid child; and do your family some credit with the money!' (i, 20). The name-calling of Amy is especially disarming; it is clearly an affectionate and disguised acknowledgement of guilt. Fanny is a very intelligent, self-knowing woman. Her dilemma is a serious one and its problems are adroitly suggested in this exchange with Mrs General:

> 'I should think so,' observed Miss Fanny, with a toss of her head, and a glance at her sister. 'But they would not have been recalled to our remembrance, I suspect, if Uncle hadn't tumbled over the subject.'
>
> 'My dear, what a curious phrase,' said Mrs. General. 'Would not inadvertently lighted upon, or accidentally referred to, be better?'
>
> 'Thank you very much, Mrs. General,' returned the young lady, 'no, I think not. On the whole I prefer my own expression.'
>
> This was always Miss Fanny's way of receiving a suggestion from Mrs. General. But, she always stored it up in her mind, and adopted it another time. (ii, 5)

Fanny's arrogant toss of the head is part of her integrity in resisting Mrs General, but it is followed by compromise. And in her determination to pay Mrs Merdle back, she again compromises by adopting the standards of the enemy. Just as she stood up for good prose only to make the choice of bad prose her own, so a wilful integrity marks her choice of Edmund Sparkler for a husband. Like Pancks she is drawn irresistibly to what she despises.

Her marriage emphasizes the similarities between her and Becky Sharp. It also points to Dickens as a far more serious and responsible artist than Thackeray. Becky's marriage in *Vanity Fair* is a fine piece of comic story-telling, a well-organized narrative *coup*. 'Taking Advice' (ii, 14), the chapter in which Fanny decides to marry Sparkler, is not nearly so dramatic – yet Fanny's account of her decision, proud because it is hers, shamefaced because she is telling Amy, is wholly beyond Thackeray's range:

> 'Short time or long time,' interrupted Fanny. 'I am impatient of our situation. I don't like our situation, and very little would induce me to change it. Other girls, differently reared and differently circumstanced

altogether, might wonder at what I say or may do. Let them. They are driven by their lives and characters; I am driven by mine.' (ii, 14)

For Dickens to grasp that internal energy can be as compulsive as fate is impressive enough. For Fanny to grasp it is astonishing. She becomes at once free and hopelessly enslaved: 'the way she had chosen lay before her, and she trod it with her own imperious self-willed step.' Fanny's freedom, moreover, like Pancks's energy, relates impressively to the major social and political themes of the novel. At the heart of her choice is a profound protest against all that Mrs Merdle and Mrs General stand for:

> 'And the dancer, Amy, that she has quite forgotten – the dancer who bore no sort of resemblance to me, and of whom I never remind her, oh dear no! – should dance through her life, and dance in her way, to such a tune as would disturb her insolent placidity a little. Just a little, my dear Amy, just a little!' (ii, 14)

'Dancing' here is vitality, instinct, the general heart, everything marble-smooth Merdleism petrifies into stiff, bodiless role-playing. Fanny intends to disturb, just a little, the placid inhumanity of the rich. And yet, marrying Sparkler will take the dancing out of her own life. Fanny's integrity, like Pancks's, savages itself; her wilfulness is brave, stupid, wrong, and inevitable.

Fanny and Pancks live at the heart of the social, political, and human dilemmas which the whole novel enacts. Their head-on encounter with the social and economic system (high finance, high society, and Westminster slums) force them into complex personal difficulties and complicated distortions of phrase and appearance, which they can only break out of at great cost. Their natural violence, the integrity and energy with which they live, drive them at times into open rebellion, at times into subversive co-operation with the system, but in the end it is all self-defeating and corrupting. In reality they are as helpless as William Dorrit.

IV

Little Dorrit, then, in its complex rejection of violent insurrection against the social system, is an astonishingly courageous statement of political despair. A problem remains, however, with Amy; her goodness seems a compromise, a sentimental attempt to assuage the pain. She is certainly a difficult character to get into focus. The sunlight is too likely to bathe her in symbolic glory, her line in allegory too feebly imitates Andersen's. And yet, in unexpected ways she is a success. When some notable misconceptions are set aside, like John Wain's suggestion that her relationship with her father leaves her 'in a permanently disabled psychological state . . .',[26] she emerges as one of Dickens's most sensitively perceived heroines. Her loneliness in Rome, like her resentment at her father's having to pay his debts 'in life and money both', has a feminine delicacy the opposite of sentimental. Yet intimations of sentimentality remain, all summed up in her nickname. It is, as Flora says, '. . . of all the strangest names I ever heard the strangest, like a place down in the country with a turnpike, or a favourite pony or a puppy or a bird . . .' (i, 23); or, it might be added, like Little Nell, or little Em'ly. But this would be to miss the point more thoroughly than Flora does, because the name Little Dorrit, and Amy's childish exterior, are meant to be misleading. She is fixed, but by phrase and appearance only, in a misleading role. She is not a child; on the contrary Dickens is repudiating very subtly his earlier faith in immaturity. The middle-class sentimentalizing of grown women into little girls produces Pet Meagles, not Amy Dorrit. Amy may have a childish form, but she has an adult personality. The point is made repeatedly in phrases like 'the Child of the Marshalsea began her womanly life', and 'she passed to and fro. . . shrinkingly now, with a womanly consciousness that she was pointed out to every one' (i, 7). One of her chief sources of pain in the novel is Arthur Clennam's failure to recognize this 'womanly consciousness' in her feelings towards him. All the other characters (except Maggie) fail in this respect even more markedly than Arthur; and when the prostitute runs away from her on finding she is not a child she is simply joining most of the other characters in the book in deliberately refusing to accept the possibility of *adult* goodness and innocence.

But Amy is also a success because she relates impressively to the novel's main themes. Against the negative passivity of Casby and Mrs General on the one hand, and the doubtfully altruistic rebelliousness of Pancks and Fanny on the other, her positive, humane, and mature calm and social usefulness are obviously important. Twice in coming out of the Marshalsea Arthur carries her 'quiet with him into the turbulent streets' (i, 35), once after their conversation about Mr Dorrit's debts, once in the closing paragraph of the novel. She is thus centrally relevant to the great problems of peace and violence posed in the novel – and yet it is difficult to place her exactly, to see her as anything but a gratuitous self-indulgence on Dickens's part, to relate her intelligently to the Circumlocution Office and the Merdle empire. She seems, in fact, out of place, miraculously unconditioned by her environment, a detached, invented evasion of the novel's problems.

Paradoxically, however, this invented quality points directly to her significance. If, in Marxist terms, the working-class 'claims no traditional status but only a human status',[27] then in Dickensian terms Amy is simply that 'human status'. The comparison, obviously, is awkward, but there are other elements in *Little Dorrit* which support it. Casby is remarkably like the 'self-satisfied private property' of Marx's *Holy Family*, enjoying his *'semblance* of human existence'; Pancks, Casby's dialectical opposite and the disturber both of Bleeding Heart Yard and his own peace, is 'the negative side of the contradiction, its restlessness within itself . . .'[28] Again their relations with the Plornishes are strikingly echoed in the Marxist claim that the bourgeoisie had destroyed 'all feudal, *patriarchal, idyllic* relations' – Mrs Plornish's 'counterfeit cottage' (ii, 13) comes easily to mind – leaving 'no other nexus between man and man than naked self-interest, than callous "cash payment".'[29] Certainly Marx's general description of the bourgeois epoch as a time of 'everlasting uncertainty and agitation'[30] matches the turbulent streets of *Little Dorrit*. Dickens's vision has subtler complexities, but both he and Marx share an overall sense of their times as being especially inhuman, and both set against them simple humanity as such without 'traditional status'.

Marx, however, believed that the proletariat would first have to undergo 'a *total loss* of humanity', thereby making neccessary 'a *total redemption of humanity*'. Amy suggests a different approach. Without explanation she is simply introduced into a totally unredeemed world as a rebuke both to smug quietism and the distortions of revolutionary anger. She is at the centre, in other words, of a literary rather than a practical appreciation of intransigent political and human problems; through her they are felt and judged; but she is not an instrument of change, a solution to the novel's problems. On the contrary, as Fanny says,

> . . . the virtues of the precious child are of that still character that they require a contrast – require life and movement around them to bring them out in their right colours and make one love them of all things . . . (ii, 24)

There is no question, in effect, of her reconciling us to the world of the novel. Rather she stands out against it, quietly in contrast to 'the noisy and the eager, and the arrogant and the forward and the vain', as they fret and chafe and make 'their usual uproar'; and because she does so peacefully and gratuitously, in poised, delicate adulthood, the novel finally asserts the complete incompatibility between humanity without 'traditional status' on the one hand, and nineteenth-century western Europe on the other.

Lionel Trilling suggests that 'the whole energy of the imagination of *Little Dorrit* is directed . . . to the search for the Will in which shall be our peace.'[31] I would argue, on the contrary, that it is directed towards disturbing the reader with the knowledge of an unbridgeable gap between humanity and human institutions. It leads him away from partial condemnations of specific evils, which fixing people and institutions in rigid categories makes possible, away from the kind of anger he is used to, and towards the kind he is afraid of. It also lures him into affection and sympathy for Amy, and then challenges him with the implications of her final happiness. And it does this effectively because it 'takes place' within the situation it describes; writing and reading the novel are public events; its tensions are not externally observed, but internally enacted and uncompromisingly acknowledged. It is because Dickens is within his situation, with his readers and therefore without historical perspective, that *Little Dorrit*, far from leading us to 'the Will in which shall be our peace', establishes instead grounds for our perpetual disquiet.

NOTES

1. J. Wain, '*Little Dorrit*', *Dickens and the Twentieth Century*, ed. by John Gross and Gabriel Pearson, London, 1962, p. 175.
2. R. Williams, 'Social Criticism in Dickens. Some problems of method and approach', *Critical Quarterly*, VI, p. 219.
3. J. Forster, *The Life of Charles Dickens*, ed. and annotated with an Introduction by J. W. T. Ley, London, 1928, p. 246.
4. *Ibid.*, p. 600.
5. J. Butt and K. Tillotson, *Dickens at Work*, London, 1957, p. 225.
6. G. Orwell, 'Charles Dickens', *Collected Essays*, London, 1961, pp. 40, 68.
7. I quote from *The New Oxford Illustrated* ed. (1953).
8. *Household Words*, xiv, no. 336, 30 August 1856, pp. 145–7.
9. E. Johnson, *Charles Dickens His Tragedy and Triumph*, London, 2 vols., 1953, II, pp. 604–5.
10. R. Williams, *op. cit.*, p. 219.
11. *Ibid.*, p. 214.
12. H. James, 'The Limitations of Dickens', *The Dickens Critics*, ed. by George H. Ford and Lauriat Lane, Jr., New York, 1961, p. 51.
13. E. Wilson, 'Dickens: The Two Scrooges', *The Wound and the Bow, Seven Studies in Literature*, Cambridge, 1941, p. 26.
14. G. Orwell, *op. cit.*, p. 82.
15. *Ibid.*, p. 37.
16. J. Forster, *op. cit.*, p. 626.
17. *Ibid.*, pp. 638–9.
18. J. Holloway, 'Introduction', *Little Dorrit*, Penguin English Library Edition, 1967, pp. 24–5.
19. L. Trilling, '*Little Dorrit*', *The Dickens Critics*, p. 293.
20. J. Forster, *op. cit.*, p. 625.
21. Ibid., pp. 412–3.
22. J. Butt, 'The Topicality of *Little Dorrit*', *U.T.Q.*, xxix, 4.
23. J. Butt and K. Tillotson, *op. cit.*, p. 226.
24. T. A. Jackson, *Charles Dickens: The Progress of a Radical*, London, 1937, p. 169.
25. L. Trilling, *op. cit.*, p. 287.
26. J. Wain, *op. cit.*, p. 176.
27. K. Marx, 'Contribution to the Critique of Hegel's Philosophy of Right', *Early Writings*, trans. and ed. by T. B. Bottomore, London, 1963, p. 58.
28. K. Marx and F. Engels, *The Holy Family, or Critique of Critical Critique*, Moscow, 1956, p. 51.
29. K. Marx and F. Engels, *Manifesto of the Communist Party*, Moscow, 1955, p. 57.
30. *Ibid.*, p. 58.
31. L. Trilling, *op. cit.*, p. 293.

V

GEORGE ELIOT:
POLITICS AND PERSONALITY

WILLIAM MYERS

I

Trollope is a very much more knowing writer than Dickens. Not only
are his descriptions of business and parliament more circumstantial,
but even the way he tackles formal problems in his novels – the use of
coincidence, for instance – is more discreet. Yet in terms of subject
matter he and Dickens can have much in common. Roger Carbury in
The Way We Live Now, for instance, matches Arthur Clennam in
Little Dorrit, Georgiana Longestaffe matches Fanny Dorrit, Lord
Nidderdale, Edmund Sparkler. The really striking resemblance is of
course between Melmotte and Merdle (both based on John Sadleir,
M.P.), but it is possible to see some similarities in Pet Meagles and
Hetta Carbury and in Amy Dorrit and Marie Melmotte – though the
latter is also quite like Fanny. Both novels, moreover, tackle a number
of similar themes – high finance, emotional honesty in working-class
men, the avidity of some girls for the freedoms of marriage, the
patience of others in frustrated love, and, of course, problems of
filial obedience, especially those of courageous daughters with corrupted fathers. Their material in fact is thoroughly conventional, a fact
Dickens ruthlessly exploits. Trollope, in contrast, smoothly conforms.

The nature of his conventionality is suggested by the marriages of
Georgiana Longestaffe and Marie Melmotte. Trollope is always careful to marry his young women off in the approved fashion, Georgiana,
therefore, having first accepted a middle-aged Jewish widower, and
then given way to the protestations of her family because he cannot
afford a town-house for her, has to be hurriedly matched at the end
of the novel. Trollope is not entirely unsympathetic to her painful

and humiliating position as an unmarried woman in her late twenties whom no one seems to like or consider; but this is swept aside in his honourable anger at the family's antisemitism and her own mercenary lovelessness. His way of exposing and punishing this, however, is unsatisfactory to the exact degree that it enforces conventional standards. Mr Breghert is justified not as a Jew but as a gentleman, and Georgiana is abandoned to a 'celibate' curate (this is supposed to be funny) rather younger than herself. Marie Melmotte's fate is equally distasteful. The most engaging character in the novel, ready to elope rather than marry a title, and yet able to win respect and perhaps even affection from the stupid young lord she abandons, her loneliness and courage in facing up to her father are quite moving; but in the end she marries an American share-pusher, because there is no one else in the novel, of her class, for her to marry. In effect Trollope submits to all the conventions, pairing off his characters without disturbing social arrangements and assumptions which kept women in a position of humiliating dependence, and prevented men of good family from marrying decent girls of no family at all.

As a result, the treatment of major social questions in Trollope's novels – Mr Melmotte's swindling, for instance – though impressive at a documentary level, is finally uninteresting. Melmotte's entertainments, his parliamentary career, his final drunken exit from the Commons, and his suicide, arouse no more than mere gentlemanly disgust at the behaviour of a cad and a boor. Trollope never questions the social and power structure itself, only Melmotte's suitability for position and prestige within it. Share-pushing, like gambling, is a sign of personal decadence, forgery, like cheating at cards, its inevitable outcome. This is the level at which he thinks and judges, the level of personal values and relationships. And so in a novel like *The Prime Minister* the two plots, linked tenuously by the figure of Lopez, have little imaginative relation to each other. It is true that Lopez is a libellous, heavily disguised characterization of Disraeli, but the attack is exclusively personal, not political. The Duke of Omnium, though Prime Minister, is seen in equally personal terms – he has a fine, sensitive distaste for practical politics, an acknowledged lack of interest in policy, and a dedicated patriotism. He is in fact a good man, reluctant to take office, and then – the human touch –

reluctant to leave it. One or two of his colleagues match him in virtue, but most are morally mediocre. They are all, however, gentlemen – unlike Lopez and Major Pountney, who are vulgarians and cads and who fail, anyway, to get into Parliament. The novel reveals Trollope's dislike of the coarser side of nineteenth century politics, but its casual dismissal of 'policies', like the retreat, in his best work, into the secure, personal world of the cathedral close, is more than a matter of private fastidiousness. It is a refusal to see human problems socially, an insistence that the only problems are personal, the only changeable factor in human affairs the individual personality. Trollope takes as fixed, and therefore ignores, the whole social and moral order, and as a result can offer only personal histories, arbitrarily (if deftly) inter-locked. The skeletal thinness of his achievement, in terms of symbol, action, and character emphasizes his failure to experience social fact with any density or complexity. He keeps safe within an exclusive and conservative interest in personality because he lacks the imagina-tive courage to challenge on any level, formal, intellectual, or moral, his readers' conventional habits of mind.

Trollope's novels suggest therefore that the consideration of political values and problems in personal terms is likely at least to limit and weaken a novelist's achievement. Such a position, however, could hardly be sustained merely on the evidence of a writer of Trollope's standing. The question can only be properly explored through the work of a novelist who is prepared to take the strain of justifying the position he has adopted. George Eliot is an obvious choice. Like Trollope she distrusts politicians and political pro-grammes, and asserts the primacy of personal factors in human affairs, but her work is marked by an earnest concern to encounter human problems whole. She doesn't disentangle herself from the trivia of political in-fighting merely out of personal distaste, but in order to grasp historical change in terms of personal growth and experience, and she writes openly as an intellectual – the disciple of Feuerbach, Spencer, and Comte. She is thus unlike Dickens, in that she detaches herself in effect from immediate involvement within society, assuming instead the distinctively intellectual stance of an observer; but she is even more unlike Trollope in her intense concern with the human fact in collective as well as individual terms.

Her distaste for politics in the narrow sense owes a great deal to her Positivism. Comte believed that even under ideal circumstances 'the intellectual mediocrity of the majority of men' and the innate self-ishness of human beings would remain potent factors in political and social life.[1] He himself turned his back on politics as such, on the great constitutional experiments of the nineteenth century and what he believed was their dangerous tendency to assert rights rather than duties; such trivia could attract only mediocre minds.[2] He asserted that society could and should be analysed scientifically, that his own Positivist philosophy had turned Government into a science as well as an art, and that politics should therefore be left to the expert. When the Rev Mr Debarry, in *Felix Holt*, remarks, '. . . If the instructed are not to judge for the uninstructed, why, let us set Dick Stubbs to make our almanacs, and have a President of the Royal Society elected by universal suffrage' (FH., Ch. 23),[3] he is taking a more or less Comtist position. It was not exactly George Eliot's, but it does represent an aspect of the conservatism which, with her approval, wins the North Loamshire election.

Her acceptance of this victory, however, arises less from a belief in experts, than from a fear of the intellectual and moral mediocrity of the majority of men. In *Middlemarch*, for instance, her hard-headed businessmen are overwhelmed by 'the confusion of a Tory ministry passing Liberal measures, . . . and of outcries for remedies which seemed to have a mysteriously remote bearing on private interest . . .' (Mm., Ch. 37). Nor is it just the commercially minded provinces that are confused: in all the later novels George Eliot treats the Reform Bill of 1832 and the political fever it engendered as a national waste of energy. This is a Comtist position: consti-tutional reform is irrelevant to the problems of newly industrialized societies. There may be times, of course, 'when faith in the efficacy of political change [is] at fever-heat', but afterwards, George Eliot insists, when 'wisdom and happiness do not follow, . . . comes a time of doubt and despondency' (FH., Ch. 16). Even in Savonarola's Florence, debates about the constitution are 'a question of boiled or roast . . .'; the decisive force – Savonarola – is 'outside the palace . . . [giving] the vague desires of [the] majority the character of a determinate will' (R., Ch. 35). This echoes the basic Comtist belief in the controlling power of public opinion, as Felix Holt calls it, 'the greatest power under heaven' (FH., Ch. 30). It was public opinion, in Comte's view, guided by a new 'spiritual power' replacing the old clergy, and not politics as such, which would create a just society, exactly the sort of alliance between intellectuals and workers in fact, which Savonarola and Felix Holt, in their different spheres, attempt to create. Just as Comte urged the French workers to leave politics to the middle-classes, to 'abdicate a political function that is either illusory or subversive', and to join the Positivist mandarins in shaming the bourgeoisie out of their 'misuse of power',[4] so Felix appeals to the workers of North Loamshire to drop politics and join him in shaping public opinion; 'ground by wrong and misery, and tainted with pollution' (FH., Ch. 10), they are intellectually and morally incapable of any other political role.

Positivist distrust of politics in George Eliot's work, however, runs deeper than this. She seems convinced that the inevitable articulation in political affairs of private and sectional interests necessarily undermines the moral standing of politicians. Romola, for instance, is deeply hurt when 'that political reform which had once made a new interest in her life' degenerates into 'narrow devices for the safety of Florence . . .' (R., Ch. 61); but her husband, Tito, positively enjoys 'his ability to tickle the ears of men with any phrases that pleased them' (R., Ch. 35), and even the upright Bernardo del Nero, in reference to Tito, accepts that there can be 'no sifting of political agents' (R., Ch. 45). The Positivists and George Eliot were agreed, in fact, that politics necessarily involved men in morally dubious choices, and they felt anyway that the desire for power (though not a more diffuse kind of political involvement) was itself corrupting. This can be seen both in Tito Milema and Harold Transome: the latter's willingness to tolerate corrupt practices ('treating' the miners) on the grounds that '[a] practical man must seek a good end by the only possible means . . .' (FH., Ch. 17), is symptomatic of a personality which is incapable, in private life, of 'any thorough understanding or deep respect' for others, and which, in public life, seeks merely 'the utmost enjoyment of his own advantages . . .' (FH., Ch. 43). It is thus doubly important for intellectuals, 'the spiritual power', to keep out of politics, a point Savonarola has grasped, at least in theory, when he tells Romola that he does not 'meddle . . . with the functions of the state' (R., Ch. 59). He is, of course, being disingenuous in saying this, since he has meddled with them already, and has thus lost for himself the independent moral perspective of the true upholder of principle. 'His need of personal predominance' (R., Ch. 25) has thus compromised the integrity of the spiritual power. Felix Holt, on the other hand, accepts his semi-sacerdotal role; he emphasizes the similarity of his position to that of the old Catholic priesthood in orthodox Positivist fashion (FH., Ch. 27), and repudiates both the middle-class scramble for power and the 'new wants and new motives' (FH., Ch. 5) that go with it.

George Eliot and Trollope, then, share a number of similar attitudes to politics. They find them morally distasteful, they distrust the whole business of appealing to people's self-interest, especially at elections, and they have no faith in political programmes. Like Trollope, too, George Eliot is nonetheless 'interested' in politics – if not, as he was, merely in the complexities of holding and distributing offices and honours. The nature of her political interest is brought into focus in the description in *Daniel Deronda* of Herr Klesmer's approach to life and politics as a 'fervour of creative work and theoretic belief [which] pierces the whole future of a life with the light of congruous, devoted purpose' (DD., Ch. 22). They key words here are 'theoretic belief': for George Eliot it was theory which gave politics their real dignity; they were not so much matters of practice as of belief. This, of course, is a centrally Comtist position: the essential mark, for Comte, of all human progress is 'the distinction between theory and practice . . . the separation of education from action . . . of morals from politics . . .'[5] Theoretical analysis, moreover, in Comte's view, reveals similar structures in the individual personality and society at large: the active class (soldiers, industrialists and politicians) correspond to the will, the speculative class (clergy and intellectuals) to the intelligence, and the affective class (the workers) to the emotions.[6] Social and moral progress are thus identical – an advance in both cases towards 'altruism' and 'rationality',[7] the struggle in the individual mind between egoism and altruism disclosing, in effect, 'the scientific germ of the struggle . . .

between the conservative and reforming spirit . . .'[8] The development of political theory, therefore, and the desire for social justice, are, *in themselves*, political events.

One does not have to attribute an over-rigorous Positivism to George Eliot to see how strongly *Felix Holt* supports this approach. The novel by-passes the political struggle between reforming and reactionary parties, and concentrates on a moral struggle between 'the conservative and reforming spirit'. And the spirit of reform, in Mr Lyon's words, is the search for that 'norm or rule for all men' which must ultimately, if human problems are to be solved, be 'written on all hearts, and be the very structure of all thought, and be the principle of all action' (FH., Ch. 13). Exactly according to Positivist prescription, a theoretical appreciation of the true and the good, acting first through the lives of individuals, eventually influences social activities and institutions; or, as Felix Holt puts it, the force to work the engines of political and social life 'must come out of human nature – out of men's passions, feelings, desires' (FH., Ch. 30).

Personality is thus the central political fact in both Positivist theory and George Eliot's novels. In *Romola*, for instance, the political condition of Florence outlined in the Proem is seen in terms of the thoughts and feelings of a typical Florentine; throughout the book phrases like 'made an epoch in the history of' are used with equal freedom of cities and people; and the major political events of the action are analysed in moral and psychological terms. The attitude of Florence to the French invaders, for instance, is shaped by 'certain moral emotions to which the aspect of the times gave the form of presentiments . . .' (R., Ch. 21), while the siege of Florence is notable for a new altruism in the people – the gates are kept open for the peasants (R., Ch. 42). The logic of such an approach is obviously to place an almost exclusive value on education; and so, in *Felix Holt*, the authentic work of reform takes place not through the ballot but in lectures to miners in a pub. (Comte, incidentally, had recommended using wine-shops for this purpose.)[9]

At the centre, therefore, of George Eliot's activity as a novelist is a theoretical exploration of human experience, since it is above all in visions and theories that historical realities are forged. This, as we shall see, has disadvantages for her work as a novelist, but it has one great advantage: because it detaches her both from the society she is writing about, and the society she is writing for, she cannot automatically assume the validity of the point of view she is adopting; she has to test and substantiate it in her work. We find her, therefore, constantly resisting her own conclusions in a way Trollope could never have attempted. On the small point of the corruptions of public life, for instance, *Middlemarch* and *Daniel Deronda* clearly attempt to modify the sanctimonious idealism of *Felix Holt*. Even in *Romola* there is the assertion that 'public spirit can never be wholly immoral, since its essence is care for a common good' (R., Proem), and in *Middlemarch* Ladislaw and Lydgate actually debate the question with interesting results. Lydgate takes the standard Comtist position, arguing that 'there is nothing more thoroughly rotten than making people believe that society can be cured by a political hocus-pocus.' Ladislaw argues against this kind of puritanism. '. . . That's my text [he says] – which side is injured? I support the man who supports their claims; not the virtuous upholder of the wrong' (Mm., Ch. 46). He argues in fact for the cause not the man, obviously because George Eliot wants to see politics as an honourable profession. In the end, however, she reverts to something like her position in *Felix Holt*, arguing for the man not the cause: Will does enter politics, but at a time 'when reforms were begun with a young hopefulness . . . which has been checked in our days . . .' The real justification for his doing so therefore, is not in the policies he supports but in his choice, since wrongs exist, to 'be in the thick of a struggle against them . . .' (Mm., Finale). It is especially significant that he should merely be in '*a* struggle' against injustice, just as the Florentine ghost cares for '*a* common good': the indefiniteness of both emphasizes the exclusively moral justification for their involvement. Nevertheless the study of Ladislaw is a serious, if not altogether successful attempt to test a particular Positivist prejudice, and explains perhaps how in *Daniel Deronda*, in many ways George Eliot's most idealistic novel, she can nonetheless present two such subtle, tolerant portraits of public men as Mr Gascoigne and Sir Hugo Mallinger – both outside her earlier range and superior to Trollope on his own ground.

This readiness to explore, test, and modify is characteristic of George Eliot's whole approach to life and thought; and in the later novels especially she seems determined to think independently of the great men who influenced her, Feuerbach and Spencer, as well as Comte. In all three there is an obsessive concern with history as an evolution of mind. For Comte, as we have seen, history is a process by which innate tendencies of human nature gradually shift towards altruism and rationality. For Spencer both evolution and history reveal a gradually developing 'correspondence' between life and its environment: the single cell's universe is identical with its physical structure; human consciousness, on the other hand, reaches far into the past and future, to stars and microbes, in increasingly extensive and complex relations with the world, the growth of culture, technology, and morality, being all part of the evolutionary process.[10] As well as sharing similar ideas, however, Comte and Spencer also shared a delight in systematizing: their language and ideas can have a merely mechanical complexity. Comte's definition of 'life' as 'a continuous and close adjustment of internal spontaneity with external fatality',[11] is typical of their dogmatic laboriousness. It was George Eliot's achievement, however, to grasp the substance behind their words, and recreate it in compact, vivid, and simple language. Thus Felix Holt, discussing 'taste' and 'opinions' with Esther Lyon, can refer quite closely to Spencer's ideas about 'correspondence' and the unity of all mental faculties, and yet never abandon, as Spencer does, the world of ordinary, concrete experience for that of mere abstraction:

> It comes to the same thing [he says]; thoughts, opinions, knowledge, are only a sensibility to facts and ideas. If I understand a geometrical problem, it is because I have a sensibility to the way in which lines and figures are related to each other; and I want you to see that the creature who has the sensibilities that you call taste, and not the sensibilities that you call opinions, is simply a lower, pettier sort of being – an insect that notices the shaking of the table, but never notices the thunder (FH., Ch. 10).

No novelist but George Eliot could bring good taste, geometry, insects, and thunder into such complex, lucid, and logical relations.

Thinking of this kind permeates her work. There is, for instance, far more than mere social documentation in her account, in the Introduction to *Felix Holt*, of the average Treby farmer, for whom 'Mail or stage coach . . . belonged to that mysterious distant system of things called "Gover'ment", which, whatever it might be, was no business of his, any more than the most out-lying nebula or the coal-sacks of the southern hemisphere . . .' Local history, wider social and economic history, scientific and technological progress, geography, psychology – all combined in a vast body of evolutionary theory, are at once assumed and illustrated in this sentence. 'Stage-coach', 'Gover'ment', 'coal-sacks', 'outlying nebula', as facts in the world and ideas in both the farmer's and the author's minds, are offered in uncomplicated syntactic relationships, and yet their actual, highly complex relations are not falsified. George Eliot's world-view may be derivative, but her understanding of it is individual and creative. This is why her comments on man and society are frequently so exact, complex, and profound. When, for instance she writes in *Romola*

> The same society has had a gibbet for the murderer and a gibbet for the martyr, an execrating hiss for a dastardly act, and as loud a hiss for many a word of generous truthfulness or just insight: a mixed condition of things which is the sign, not of hopeless confusion, but of struggling order. (R., Ch. 57)

her favourite abstraction, 'meliorism', could hardly be better explained. There is an exact blending of abstract and concrete in her best writing which ensures that phrases like '*a* common good' and '*a* struggle against wrong' suggest not indefiniteness but a strenuous search for exactness.

A basic factor in this search is the belief that one set of ideas and experiences is 'translatable' into another. In *Romola*, for instance, art, politics, and religion are each expressive of the other, the symbol of their unity being the architecture of the city:

> as the campanile in all its harmonious variety of colour and form led the eyes upward, high into the clear air of this April morning, it seemed a prophetic symbol, telling that human life must somehow and some time shape itself into accord with that pure aspiring beauty. (R., Ch. 3)

George Eliot : Politics and Personality

The basic idea behind this passage is given perhaps its most sophisticated expression in Klesmer's encounter with his rival for Miss
Arrowpoint, the rising party man, Mr Bult, in *Daniel Deronda*. Mr
Bult is very confused by Klesmer's dinner-table diatribe against
'the lack of idealism in English politics, which left all mutuality
between distant races to be determined by the need of a market . . .'
(DD., Ch. 22). Bult assumes that Klesmer is 'in a state of political
refugeeism which . . . obliged him to make a profession of his
music . . .'; but afterwards, in the drawing room, Klesmer insists on
his own political significance in his role as artist:

> . . . We help to rule the nations [he asserts] and make the age as much as
> any other public men. We count ourselves on level benches with
> legislators. And a man who speaks effectively through music is compelled
> to something more difficult than parliamentary eloquence.

Music and politics are thus, in Klesmer's view, aspects of each other,
and their interaction in the 'mind' of a society – in its culture – 'make
the age'. By the same token political ideas make the man. Political,
philosophical or ethical theories, in other words, like art and ritual,
work on the affective life independently of their purely intellectual
value. Even this recognition of their double function has a moral as
well as a theoretical significance. Klesmer's statement of faith is thus
a sign of his personal development, just as his qualities as a man
confirm on inclusive human grounds the validity of his sense of the
musician's political role. It is George Eliot's sensitive appreciation of
this which gives meaning to the comedy of Bult encountering
Klesmer at the piano, with Miss Arrowpoint standing by:

> 'I had no idea you were a political man.'
> Klesmer's only answer was to fold his arms, put out his nether lip, and
> stare at Mr. Bult.
> '. . . From what you said about sentiment, I fancy you are a Pan-
> slavist.'
> 'No; my name is Elijah. I am the Wandering Jew,' said Klesmer,
> flashing a smile at Miss Arrowpoint, and suddenly making a mysterious
> wind-like rush backwards and forwards on the piano . . .
> 'Herr Klesmer has cosmopolitan ideas,' said Miss Arrowpoint . . .
> 'He looks forward to a fusion of races.'

115

'With all my heart,' said Mr. Bult, . . . 'I was sure he had too much talent for a mere musician.'

This certainly suggests some human limitations in Klesmerism; but also reinforces the musician's claim to have his public life taken seriously. It does so above all in the delicacy and intelligence of Miss Arrowpoint's appreciation of his beliefs and in her love for the man. Music and politics thus give each other an identical human value in terms of individual human personalities; and the achievement of defining that value is wholly George Eliot's. Comte may have argued for the proposition that the central political reality is the human personality; but George Eliot has grasped what this means with an intelligence quite outside Comte's – never mind Trollope's – range.

II

George Eliot's thinking on history and politics, at its best, then, is both original and magnificently precise. It can, however, also be remarkably ill-disciplined. In *Romola*, for instance, there is the suggestion that 'fear' will lose its moral value 'only when all outward law has become needless – only when duty and love have united in one stream and made a common force' (R., Ch. 11). In what sense, metaphorically or positively, 'love' and 'duty' are 'forces' in human history is, however, left deliberately unclear. More serious is a misuse of religious vocabulary in *Romola*. When Savonarola tells Romola that her life is below that 'of the believer who worships that image of the Supreme Offering, and feels the glow of a common life with the lost multitude for whom that offering was made, and beholds the history of the world as the history of a great redemption . . .' (R., Ch. 40), the fact that, historically, '*a* common life' would in practice mean '*the* Catholic Church', is conveniently blurred. To establish a common ground between Catholicism and Positivism, phrases are made abstract and inclusive which in fifteenth century Florence could only have been specific and exclusive. Of course if George Eliot had made her meaning clearer, her English Protestant readers would certainly have objected to both Savonarola's views and her own. As it is they are left to interpret the words as they see fit. In notable contrast to Dickens, in fact, she deliberately seeks ways of *not* challenging her readers' convictions, a tendency especially noticeable in her treatment of political ideas. Ladislaw, for instance, is described by Mr Brooke as 'a kind of Shelley . . . I don't mean as to anything objectionable – laxities or atheism, or anything of that kind, you know . . . But he has the same kind of enthusiasm for liberty, freedom, emancipation . . .' (Mm., Ch. 37). Mr Brooke's vague vocabulary is amusingly confused, but in fact George Eliot hardly examines Ladislaw's beliefs with any greater precision herself. On the contrary she uses virtually Mr Brooke's methods to keep the novel's political and religious themes as indefinite as possible.

The indefiniteness in her political writing arises naturally out of her conviction that the real causes of history are 'cultural', in the spirit behind events, not in the events themselves. Georg Lukács criticizes Comte's great mentor, Saint Simon, for taking up just this position, for seeing 'the really decisive factor, that which really changes things, . . . [in] art, science, technology, religion, morality and world-view.'[12] It is a position which comfortably evades the challenge of slums, crime, disease, and violence that Dickens was prepared to face. To insist, as Deronda and Mordecai do, that it is the visionaries who are 'the creators and feeders of the world – moulding and feeding the more passive life which without them would dwindle and shrivel into the narrow tenacity of insects . . .' (DD., Ch. 55), is to ignore the concrete factors in social and economic life which make people passive and narrowly tenacious. Similarly, the description of the United States as 'a polity' formed from nothing 'but memories of Europe, corrected by the vision of a better' (DD., Ch. 42), takes no account of all the material factors which go into building a nation.

George Eliot habitually psychologizes social fact. For her, 'railways, steamships and electric telegraphs' influence human life primarily by 'making self-interest a duct for sympathy'.[13] Her approach is typified by the description in *Daniel Deronda* of 'the grand dim masses or tall forms of buildings which were the signs of world-commerce' (business may be sordid but its 'forms' are grand) entering into Mordecai's mood, 'as a fine symphony *to which we can hardly be said to listen* makes a medium that bears up our spiritual wings' (DD.,

Ch. 38 – italics mine). The acknowledged inattention is highly suggestive, bringing to mind all those grand dim masses of emotional prose associated with Mordecai himself. They have frequently been blamed on a residual immaturity in George Eliot, but in fact they follow naturally from the logic of her position. To assert the unity of aesthetic, moral, religious, and political experience, and to stress the overriding importance of the resulting vision, is inevitably to undervalue detailed observation and thought. It is significant that Ladislaw should argue that to insist on logic in the reform bill would make Mr Brooke 'a revolutionist' (Mm., Ch. 51). George Eliot would rather commerce should melt into music, and logic into dreams than that.

It is typical of her intellectual alertness, however, that she should recognize both this tendency to formlessness in her political thought, and the resulting need for something more concrete than vision in the real world. Into Mordecai's dream, therefore, there intrudes 'a blooming human life, ready to incorporate all that was worthiest' in his existence – Daniel Deronda. In a famous letter to Frederick Harrison George Eliot talks of the great difficulty she had in making 'ideas thoroughly incarnate' in her novels,[14] and the word 'incarnate' expresses exactly her method of giving positive historical reality to her thought. She seeks literally for affirmation of her ideas in her characters' flesh and blood. Savonarola is a notable example:

> Then he stretched out his hands, which, in their exquisite delicacy, seemed transfigured from an animal organ for grasping into vehicles of sensibility too acute to need any gross contact: hands that came like an appealing speech from that part of his soul which was masked by his strong passionate face . . .
>
> After the utterance of that blessing, Savonarola himself fell on his knees and hid his face in temporary exhaustion. Those great jets of emotion were a necessary part of his life; he himself had said to the people long ago, 'Without preaching I cannot live.' But it was a life that shattered him. (R., Ch. 62)

The historical forces which made and broke the Catholic spiritual power are seen here virtually in physiological terms. Savonarola's bodily sensitivity (he is terrified of the fire) participates in the sensitivity of his 'soul'; the great jets of emotion which make his preaching effective create appetites which shatter his body. They are the physiological components of his self-destructive need to dominate. Yet, as Tito points out after the blessing, he is 'a man to make one understand that there was a time when the monk's frock was a symbol of power over men's minds . . .'; in short he is the Catholic spiritual power – literally incarnate.

Romola herself is another such incarnation, representing, in George Eliot's own words, '*some* out of the normal relations'.[15] She is an attempt, and in many ways a perceptive one, to envisage the historical destiny of the human personality in Positivist terms. As she longs 'for that repose in mere sensation which she had sometimes dreamed of in the sultry afternoons of her early girlhood, when she had fancied herself floating naïad-like in the waters' (R., Ch. 61), and later, when she allows the agitating past to glide away as the 'soft warmth' of the sun penetrates her 'young limbs' (R., Ch. 68), Romola is a complex, substantial human being. The extremes of moral and physical experience are seen in intricate and fascinating proximity. And yet as a character she is a failure; she remains unreal, out of focus, bringing to mind Lukács's criticism of Flaubert's *Salammbô*, with its over-concentration on 'purely private, intimate and subjective happenings'.[16] In *Romola*, admittedly, George Eliot gives us something more than 'the hysterical longings and torments of middle-class girls in large cities',[17] which is all Lukács can find in *Salammbô*, because she has at least set out to discover public, historical significance in private, personal events. Nevertheless the reasons behind her decision to write an historical novel were probably similar to Flaubert's. A story about nineteenth-century politics would have stirred up the reader's prejudices and distracted his attention from 'the normal relations' which the novel depicts. Dickens was quick to exploit such prejudices, but George Eliot, convinced of the ultimate insignificance of day to day politics, found them irrelevant. Hence the choice of Savonarola's Florence as the setting for 'some out of the normal relations'; against such a background the reader can share her effortless recognition of the shallowness of great political disputes and petty political intrigues. He can stand with her above politics, above history. Like Flaubert, in fact, according to Lukács's diagnosis, George Eliot has set herself 'a consistent programme: to reawaken a vanished world of no concern to us.'[18] The result is to detach Romola herself from any significant connection with the world about her, to make her, and incidentally the reader, 'superior to society' in the classic Marxist sense. This is an inevitable result of regarding 'the theoretical as the only genuinely human attitude'[19]; it assumes that the teacher (and so his pupils) can gain access to 'the truth' independently of the pressures of history.

This of course is what is wrong with Felix Holt too. The only 'master craftsman' in the novel, he dissociates himself from Tory landlords, dissenting tradesmen and dispossessed workers alike, and is finally isolated from all real, practical problems, when he settles down with Esther Lyon on £2 a week from the Transome estate and a pension for his mother. Instead of suggesting practical solutions to North Loamshire's political problems, the plot merely offers us a curiously unexciting solution to the hero's personal problems, and a vague hope that his ability as a teacher will help the Sproxton miners. In both *Romola* and *Felix Holt*, in fact, the whole emphasis on education, as a way of changing people first and society afterwards, means that the central characters escape from specific, historically determined relationships into vague morally determined ones. Whatever the intrinsic merits of such a point of view, it is a dangerous position for a novelist, taking politics as a major theme, to adopt.

This can be seen especially in the influence on George Eliot's most obviously political novels, *Romola*, *Felix Holt*, and *Daniel Deronda*, of the fundamental arbitrariness which characterized Positivist political theory. Comte argued that his spiritual power would form 'a wholly new class', the advent of which would be 'essentially spontaneous, since its social sway can arise from nothing else than the voluntary assent of men's minds.'[20] He believed also that women would decide, with a similar spontaneity, that practical decisions were best left to men, since their social position was really 'very similar to that of philosophers and the working classes. . . . It [was] their combined action which [constituted] the modifying force of society.'[21] In line with this, the modifying force in North Loamshire turns out to be a-political miners on the one hand, Esther Lyon on the other, and, presiding over both, the novel's husband–philosopher, Felix Holt himself. To bring this about George Eliot has to fix the social situation – so that Felix can have enough to live on – and the psychological situation also – so that his mind can have a messianic authority which nothing in his background can account for. The personal and political problems in the novel are thus arbitrarily dovetailed and resolved with exactly that magical spontaneity which in Comte's scheme of things was going to produce new social institutions. The same tendency is evident in *Daniel Deronda*. Personal and political problems (Daniel's parentage and his search for a political cause) are first of all merged and then jointly and magically solved by the discovery of his Jewish heritage; and as in *Romola* and *Felix Holt*, heavy use of coincidence is needed to produce a solution. Whereas in *Middlemarch*, a far less political novel, the use of coincidence hardly matters, in *Daniel Deronda* the whole novel has to be distorted so that an English gentleman can find a satisfactory political vocation in the Middle East, that is, in a sort of primaeval a-political hinterland, utterly remote from the social, political, and economic world of the novel, and therefore from those morally limiting, practical problems which engaging in European politics would entail. Plot is thus unjustifiably used to enforce a particular political point of view. This would not, perhaps, be in itself all that serious but for the fact that the central characters, cut off from society, are thereby turned into mere puppets. The conviction that personality determines history has paradoxically deprived George Eliot's major characters of distinctive personalities in their own right. Like Amy, in *Little Dorrit* they are encapsulated psychologically from the world. With Dickens, however, this gratuitousness enforces a serious judgement on society; in George Eliot it weakly asserts a naive, unearned optimism.

It is typical of her intellectual persistence however that she should recognize even these logical and imaginative weaknesses in her position and try to meet them. She remains of course determined to find solutions to human problems in personal terms (to think otherwise would be to turn herself into 'a revolutionist'), but she quickly recognizes also the need to keep her characters, somehow, in and of society. There is a clear sense of the problem in *Romola*; indeed Savonarola blames Romola for living apart from her fellow-Florentines 'with those who sit on a hill aloof, and look down on the life of their fellow-men ...' (R., Ch. 40). The attempt to incorporate Romola into society by giving her a plague-stricken village to look after fails of course for reasons we have already considered: it is a device of plot to escape from the problems of history. But George Eliot turns to the problem once again in *Daniel Deronda*, and gives it subtle and extensive attention. It is for Daniel an acute personal problem as well as a general moral one: he despises 'the feeble, fastidious sympathy which shrinks from the broad life of mankind ...' (DD., Ch. 33), but he can find no justification for taking sides and so involving himself in one set of problems at the expense of others. He longs to be, nonetheless, 'an organic part of social life, instead of roaming in it like a yearning disembodied spirit ...' (DD., Ch. 32). He feels in other words in personal terms that very isolation which George Eliot's approach to social and political problems inevitably places him in. Somehow, however, the political visionary must be seen, and must see himself, as the product of society and not merely as the isolated consciousness which initiates change within it. This requires the discovery of a principle of change in human affairs which is distinct from individual consciousness, which all men participate in, but which first of all operates on the individual, and through him on society at large.

When Deronda enters a synagogue for the first time he quickly surrenders 'to that strongest effect of chanted liturgies *which is independant of verbal meaning* ...' (DD., Ch. 32, italics mine).

> The most powerful movement of feeling with a liturgy [George Eliot explains] is the prayer which seeks for nothing special, but is a yearning to escape from the limitations of our own weakness and an invocation of all Good to enter and abide with us; or else a self-oblivious lifting up of gladness, a *Gloria in excelsis* that such Good exists ...

This carries one stage further her basic conviction that religious, aesthetic, and political experiences are interchangeable – it suggests a pre-verbal reality, where the real shaping forces of human life operate, prior to their manifestation in speech, art, and action. An idea related to this emerges during the debate in The Hand and Banner, when the orthodox Positivist position of Miller, that '... The laws of development are being discovered, and changes taking place to them are necessarily progressive', is challenged by Deronda, who points to 'the danger of mistaking a tendency which should be resisted for an inevitable law . . .' Mordecai agrees: '. . . I believe', he says, 'in a growth, a passage, a new unfolding of life whereof the seed is more perfect . . .' (DD., Ch. 42). Human progress, in effect, is a matter, first of all, of *organic* transformation. Where these ideas are leading becomes clear when Daniel discovers his Jewish ancestry. The soul's yearnings, he then realizes, are inherited:

> . . . Suppose the stolen offspring of some mountain tribe brought up in a city of the plain, or one with an inherited genius for painting, and born blind – the ancestral life would lie within them as a dim longing for unknown objects and sensations, and the spell-bound habit of their inherited frames would be like a cunningly-wrought musical instrument . . . quivering throughout in uneasy moanings of its intricate structure that, under the right touch, gives music . . . (DD., Ch. 63)

This complex of unconscious impulses within 'the inherited frame' literally embodies 'the ancestral life'; it is here that progress is initiated, and, since the individual personality is grounded in unconscious, racial impulses, such change is simultaneously social and personal. The authentic human community derives not from a visible, shared life in work, art, and politics, but in the invisible, unconscious impulses of race. Here the visionary receives his vision, and, in his racial ties with other men, the politician finds his social function, that 'social captainship' which Deronda longs for, and through which he can feel himself to be 'the heart and brain of a multitude' (DD., Ch. 63).

This is the position George Eliot worked towards with enormous intellectual effort and finally achieved in her last novel. Its ironies are terrible. An earnestly Zionist work urges the view that the growth points of human history are inherited, unconscious racial impulses, and that these lead naturally to what is, in effect, a kind of *Führerprinzip*. These proto-fascist ideas, of course, are as innocent as the dream of Palestine as a Belgium of the East, 'a halting-place for enmities' (DD., Ch. 42); they are the result simply, of a failure to grasp human events in other than personal terms. Indeed paradoxically it is a sign of George Eliot's acute intelligence and integrity that this belief in personal solutions to human problems, a thoroughly comfortable, ordinary, Trollopian attitude, should have forced her towards such complex, if doubtful conclusions. She at least saw the problems inherent in personalizing history and politics, and with all her formidable talents as a novelist and thinker tried to meet them. The attempt may have made a weak position a dangerous one, but the intelligence and honesty of the effort are not to be questioned.

III

Most of what has been said up to now relates to George Eliot's less successful writing, but it has its relevance to her very finest work, though in some cases the specifically political interest is only peripheral. In the 'Prelude' to *Middlemarch*, for instance, the brief picture of Saint Teresa and her brother going to look for martyrdom 'with human hearts, already beating to a national idea . . .' is clearly of central relevance to the study of Dorothea: the heart, distinctively human precisely because it participates in 'a national idea', and yet deprived of any effective field of action, is one of the novel's main themes. Dorothea of course never does solve the problem. Comte might have thought her ultimate social role as wife and mother highly suitable, but the 'Finale' sounds a more complex, regretful note. This one would expect, since it is in this area, the free exploration of the difficulties encountered by distinctively human hearts in adjusting themselves to the deficiencies of ordinary social life, that George Eliot achieves her great successes. Dorothea's reaction to Lydgate's account of why Bulstrode's unpopularity is going to make for difficulties in his plans for the hospital is typical:

> 'People don't like his religious tone,' said Lydgate . . .
> 'That is all the stronger reason for despising such an opposition,' said Dorothea, looking at the affairs of Middlemarch by the light of the great persecutions.' (Mm., Ch. 44)

The exact sense of the disparity between the ideal and the real here, and the finely judged valuation of both, suggest an achieved common-sense in George Eliot's attitude to public affairs, utterly remote from the merely conventional common-sense which dismisses or patronizes the misjudgements of enthusiasm.

Mrs Transome represents another study, in George Eliot's most brilliant manner, of the relationship between individual and environment, and in her case politics are strikingly relevant. If, in Comte's phrase, the mental struggle between egoism and altruism 'discloses the scientific germ of the struggle . . . between the conservative and reforming spirit . . .', then Mrs Transome may be said to incarnate the spirit of reaction. She wants rule, respect, and the public ritual deference which Denner gives her in private. Her religion therefore, according to Feuerbachian formula, is a projection of irrational egotistic impulses, 'a view of this world and the next [which preserves] the existing arrangements of English society quite unshaken, keeping down the obtrusiveness of the vulgar and the discontent of the poor' (F H., Ch. 7). This desire to conserve existing arrangements for the sake of her own private happiness is like a great charge of energy in her mind and body, but industrialized England has no place for feudal *châtelaines*. And so this clever, intense woman is trapped in a house and a way of life that are falling into shabby disuse. At the end of the novel she is left 'in the midst of desecrated sanctities, and honours that [look] tarnished in the light of monotonous and weary suns' (F H., Ch. 40), a hardened, lonely, selfish old woman. In a sense however she is not to blame for this – life has determined her in one direction and history has determined society in another. She may be an adultress and the spirit of reaction incarnate, but she reveals nonetheless, in her strength and dignity, the tragic gap between the distinctively human and the vast, impersonal processes of history.

Gwendolen Harleth in many respects stands between Dorothea and Mrs Transome, a virginal Mrs Transome with some of Dorothea's talent for love. We see her, moreover, not only when the options for change within herself are still open, but also at a time of major social and political change. Repeatedly her consciousness is set against the background, specifically, of the American Civil War:

> Could there be a slenderer, more insignificant thread in human history than this consciousness of a girl, busy with her small inferences . . . ? – in a time, too, . . . when women on the other side of the world would not mourn for husbands and sons who died bravely in a common cause, and men stinted of bread on our side of the world heard of that willing loss

and were patient: a time when the soul of man was waking to pulses which had for centuries been beating in him unfelt. . . .

What in the midst of that mighty drama are girls and their blind visions? (DD., Ch. 11)

This is a brave question for George Eliot to ask, for though she answers herself with the assertion that they are the 'delicate vessels' in which 'is borne onward through the ages the treasure of human affections', Gwendolen is completely devoid of any public concern or generosity. 'Inwardly rebellious', she has nonetheless no 'speculations', and she satirizes 'practically reforming women':

> her horizon was that of the genteel romance where the heroine's soul poured out in her journal is full of vague power, originality, and general rebellion, while her life moves strictly in the sphere of fashion . . . (DD., Ch. 6)

She is, in short, a 'queen in exile' (DD., Ch. 4), one of those girls whom Lukács finds depicted in *Salammbô*, middle-class girls who need a setting which will enable them to express 'the subjectivity more fully than . . . a contemporary subject would permit.'[22] Rex asks her, in fact, what she would like to do

> Oh, I don't know! [she replies] – go to the North Pole, or ride steeple-chases, or go to be a queen in the East like Lady Hester Stanhope. (DD., Ch. 7)

The study of Gwendolen Harleth thus sets out explicitly to explore the problem which is so carefully evaded in *Romola*; it seeks to establish a relationship between, on the one hand history and politics in the largest, simplest sense of both words, and on the other, the 'hysterical longings and torments' of a middle-class girl. Dr Leavis has pointed out how intimately the Zionist and English parts of *Daniel Deronda* are related.[23] Politics is not the least important of the connections between them.

Another is suggested by the reference, in the passage I have just quoted, to 'pulses which had for centuries been beating in [man] unfelt . . .' In Deronda such hidden impulses are simply 'the ancestral life'; in Gwendolen, more ambiguously, they are 'dark rays doing their work invisibly in the broad light' (DD., Ch. 48).

Her marriage makes them startlingly visible. Behind the obvious forces which lead her to betray Mrs Glasher are impulses of compelling strength which find their counterparts in Grandcourt, and their full expression in the restrained sexual perversity of their relationship. The twin themes of the serpent and torture which haunt the figure of Gwendolen, 'the undefinable stinging quality' which suggests 'a trace of demon ancestry' in her make-up (DD., Ch. 7), her feeling of 'physical repulsion, to being directly made love to' – all blend disturbingly with the pleasure Grandcourt takes in her knowing things which make 'her start away from him' and in his own ability nonetheless to 'triumph over that repugnance . . .' (DD., Ch. 27) and force her 'to kneel down like a horse under training for the arena . . .' (DD., Ch. 28). Her fierce maidenhood, so full of physical and nervous vitality, instinctively *submits* to the 'benumbing effect' of Grandcourt's will, which 'like that of a crab or a boa-constrictor . . . goes on pinching or crushing without alarm at thunder' (DD., Ch. 35). It is perhaps significant that 'submission' – a key word in Positivism – was for Comte the fundamental impulse behind religion. Certainly the very forces of mind and body which drive Gwendolen into and through her marriage are active also in the final delicacy of her relations with her mother, her humble acceptance of spiritual advice from Deronda, her femininity, and her sheer talent as a person. George Eliot, in short, tries, through Gwendolen, to relate the unconscious as well as the consciousness of an hysterical girl to the historical process, and she has the courage to recognize that frightening ambiguities at work in the delicate vessel of a young girl's constitution may in fact help to carry through the ages 'the treasure of human affections' and indeed the religious impulse itself.

We may take it that George Eliot was the 'one very dear to me' who taught George Henry Lewes to regard Comte's predictions for a Positivist social order as 'a utopia, presenting hypotheses rather than doctrines . . .'[24] In *Daniel Deronda*, Deronda himself is the 'hypothesis'; Gwendolen, however, if the word can properly be applied to a study so carefully inconclusive, is the 'doctrine'. Her story (especially in the conversations with Deronda which follow so closely the familiar outline of a patient's relations with his analyst) has a cool, objective, quality about it, all that is best in fact in a truly positivist approach. What makes it really remarkable, however, is not its analytical precision, but the imaginative courage that goes into it, and the integrity which compels George Eliot to leave Gwendolen with the last and greatest problem unsolved. Gwendolen stands at the end of the novel trapped between the complexities of her own inner life and the complexities of global politics; her victory is that she is able to accept, *to submit to*, her own helplessness:

> 'I am going to the East . . .' said Deronda . . . 'The idea that I am possessed with is that of restoring a political existence to my people. . . .'
> There was a long silence between them. The world seemed to be getting larger round poor Gwendolen and she more solitary and helpless in the midst. . . . There comes a terrible moment to many souls . . . when the slow urgency of growing generations turns into the tread of an invading army. . . . Often the good cause seems to lie prostrate under the thunder of unrelenting force. . . . *Then it is that the submission of the soul to the Highest is tested*, and even in the eyes of frivolity life looks out from the scene of human struggle with the awful face of duty, and a religion shows itself which is something else than a private consolation.
> That was the sort of crisis which was at this moment beginning in Gwendolen's small life: she was for the first time . . . being dislodged from her supremacy in her own world . . . (DD., Ch. 69, italics mine)

No passage could more typify George Eliot's manner; style thought, metaphor, even the use of the indefinite article, are completely characteristic. It is to place her achievement as a novelist rather precisely, therefore, to point out that she here faces, as no other writer of her age could have faced, the overwhelming human importance of history and yet its indifference to the individual. There is a great deal of evasiveness and easy wish-fulfilment in *Daniel Deronda*; nevertheless the image of Gwendolen Harleth at the end of the novel, solitary and helpless in the midst of a larger world, seems to me to be nearly as potent and significant as the image of Amy Dorrit and Arthur Clennam, together and at peace in the restless world of *Little Dorrit*. There is certainly no other Victorian novelist than Dickens with whom, in terms of imaginative courage, George Eliot can sensibly be compared.

George Eliot : Politics and Personality

NOTES

1. A. Comte, *The Positive Philosophy of Auguste Comte*. Freely translated and condensed by Harriet Martineau, London, 2 vols., 1853, ii, p. 141.
2. *Ibid.*, ii, pp. 32–34.
3. I quote from the Standard Edition of *The Works of George Eliot*, 21 vols., Edinburgh, 1878–80. Cue titles: FH., *Felix Holt, the Radical*; R., *Romola*; Mm., *Middlemarch*; DD., *Daniel Deronda*.
4. A. Comte, *System of Positive Polity*, London, 4 vols., 1875–7, i, p. 109.
5. *Ibid.*, i, p. 71.
6. *Ibid.*, i, pp. 101–09.
7. *Ibid.*, i, pp. 78–80.
8. A. Comte, *The Positive Philosophy*, ii, p. 132.
9. A. Comte, *System of Positive Polity*, i, p. 156.
10. H. Spencer, *The Principles of Psychology*, London, 1855, pp. 339–487.
11. A. Comte, *System of Positive Polity*, i, p. 335.
12. G. Lukács, *The Historical Novel* translated from the German by Hannah and Stanley Mitchell, London, 1962, p. 210.
13. George Eliot, 'The Influence of Rationalism', *Fortnightly Review*, i, p. 45, May 1865.
14. *The George Eliot Letters*, ed. by Gordon S. Haight, London, 7 vols., 1954–6, iv, p. 300.
15. *Ibid.*, iv, p. 301.
16. G. Lukács, *op. cit.*, p. 199.
17. *Ibid.*, p. 189.
18. *Ibid.*, p. 185.
19. K. Marx, 'Theses on Feuerbach', reprinted (in English) in K. Marx and F. Engels, *On Religion*, Moscow and London, n.d., p. 68.
20. A. Comte, *The Positive Philosophy*, ii, p. 467.
21. A. Comte, *System of Positive Polity*. i, p. 170.
22. G. Lukács, *op. cit.*, p. 231.
23. F. R. Leavis, 'George Eliot's Zionist Novel', *Commentary*, xxx, p. 318, October, 1960.
24. G. H. Lewes, 'Auguste Comte', *Fortnightly Review*, iii, p. 404, January 1866.

VI

GEORGE MEREDITH: 'DELICATE' AND 'EPICAL' FICTION

DAVID HOWARD

1. *The Italian Novels*

'but one doesn't die for good manners'

I

Sandra Belloni or *Emilia in England* (1864) is one of Meredith's best novels and there is justification enough in attempting to present its, somewhat neglected, quality. This quality emerges strongly if the novel is read along with its sequel *Vittoria* or *Emilia in Italy* (1866)[1] and the two novels seem to me to be very important for an understanding of *Beauchamp's Career* (1874).

The last named is the most obviously 'political' of the three, and is also the most contemporary. The two Italian novels deal with events in the 1840s although of course the success of the Italian Risorgimento was very contemporary in the 1860s. Then, as for many years before, it was an important political and cultural presence in England. It affected English politics, it formed a fascinating part of the English image of Italy, it affected the English image of political possibility. One of the advantages of considering both novels, and of connecting them with *Beauchamp's Career*, is that this English concern emerges. The analysis of English society in *Emilia in England* provides a way of reading *Emilia in Italy*. They are both English novels as well as being both Italian novels. Of course, Meredith had a real interest in Italian life and politics. He was one of the least insular of

Victorian writers. And the 'accuracy' of *Emilia in Italy* has often been noted. But what I would stress in the two novels is that the 'reality' of Italy there, the 'reality' most importantly of their herione Emilia, is most significant in relation to an English need – I should say at this stage, more cautiously, in relation to Meredith's analysis of an English need, or, more cautiously still, in relation to Meredith's need.

For one primary and irresistible reaction to *Emilia in Italy* is that it illustrates Meredith's case as a writer and a man, a case clarified by the perspective of *Emilia in England*. The two novels belong naturally together but they are also, perhaps more fundamentally, yoked together, with false continuities of character, event, and implied sequel. And whatever else has to be taken into account – in particular, the changes in Meredith's circumstances, I would think – one can't avoid the sheer difference in quality. There are two Merediths here and one writes much less well than the other. But to bring out this difference along with others can become also a way of grasping an essential continuity, a continuity that takes one into the greater achievement of *Beauchamp's Career*, where that foreseeable badness of *Emilia in Italy* is wonderfully exploited.

Towards the end of *Emilia in England* Meredith looks forward to writing a sequel:

He [the Philosopher] maintains that a story should not always flow, or, at least, not to a given measure. When we are knapsack on back, he says, we come to eminences where a survey of our journey past and in advance is desirable, as is a distinct pause in any business, here and there. He points proudly to the fact that our people in this comedy move themselves – are moved from their own impulsion – and that no arbitrary hand has posted them to bring about any event and heap the catastrophe. In vain I tell him that he is meantime making tatters of the puppets' golden robe – illusion; that he is sucking the blood of their warm humanity out of them. He promises that when Emilia is in Italy he will retire altogether; for there is a field of action of battles and conspiracies, nerve and muscle, where life fights for plain issues, and he can but sum results. Let us, he entreats, be true to time and place. In our fat England, the gardener Time is playing all sorts of delicate freaks in the hues and traceries of the flower of life, and shall we not note them? If we are to understand our species, and mark the progress of civilization at all, we must. Thus the Philosopher. Our partner is our master, and I submit, hopefully looking for release with my Emilia, in the day when Italy reddens the sky with the banners of a land revived. (Chap. XLIV, p. 483)

I shall need to return to the question of tone, but for the moment I want to stress the two kinds of fiction sketched here: the fiction of action, heroics, 'plain issues', and the fiction of 'delicate' analysis. This distinction as far as it goes certainly applies to the difference between the two novels. *Emilia in Italy* is full of rather frantic, although confused, action, a panorama of the heroics of both sides; *Emilia in England* is full of delicate probing of 'fat England', the 'Nice Shades' and 'Fine Feelings' of its middle class. The tone of this passage would seem to be one of ironic depreciation of the more delicate kind of fiction, the kind of fiction which, without much hope of appreciation, Meredith really excelled in. This would seem to confirm the common judgement on Meredith, when he is considered seriously at all, that his strength lies in psychological subtlety, and, as again the passage reveals, in 'comedy'. The distinction is between comic and epic fiction.

But elsewhere we have to take this 'hopefully looking for release' without irony. Here are the two kinds of fiction again, in letters Meredith wrote while completing *Emilia in Italy* or *Vittoria*. Nathaniel Hawthorne, it might be useful to note, had in 1860 published his Italian novel, *The Marble Faun* or *Transformation*, where, if anything, the possibilities of action, of 'plain issues', are even more inhibited than in his earlier fiction:

Hawthorne has just the pen to fascinate you. His deliberate analysis, his undramatic representations, the sentience rather than the drawings which he gives you of his characters, and the luscious, morbid tone, are all effective. But I think his delineations untrue: their power lies in the intensity of his egotistical perceptions, and are not the perfect view of men and women . . . I am very hot upon *Vittoria*. Lewes says it must be a success; and it has my best writing. I fancy I begin in the *Fortnightly* in February. Perhaps I have given it too historical a character to please the brooding mind of Fred. But, we shall see. I think one must almost love Italy to care for it and the heroine. There are scenes that will hold you; much adventure to entertain you; delicate bits and fiery handling. But there is no tender dissection, and the softer emotions are not kept at half gasp upon slowly-moving telescopic objects, with their hearts seen beating in their frames.

As regards Hawthorne, little Meredith admits that your strokes have truth. I strive by study of humanity to represent it: not its morbid action. I have a tendency to do that, which I repress: for, in delineating it, there is no gain. In all my, truly, very faulty works, there is this aim. Much of my strength lies in painting morbid emotion and exceptional positions; but my conscience will not let me so waste my time. Hitherto consequently I have done nothing of mark. But I shall, and *Vittoria* will be the first indication (if not fruit) of it. My love is for epical subjects – not for cobwebs in a putrid corner; though I know the fascination of unravelling them.[2]

Here the commitment, although not a wholly convincing one, is to the second kind, the 'epical' kind of fiction, which will be embodied in *Emilia in Italy*. Of course one can make a lot of the uncertainty of the self-criticism here, particularly in relation to Meredith's circumstances. Brooding Fred, to whom the letters are addressed, is Captain Maxse, Meredith's lifelong friend, who became the model for Nevil Beauchamp. And as the rest of the second letter shows, Meredith is having to defend himself against charges of evasiveness and lack of commitment on questions of the day and 'the deepest questions of life'. In spite of making a strongly worded defence of himself – 'They (the deepest questions) are to be thought over very long and very carefully before they are fought over' – he does, through the remarks on fiction, seem to accept the charge. He seems, that is, under this kind of pressure, to force himself towards an 'epical' self.

Another kind of pressure could be behind this move. At this time, even more than usual, Meredith was short of money. None of his books had sold particularly well. He had recently married again, and there was the increasing expense of his son's education. The letters mentioning *Rhoda Fleming* (1865) are particularly revealing in this respect. Meredith felt that he was capable of writing popular fiction, fiction that would sell, and he identified the popular with plainness and action. So he could please both his 'activist' friends and a wider audience. Nevertheless I think we have to understand this urge for epic, 'plain issues', action, as something natural to Meredith. Throughout his life there is this preoccupation with 'noble', simple, fine action, which often manifests itself as an obsession with an image of the aristocracy and its code of honour, an obsession in particular with the insult and the duel, as well as with individual heroics in battle. This can be and has been explained in terms of Meredith's low birth and family situation. Although important, I find this can lead to an oversimplified emphasis on the aristocratic element in Meredith, when the significance of that element lies in it as an image of direct purposeful action. As a child and as a father, Meredith was obsessed with vigorous, healthy, physical action, as a necessary complement to meditation and bookishness.

All this, of course, sounds very Victorian in the most obvious way. Meredith's preoccupation with action partakes of the general Victorian preoccupation with games, fitness, something to prevent 'morbidity'. And the call to action, away from thought, introspection, art, is one of the most persistent and hackneyed themes in Victorian literature. Meredith's phrasing in his letters recalls one of the most obvious texts – Arnold's preface to his *Poems* (1853) where the earlier self which wrote *Empedocles on Etna* and gave no hope of 'action' is similarly dismissed. A more relevant text for the purposes of this essay is Clough's *Amours de Voyage*, one of the few interesting texts to come out of the English preoccupation with the Risorgimento. There, in the situation of the beleaguered Roman Republic in 1849, the call to action for the diffident English intellectual is very much one of the themes:

Now supposing the French or the Neapolitan soldier
Should by some evil chance come exploring the Maison Serny
(Where the family English are all to assemble for safety),
Am I prepared to lay down my life for the British female?
Really, who knows? One has bowed and talked, till, little by little,
All the natural heat has escaped of the chivalrous spirit.
Oh, one conformed, of course; but one doesn't die for good manners,
Stab or shoot, or be shot, by way of graceful attention.
No, if it should be at all, it should be on the barricades there;
Should I incarnadine ever this inky pacifical finger,
Sooner far should it be for this vapour of Italy's freedom,
Sooner far by the side of the d——d and dirty plebeians.[3]

And Meredith in his scorn for 'fat England' is very near to part of the reasoning in Tennyson's *Maud*, where the selfish commercial society can purify itself in the noble cause of the Crimean War (although later in the opening pages of *Beauchamp's Career* Meredith attacks Tennyson as the Laureate of this mood).

The Italian struggle, then, could offer images of heroic action, of meaningful violence. But this is a crude placing of Meredith. It cannot really account for Emilia in either novel, although it does, along with the other factors mentioned, go towards explaining the direction and the decline in the two novels. The Emilia possibility is a distinctive one, offering both crude and subtle alternatives to fat England. And it is, in a curious way, a political possibility.

II

But firstly I must attest in some small way to the obvious strength and success of *Emilia in England*, in its satirical presentation of middle-class England. Whatever else Emilia is, she is the foreign element who reveals by her very difference the nature of the world she intrudes on. 'Emilia had been a touchstone to this family' (p. 605).

Her entry into the world of the Poles, her 'rise', gives the novel a familiar pattern in the English tradition. One can look back at it through Forster's use of an Italian element to show up the qualities of English bourgeois life. More usefully perhaps, one could think in terms of Sissy Jupe in the Gradgrind family in *Hard Times*, or of Fanny Price and the Bertrams' in *Mansfield Park*. In both these novels the patronized dependent becomes the saviour of the family.

This is the outline of *Emilia in England*. The Poles take up Emilia, but instead of being submissive, grateful, and assimilated, she becomes their destroyer and preserver. For the obvious strength of the novel, however, the preservation aspect is not so relevant as Emilia's agency of revelation. She is not the only agent, of course, but she is the heroine of the force of frankness in the novel. The un-masking of the Poles and their friends is not necessarily regenerative. It is potentially so, but in many ways the predominant note is shock and dismay, of which Adela Pole's thought at one point is typical: 'Well! if all we do is to come into broad daylight!' (p. 290) It is in this unmasking then that the most secure achievement of the book lies.

George Meredith : 'Delicate' and 'Epical' Fiction

Through the Poles and their connections Meredith represents a
middle-class England economically secure enough to want to forget
its origins, to devote itself to refinement, manners, social success, and
art, to the realms of 'Fine Shades and Nice Feelings'. This stage, or
rather the middle-class consciousness of it, Meredith calls 'sentimentalism'. The elaboration and subtlety of his exploration of this
condition is striking, and so too is the quality of his sympathy for it.
Wilfred and his sisters are not caricatures (although the same might
not be said for Mr Pole and Mrs Chump), nor are Lady Charlotte,
Sir Purcell Barrett, Merthyr Powyrs and his sister. The complexity
of their sentimentalism, its convincing human depth, is partly the
point. In the same way Emilia's simplicity is treated comically too,
in herself alone, and through the association of her 'vulgarity' with
that of the two more obviously comic outsiders, Mrs Chump and
Mr Pericles. If she represents the claims of life and art, a challenge to
the values of the Poles, so do they, and their claim, on one level at
least, muffles hers. A quality of ruthless sympathy hangs over the
novel, the double or alternate invitation to share and judge experience.
In his occasional discussions of his method Meredith has a novelist
debate with a 'philosopher', and the key question is how much
detachment and sympathy there is going to be. Similarly the method
of the novel ranges from delicate psychological notation and subtle
conversational drama to semi-farce, such as Wilfred dousing himself
with Mrs Chump's dead husband's perfume, 'Alderman's Bouquet'–
'The smell of ye's comfortin' she says (Chap. LIII). Frequently the
methods are mixed, so that it is difficult to tell them apart, indeed one
becomes another. The trivial is elevated, the crucial diminished,
toast challenges suicide.

To a certain extent Meredith is playing on ready-made sympathies,
the sympathies of the 'sentimental' reading public for one; but he
also plays on the sympathies that are aroused with the kind of novel
Emilia in England impersonates (again the obvious example would be
the novels of Jane Austen), the novel of aspiring English middle-class
sisters and daughters, the novel that is so obviously for its readers
because it is about its readers. The temptations to toughness of such
a novel with all its potential of sentimentalism, of indrawn domestic
'drama', are obvious, especially if you bear in mind, as Meredith

137

did, the possibility of crossing from this world of 'little people' to the epic of a national struggle.

I don't offer this as a defence of the sometimes 'sketchy' nature of Meredith's writing (that is part of the larger argument) but as a suggestion to involve in the question of Meredith's sympathy and tone. *Emilia in England* begins with an analysis of the Poles, before they are created, but in the sense I have indicated they are already there, forever reading that book about themselves. What is indisputably there in the 'Prelude' is Meredith's precision of analysis of the Pole sisters. The toughness, the detachment of consciousness is immediate. The voice in the wood is 'a surprise furnished for their amusement . . . Music was now the Art in the ascendant at Brookfield . . . the ladies were scaling society by the help of the arts . . . They went on perpetually mounting . . . Sentimentalists are a perfectly natural growth of a fat soil. Wealthy communities must engender them . . . our sentimentalists are a variety owing their existence to a prolonged term of comfortable feeding' (p. 1). Two other elements apart from this stringency of tone should be stressed in the first chapter. One is indicated by the last fragments of quotation. There is a note of determinism, of dialectic, in the presentation of the Poles. They are a 'natural growth' and 'in their way they help to civilize us'. As a counter to the general satirical portrait they are offered as a necessary middle stage to some better condition, half-way people, just as Wilfred is later described as a half-man. There will be more to say of this but for the moment one can notice it in relation to the general doctrine emerging from Meredith's fiction of ordeal, ordeal for individual, class, or nation, consequent on inevitable mistakes which both bring disaster and promise (although not inevitably) betterment.

The other thing to notice here, although again I want to postpone any attempted assimilation of it, is a certain repellent element in Meredith's tone. There are certain elements of style which convey a wilful, self-congratulatory, patronizing, detachment; vocabulary like 'damsels', 'panoply', constructions like

> Nor let the philosopher venture hastily to despise them as pipers to dilettante life
> And I maintain it against him, who have nevertheless listened attentively to the eulogies pronounced by the vendors of prize bacon. (p. 6)

There is something literary and second-hand here, something forced and clever. This is the notoriously irritating Meredith surface (especially pronounced in his first chapters) which I shall for the moment ignore, until I come to another style in the book which is this style's resolute ghost and residue.

The Poles' pretensions to refined comprehension include then a pretension to the comprehension of art. Emilia, the beautiful voice in the wood, is immediately assimilated. It is an opera singer sent down by Pericles as a surprise amusement for them. And when this turns out to be a mistake, she is then made a 'discovery', something to be taken up and displayed in their circle. As a brilliant later phrase has it, 'The parasite completes the animal, and a dependent assures us of our position' (p. 60). They are sincerely enchanted by Emilia's voice but that is secondary to their use of her. Eventually of course it is they and their England who become parasites on the animality of Emilia.

From the beginning of the book the sentimental comprehension of the Poles is subject to shock and exposure, the shock and exposure increasing as their ambitions mount: to move and impress in a more fashionable circle, to acquire the big house and estate of Besworth, to jettison their early unworthy aquaintances, to marry into society. Both the ambition and the exposure relate to the uncomfortable fact of money. Mr Pole is forced to speculate, partly with Mrs Chump's money, in order to back these ambitions. It is one of the continuous symbolic comedies of the novel that Mrs Chump is despised by the sisters as representing the world they are escaping from, but at the same time has to be accepted as a means to that escape. Money is needed to forget money. Meredith details this comic ordeal with great skill, and the process of being agonizingly nice to Mrs Chump ends brilliantly, after the sisters and Wilfred have ejected her from the house, with Adela impersonating her brogue in letters to Mr Pole to deceive him into thinking she is on board Wilfred's yacht; is still, that is, one of them.

I want to illustrate Meredith's presentation of the Poles and money through Chapter XVI. The sisters have been told by Wilfred that Mr Pole is in financial trouble and that they must face up to the possibility of him needing to marry Mrs Chump. They decide to put up with Mrs Chump for the moment but to escape from the circle of which she might be a part. This 'escape' is typically muffled in their consciousness: 'By means of Fine Shades it was understood that Brookfield was to be abandoned. Not one direct word was uttered.' The horror of what they are to escape from freshened by a sentimental evocation of their dead mother, successfully obscures what they are proposing for themselves: the escape from a marriage for money by means of marriages for money. Here is Adela contemplating and escaping the horror at the same time:

> 'Suppose that after all Money! . . .' Yes, Mammon has acted Hymen before now. Nothing else explained Mrs. Chump; so she thought in one clear glimpse. Inveterate sentimental habit smeared the picture with two exclamations – 'Impossible!' and 'Papa!' I desire it to be credited that these simple interjections absolutely obscured her judgment. Little people think either what they are made to think, or what they choose to think; and the education of girls is to make them believe that facts are their enemies – a naughty spying race, upon whom the dogs of *Pudeur* are to be loosed, if they surprise them without note of warning. Adela silenced her suspicion easily enough; but this did not prevent her taking a measure to satisfy it. Petting her papa one evening, she suddenly asked him for ninety pounds.

Adela here is not simply concerned with the question of whether her father is short of money. The real question, the hostile yet enticing fact of life, is that of marrying for money, for herself as well as for her father.

Mr Pole reluctantly promises the sum. Later, in the middle of the night, Cornelia in search of an 'intellectual sedative' from the library, and having dropped her candle, bumps into him.

> She had to find her way back in the dark. On the landing of the stairs, she fancied that she heard a step and a breath. The lady was of unshaken nerves. She moved on steadily, her hand stretched out a little before her. What it touched was long in travelling to her brain; but when her paralysed heart beat again, she knew that her hand clasped another hand. Her nervous horror calmed as the feeling came to her of the palpable weakness of the hand.
>
> 'Who are you?' she asked. Some hoarse answer struck her ear. She asked again, making her voice distincter. The hand now returned her

pressure with force. She could feel that the person, whoever it was, stood collecting strength to speak. Then the words came –

'What do you mean by imitating that woman's brogue?'

'Papa!' said Cornelia.

'Why do you talk Irish in the dark?'

This is one of many scenes in the novel where the sentimental consciousness gropes in the dark, literally here, half-discovering and half-impersonating the realities it fears. The money reality has here of course become the sex reality. For much of the book they are the the same fact of life (Emilia likes to define what she is worth in terms of money). What Pole is actually up to is stealing the money from Mrs Chump's room to give to Adela in the morning. Equally he might be visiting her to 'talk Irish in the dark'. These acts of darkness become one. The sisters have been symbolically engendered.

The chapter goes on with Mr Pole in the role of country squire reading morning prayers to the assembled household, to be interrupted by Mrs Chump with her cries about her stolen money. Again the voice of a despised reality interpenetrates the genteel world.

As I have suggested, Mrs Chump represents both the shock of money and of sex. This is well caught in a later scene in the book when Mrs Chump is about to be ejected by the Pole children after the social disasters of the Besworth party. She desperately defends her interest in Pole and tries to account for their hostility:

'Dear Hearts!' she addressed her silent judges, in mysterious guttural tones, 'is it becas ye think there's a bit of fear of . . . ?'

The ladies repressed a violent inclination to huddle together, like cattle from the blowing East.

'I assure ye, 'taint possible', pursued Mrs. Chump . . . (p. 341).

One of the key words for this area of the book is 'animal'. The sentimentalists try to suppress the sense of an animal self, of appetite. One of their most frequent responses to Emilia is to find her 'animal'. 'A creature without ideas and a decided appetite' (p. 23), is one of the first reactions of the sisters.

In questions of money Wilfred is more realistic than his sisters but in his relations with Emilia and Lady Charlotte he is a fully sentimental figure. He cannot escape from the image of himself as heroic, or pathetic, or tragic lover. And the real continually intrudes on and destroys this image. An early scene with Emilia illustrates this neatly. There has been a romantic episode by moonlight. 'Love, with his accustomed cunning, managed thus to lift her out of the mire and array her in his golden dress: to idealize her as we say.' They arrive back at the house:

> 'Do I love her?' thought Wilfred, as he was about to pull at the bell, and the thought that he should feel pain at being separated from her for half-a-dozen hours, persuaded him that he did. The self-restraint which withheld him from protesting that he did, confirmed it.
> 'To-morrow morning,' he whispered.
> 'I shall be down by daylight,' answered Emilia.
> 'You are in the shade – I cannot see you', said he. The door opened as Emilia was moving out of the line of shadow. (Chap. XII, p. 110)

Once again Emilia steps out, in the act of offering herself, from the romantic shade where he can formulate her. She continually comes into the light. And that promised 'daylight' will reveal to Wilfred the physical vulgarity of a black eye received in protecting Emilia in a village brawl. He doesn't keep the appointment.

The sentimental agonies of the English 'lovers' in the novel are very well done. The portrait of Lady Charlotte is particularly fine I think, especially in her conversations with Wilfred, where there is a delicate balance of deception, self-deception, sophistication, and, also, a real pathos, of the woman who wants to give herself but can't:

> The flush of her face, and tremour of her fingers, told of an unimagined agitation hardly to be believed, though seen and felt. Yet, still some sign, some shade of a repulsion in her figure, kept him as far from her as any rigid rival might have stipulated for. (Chap. XXXVI, p. 386)

But I want to dwell on the most 'tragic' of the lovers, Sir Purcell Barrett, because his despair and suicide in their contrast with Emilia's despair can lead me directly to Emilia's presence in the book.

The chapter 'The Tragedy of Sentiment' offers a fine account of the more morbid kind of sentimentalist. He has made Cornelia into an impossible ideal as a test of the life which has so far maltreated him. This is a reciprocal affair. In 'our world, where all things must move' (p. 560), Cornelia accepts willingly the role of ideal or 'idol'. Over this relationship, as over Lady Charlotte, hangs the missed opportunity of decisive action, physical commitment. Both get trapped into a self-regarding posture of impossible love. Sir Purcell moves inevitably towards the melancholy relish of suicide, and even this is given into the hands of fate – he won't know which gun is loaded of the two he takes with him. But the really striking part of the chapter is the detail of Sir Purcell's last morning. Before he can get down to Brookfield and straight from his dreams of Cornelia lifting his corpse into its grave, he has to face 'his landlady's little female scrubber ... working at the grate in his sitting-room', and a prolonged absurd debate with her and the landlady about toast and 'aig' for breakfast. This unideal femininity and the reminders of undeceased appetite are ruthlessly placed, as are the comfortable circumstances of this hater of life. And it is this elaboration of breakfast which clinches the connection with Emilia's despair and near suicide which comes before in the novel. It is one of the signs of Emilia's natural, unforced despair after her final rejection by Wilfred, that throughout her wanderings in London she is concerned with food. So that in the end she is not dying for sentiment or art but simple want of food. She has moved back into that nether world from which she came, and where the fundamental reality was potatoes. 'I suppose', she says to Wilfred early in the novel, 'you have never lived upon potatoes entirely?'

Over the sentimental agonies and evasions, then, always hovers the hint of something other in Emilia. Again and again the sentimentalists are defined or define themselves in relation to her. When it is said of Cornelia that 'Posture seemed always to triumph over action' (p. 552) or when Wilfred is presented as one of those 'men of murdered halves' who 'know that they do not embrace life' (p. 297) it is Emilia they are measured against. She begins as the parasite of the book, the condescendingly taken up outcast; but as the book progresses the sentimentalists begin to feed on her vitality, confusedly and reluctantly. Lady Charlotte, who has a 'proper fear' of the word love, 'saw there something she had not' (p. 288). Reading Wilfred's love note to Emilia, itself parasitic upon Emilia's own frank style,

'It's villainy', she said. But more and more frequently a crouching abject longing to call the words her own – to have them poured into heart and brain – desire for the intoxication of the naked speech of love usurped her spirit of pride, until she read with envied tears, half loathing herself, but fascinated and subdued: 'Mine! my angel! You will see me tomorrow. – YOUR LOVER'. (Chap. xxxiv, p. 348)

Wilfred becomes more desirable because he has been involved in the unknown mystery of love. 'The heat of Emilia's love played round him and illumined him. This borrowing of the passion of another is not uncommon' (p. 398). Similarly Georgiana Ford with the example of Emilia's love for Wilfred before her 'almost conceived what this other, not sisterly love might be' (p. 406). Sir Purcell too, feeds his melancholy on her capacity for hope.

None of this of course is straightforward. Emilia is 'borrowed' and attacked at the same time. Charlotte and Georgina are continually finding her to be 'animal' and vulgar. They fight and denounce her vitality. In a brilliant chapter (xxvi) where Emilia visits Mr Pole to persuade him not to object to her marrying Wilfred there is a grotesque version of the sentimentalist confronting, evading, secretly feeding on Emilia.

'Oh! bless my love for him. You have only to know what my love for him is! The thought of losing him goes like perishing cold through my bones; – my heart jerks, as if it had to pull up my body from the grave every time it beats . . .

'God in heaven!' cried the horrified merchant, on whose susceptible nerves these images wrought with such a force that he absolutely had dread of her . . . 'What's that your heart does?' (p. 266)

The shock to Mr Pole here is also an articulation of his approaching stroke. He borrows the force of her language at the same time as resisting what that force expresses. 'What's that your heart does?' It could serve as an epigraph for the book.

That phrase should remind us that Emily is almost as absurd as Pole in this scene. Her passion becomes physicalized by the connection with Pole's condition; they are both hypochondriacs. And throughout the novel her opposition to the sentimentalists is not allowed an easy claim. She is frequently made to appear absurd, ignorant, vain, theatrical, 'animal'. 'Doggies make that noise' thinks Lady Charlotte on one occasion when she moans at having to leave Wilfred. There the endorsement of her through Charlotte's contempt seems clear enough. But elsewhere an ambiguity about her persists outside of other characters' comments on her. The possibility of becoming Pericles' mistress, her final revenge on Lady Charlotte, these are episodes where the endorsement of her passionate nature seems somewhat hedged.

This is partly a tribute to the way Meredith makes her both simple and unpredictable. One has to remember that the novel is about her growth as well as anything else, her adolescence and finding of herself. So that she can never be an uncomplicated representative of life-joy. She makes mistakes and pursues illusions, undergoes her ordeal, in parallel with the sentimentalists. And there is no certainty of the result. Meredith writes of her just before her episode as outcast in London, 'the great result of mortal suffering – consciousness – had fully set in; to ripen; perhaps to debase; at any rate, to prove her' (p. 420). And that reference to her mental growth is instructive. She is not offered as an unconscious passionate presence, an unthinking challenge to the Nice Shades and Fine Feelings, although this is to a certain extent true of her in the early part of the book.

The crucial difference between her and the English world she penetrates, whether she is thinking or not, is the force and fullness of her experience. The key word on her side is 'passion' as opposed to 'sentiment': 'such timorous little feather-play of feminine emotion she knew nothing of: in her heart was the strong flood of a passion' (p. 170). She has 'the capacity to concentrate all animal and mental vigour into one feeling, this being the power of the soul' (p. 263). She is 'a voice of nature', 'brave of heart'. The Philosopher says in Chapter XLIV

Passion . . . is *noble strength on fire* and [he] points to Emilia as a representation of passion. She asks for what she thinks she may have; she claims what she imagines to be her own. She has no shame, and thus, believing in, she never violates, nature, and offends no law, wild as she may seem. Passion does not turn on her and rend her when it is thwarted. She was never carried out of the limit of her own intelligent force, seeing that it directed her always, with the simple mandate to seek that which belonged to her. She was perfectly sane, and constantly just to herself, until the failure of her voice, telling her that she was a beggar in the world, came as a second blow, and partly scared her reason. (p. 482).

This quality of passion is opposed to a typically parasitic description of the sentimentalist: '(he) goes on accumulating images and hiving sensations, till such time as (if the stuff be in him) they assume a form of vitality, and hurry him headlong. This is not passion, though it amazes men, and does the madder thing.'

The opposition in outline is clear enough but there are difficulties in closely defining her passionate possibility – notice the word 'intelligent' again – and there is the more important question how far Emilia exists apart from such comments on her. One is tempted to say she exists mainly as a possibility, a possibility that emerges strongly if negatively through the elaborately realized condition of the sentimentalists. But she does have an actual presence in the book and the difficulties of the Philosopher's language in talking about what she represents are helpful in defining that presence. What is striking in that language is the attempt to desentimentalize 'passion', to bring together words like 'law' and 'wild', to speak of 'intelligent force', to make passion something practical almost – 'She asks for what she thinks she may have.'

The literary critical temptation is obvious. She was sane and true to herself, 'until the failure of her voice'. Her voice is her art. Emilia's passion, her possibility, is the vital possibility of art beyond the dimension of life. In her singing and only in her singing all becomes harmonious. Her appetite for life is a preparation, a qualification for art. She is like the Queen of Song, 'intensely human ... indifferent to finesse and despising subtleties: gifted to speak, to inspire, to command all great emotions ... (who) could, as a foremost qualification for Art, feel harmoniously' (p. 441).

To read the novel, and *Emilia in Italy*, as a study of the artistic temperament, an affirmation of art, makes sense. Much of what I have already noted of Emilia would fit a conventional apologetic in the nineteenth century for the artist. Her peculiar combination of passion and hardness, her frankness, her vanity, her openness of appetite, even the things Meredith seems to muffle, her capacities for revenge and unconventional sexual behaviour, all these can be

mobilized for such an account. Add to these the attention the book
pays to the necessity of practice and study – she has to learn that her
voice is too natural, too subject to her own emotional state. The loss
of her voice indicates that disabling dependence (although it's a
dependence that seems an inevitable preliminary) and initiates the
necessary concentration on the impersonality of her art, her objective
worth, 'acting as if the rich warm blood of self should have ceased to
hug about us' (p. 431). This is the stage at which she is most puzzling
and most contemptible to her English friends like Georgiana Ford –
coldly establishing that she is physically desirable, that she is worth
something on the market. After this the voice returns.

Add also the Italian element. She several times identifies herself
or is identified as Italy. Meredith makes use of the most persistent
part of the image of Italy in England, the Italians as 'an artistic
people'. But one of the commonest companion parts in that image
was their political incapacity. When Merthyr Powys returns wounded
from an abortive uprising Meredith's caricature of an Englishman
presents this image very succinctly, 'Let them paint, and carve
blocks, and sing. They're not fit for much else, as far as I can see'
(p. 600).

Through the figure of Emilia then Meredith presents not simply
the artistic temperament but the connection of art and politics. And
with this additional dimension the affirmation of art is by no means
clear. Partly it is that a purist conception of art is caricatured through
this 'stout Briton' and more importantly for the book through the
millionaire patron Pericles. But far more fundamental to the experience of the novel are the two voices of Emilia.

One voice is of course the voice we have to take on trust, her
marvellous singing voice, which appeals to all individuals and classes.
It appears at various moments in the novel apparently as an escape
from or harmonious enchantment of the struggles and deformities of
human life. Its first occurrence is typically in a 'desolate' part of the
wood, the same part where Sir Purcell (himself a musician) will
later commit suicide.

But the very fact of the unrealizable nature of that voice throws
attention on the voice which is realized, her speaking voice in the novel.
It is a very distinctive voice and it is what we have to go on. When

he interiorizes, Meredith usually does so with the sentimentalists. Even in the outcast episode the representation of Emilia's inner state is curiously remote. I think this is intentional because there is a sense in which we can never know Emilia in the same way we can know Wilfred or his sisters. The force of impersonality she comes to stand for is enacted by the technique of the book. There is an 'alienation' effect with the central figure which is characteristic of Meredith's fiction.

But the voice is there and emerges more and more distinctly as the book progresses. It begins as the voice of simplicity, frankness, vivid experience, immaturity:

> She felt his arm dreamily stressing its clasp about her, and said: 'Now I know you love me. And you shall take me as I am. I need not be so poor after all. My dear! my dear! I cannot see beyond you.'
>
> 'Is that your misery?' said he.
>
> 'My delight! my pleasure! One can live a life anywhere. And how can I belong to Italy, if I am yours? Do you know, when we were silent just now, I was thinking that water was the history of the world flowing out before me, all mixed up of kings and queens, and warriors with armour, and shouting armies; battles and numbers of mixed people; and great red sunsets, with women kneeling under them. Do you know those long low sunsets? I love them. They look like blood spilt for love. The noise of the water, and the moist green smell, gave me hundreds of pictures that seemed to hug me. I thought – what could stir music in me more than this? and, am I not just as rich if I stay here with my lover, instead of flying to strange countries, that I shall not care for now? So, you shall take me as I am. I do not feel poor any longer.' (p. 200)

That is the note of the vulnerable, 'innocent' lover of Wilfred, the Wilfred who 'was screwed up to feel' something at this particular utterance. The later note is that of the Emilia who does belong to Italy, but more importantly in a general sense can 'see beyond you'. The later voice is that of a new, hardened, inviolate self. Something she says to Tracy Runningbrooke has the characteristic ring, and is very apposite to her new condition, 'I seem to have got to the other side of you' (p. 580). Again, 'I want something more than our way of talking' (p. 577), and 'I could not see through it before' she says to Georgiana of her promise to Wilfred not to go to Italy if he will not join the Austrians. As that scene (Chap. LVI) shows, the new self and voice is still an impassioned one (again to the contempt of the sentimental English listener).

In what I find to be an impressively fragmentary way this new voice emerges at the end of the novel. Meredith adroitly keeps back its full flow until the last pages, in her letter to Merthyr, where indeed her voice, because it is the last voice, becomes the voice of the novel. That other voice too, the beautiful voice of art, has also had its celebration of a new-found perfection and impersonality in the penultimate chapter. It is not a very successful scene – it is far too cluttered – but it does register Emilia's success in the presence of Wilfred and her rival for him, Lady Charlotte, in separating her voice from personal involvements. In an earlier, matching scene, she couldn't sing before Wilfred in moonlight. And she also sings to detach him from his Austrian sympathies, although inevitably this looks to Charlotte like a 'savage's' vengeance. But this is the last voice, the daylight voice as it were:

My friend! the Poles were at the mercy of Mr. Pericles: Wilfred had struck him: Mr. Pericles was angry and full of mischief. Those dear people had been kind to me, and I heard they were poor. I felt money in my breast, in my throat, that only wanted coining. I went to Georgiana, and oh! how truly she proved to me that she loves you better than I do. She refused to part with money that you might soon want. I laid a scheme for Mr. Pericles to hear me sing. He heard me, and my scheme succeeded. If Italy knew as well as I, she would never let her voice be heard till she is sure of it: – Yes! from foot to head, I knew it was impossible to fail. If a country means to be free, the fire must run through it and make it feel that certainty. Then – away the whitecoat! I sang, and the man twisted, as if I had bent him in my hand. He rushed to me, and offered me any terms I pleased, if for three years I would go to the Conservatorio at Milan, and learn submissively. It is a little grief to me that I think this man loves music more deeply than I do. In the two things I love best, the love of others exceeds mine. I named a sum of money – immense! and I desired that Mr. Pericles should assist Mr. Pole in his business. He consented at once to everything. The next day he gave me the money, and I signed my name and pledged my honour to an engagement. My friends were relieved.

It was then I began to think of you. I had not to study the matter long to learn that I did not love you: and I will not trust my own feelings as they come to me now. I judge myself by my acts, or, Merthyr! I should sink to the ground like a dead body when I think of separation from you for three years. But, what am I? I am a raw girl. I command nothing but raw and flighty hearts of men. Are they worth anything? Let me study three years, without any talk of hearts at all. It commenced too early, and has left nothing to me but a dreadful knowledge of the weakness in most people; – not in you! If I might call you my Beloved! and so chain myself to you, I think I should have all your firmness and double my strength. I will not; for I will not have what I do not deserve. I think of you reading this, till I try to get to you; my heart is like a bird caught in the hands of a cruel boy. By what I have done I know I do not love you. Must we half-despise a man to love him? May no dear woman that I know ever marry the man she first loves! My misery now is gladness, is like raindrops on rising wings, if I say to myself, 'Free! free! Emilia!' I am bound for three years, but I smile at such a bondage to my body. Evviva! my soul is free! Three years of freedom, and no sounding of myself – three years of growing and studying; three years of idle heart! – Merthyr! I throb to think that those three years – true man! my hero, I may call you! – those three years may make me worthy of you. And if you have given all to Italy, that a daughter of Italy should help to return it, seems, my friend, so tenderly sweet – here is the first drop from my eyes!

I would break what you call a Sentiment: I broke my word to Wilfred. But this sight of money has a meaning I cannot conquer. I know you would not wish me to for your own pleasure; and therefore I go. I hope to be growing; I fly like a seed to Italy. Let me drill, and take sharp words, and fret at trifles! I lift my face to that prospect as if I smelt new air. I am changing – I have no dreams of Italy, no longings, but go to see her like a machine to do my work. Whoever speaks to me, I feel that I look at them and know them. I see the faults of my country – Oh, beloved Brescians! not yours, Florentines! not yours, dear Venice! We will be silent when they speak of the Milanese, till Italy can say to them, '*That* conduct is not Italian, my children.' I see the faults. Nothing vexes me . . .

Above all, this is the voice of exhilaration, an exhilaration embracing and transforming the miseries of herself and her friends. It is the voice of movement and energetic change itself ('in our world, where all things must move'), congested with meanings, its transitions and associations abrupt, even obscure, yet serene in its confidence, the seed in flight. It 'breaks' sentiments, it casts a cold but impassioned eye. And it is not the voice of art. Crucially for this question she says of Pericles, 'this man loves music more than I do'. In that same paragraph the musical voice is transformed into the political voice. The training for the impersonal, the achieved voice of art, is also the training for impersonal, that is to say considered and intelligent and still passionate involvement in the political struggle.

Throughout the novel the images of the vitality of art and of the vitality of Emilia herself have been accumulating for this transformation. And what too, I would suggest has been waiting for transformation is that repellent quality in Meredith's tone which I noted near the beginning of the essay; that strained and unsure detachment leaves the book to, is gathered into, this sure and enlivening impersonality. It is in its way the most moving parasiticism in the novel.

III

Fine as *Emilia in England* is there are signs in it of what will go wrong with *Emilia in Italy*. The following is part of a scene where Merthyr and Georgiana are contemplating the sacrifices and horrors involved in the Italian struggle. They are talking about an Italian girl they know well to whom 'it was whispered . . . that her beauty must serve':

'Giulietta?' breathed his sister.
'I would put my life on the truth of that woman's love. Well! – '
'Yes?'
'She abandons herself to the commandant of the citadel'.
A low outcry burst from Georgiana. She fell at Merthyr's knees sobbing violently. He let her sob. In the end she struggled to speak.
'Oh can it be permitted? Oh! can we not save her? Oh, poor soul! my sister! Is she blind to her lover in heaven?'
Georgiana's face was dyed with shame.
'We must put these things by,' said Merthyr. 'Go to Emilia presently, and tell her – settle with her as you think fitting, how she shall see this Wilfred Pole. I have promised her she shall have her wish.'
Coloured by the emotion she was burning from, these words smote Georgiana with a mournful compassion for Merthyr.
He had risen, and by that she knew that nothing could be said to alter his will.

A sentimental pair likewise, if you please; but these were sentimental-ists who served an active deity, and not that arbitrary projection of a subtle selfishness which rules the fairer portion of our fat England. (Chap. XLVIII, p. 509)

This is not really saved by that final categorization of their posturing as sentimental. Through them Meredith is braving the English shock at the horrors of revolution, but the thing which shocks, this image of the 'reality' of the Italian struggle is entirely stiff, theatrical, and unconvincing, not simply in their version of it but in itself. And the parallel between Giulietta and Emilia, with her 'Austrian' Wilfred, seems intended without irony as other scenes in the last part of the novel confirm. At this point we can glimpse the Emilia of *Vittoria* in a world which resounds with phrases and situations like 'She abandons herself to the commandant of the citadel'.

Emilia in Italy is a great disappointment. Having experienced this possibility of a cool and energetic political consciousness – 'I see the faults. Nothing vexes me' – we enter a world of personal and pointless heroics, of elaborate strategems, feuds, and manners. And almost continuously this false world of 'action' is conveyed through a false rhetoric. This is the Countess Ammiana on learning that the Milan revolt has been postponed and that the danger to her son has therefore been postponed also:

The news sent her heart sinking in short throbs down to a delicious rest; but Countess Ammiana disdained to be servile to the pleasure, even as she had strengthened herself to endure the shocks of pain. It was a conquered heart that she and every Venetian and Lombard mother had to carry; one that played its tune according to its nature, shaping no action, sporting no mask. If you know what is meant by that phrase, a conquered heart, you will at least respect them whom you call weak women for having gone through the harshest schooling which this world can show example of. In such mothers Italy revived. The pangs and the martyrdom were theirs. Fathers could march to the field or to the grey glacis with their boys; there was no intoxication of hot blood to cheer those who sat at home watching the rise and fall of trembling scales which said life or death for their dearest . . . Their least shadowy hope could be but a shrouded contentment in prospect; a shrouded submission in feeling. What bloom of hope was there when Austria stood like an iron wall, and their own ones dashing against it were as little feeble waves that left a red mark and no more? But, duty to their country had become their religion; sacrifice they accepted as their portion; when the last stern evil befell them they clad themselves in a veil and walked upon an earth they had passed from for all purposes save service of hands. Italy revived in these mothers. Their torture was that of the re-animation of her frame from the death-trance. (Chap. XVI, p. 186)

The inflation of the rhetoric here destroys the attempt to portray an intelligent suffering feminine consciousness which bears a ghostly resemblance to Emilia's consciousness at the end of *Emilia in England*. And this is the book's rhetoric, not Meredith's local impersonation of the necessarily gross images available to patriotic mothers. One has to make the point here which one is forced to make again and again in reading the novel: we are offered a counter to crudeness – she 'disdained to be servile to the pleasure' – which is itself crude.

Here is another example, on Mazzini:

Watching over his Italy; her wrist in his meditative clasp year by year; he stood like a mystic leech by the couch of a fair and hopeless frame, pledged to revive it by the inspired assurance, shared by none, that life had not forsaken it. A body given over to death and vultures – he stood by it in the desert. Is it a marvel to you that when the carrion-wings swooped low, and the claws fixed, and the beak plucked and savoured its morsel, he raised his arm, and urged the half-resuscitated frame to some vindicating show of existence? Arise! he said, even in what appeared most fatal hours of darkness. The slack limbs moved; the body rose and fell. The cost of the effort was the breaking out of innumerable wounds, old and new; the gain was the display of the miracle that Italy lived. She tasted her own blood, and herself knew that she lived . . . (Chap. XVII, p. 200)

And so the ludicrous image goes on, and the desperate, hollow, violence of language. In the next paragraph 'Austrians marched like a merry flame down Milan streets, and Italians stood like the burnt-out cinders of the fire-grate'. In an earlier chapter, there is a particularly prize image, 'The blood forsook Count Medole's cheeks, leaving its dead-hue, as when blotting-paper is laid on running-ink.' (A just possible joke about blue blood?)

153

Any account of the literary personality of Meredith would have to deal at large with his characteristic resort to imagery of grotesque animation – puppetry, risen corpses, and the like. It would be easy to suggest that these are the frantic gestures of one of 'those who know that they do not embrace life'. Here I would merely underline that this kind of language exhibits continually the defeat of the attempt to realize epical action, to work up the machinery of passion and 'plain issues'.

The Emilia of the earlier novel is almost entirely lost sight of. This is nearly literally true – she can't emerge from the frantic to-and-fro of the action, she is lost in the large 'cast'. And what presence she has is as one of the operatic, heroic postures. The themes of *Emilia in England* are inertly repeated, love of art and love of country, personal relationships and public duty, women in politics. It is all on the level of 'abandoning oneself to the commandent of the citadel', which in fact Emilia does in a substitute way, as expected, by making a sort of love to Wilfred, turning him into almost a traitor.

In that sense Emilia is one of the English in Italy – like Wilfred and Powys she does not participate fully in the violences and vengeances of the Austrians and Italians.

There is an occasional glimpse of a different Emilia:

> He had read Tuscan poetry to her in old Agostino's rooms; he had spoken of secret preparations for the revolt; he had declaimed upon Italy – the poetry was good though the declamation may have been bad – but she had always been singularly irresponsive, with a practical turn for ciphers. A quick reckoning, a sharp display of figures in Italy's cause, kindled her cheeks and took her breath . . . (Chap. XV, p. 174)

There is a touch there certainly of the impassioned practicality of the earlier self, but on the whole she is presented much more grossly:

> but how, thought Carlo, how can a mind like Vittoria's find matter to suit her in such sentences? He asked himself the question, forgetting that a little time gone by, while he was aloof from the tumult and dreaming of it, this airy cloudy language and symbolism, had been strong sustaining food, a vital atmosphere, to him. He did not for the moment (though by degrees he recovered his last night's conception of her) understand that among the nobler order of women there is, when *they*

plunge into strife, a craving for idealistic truths, which men are apt, under the heat and hurry of their energies, to put aside as stars that are meant merely for shining. (Chap. XVI, p. 188)

This passage refers to the previous one, the 'he' in both cases being Carlo Ammiana. In the second we have lost the practical Emilia completely. She is reduced to the 'noble' woman needing sugared politics, and we are once more in a familiar inert 'problem' in the novel – male and female attitudes to war and political struggle.

The hollowness of the prose and of Emilia are confirmed if we look at the novel as an account of the events in Italy in 1848–49. It has often been noted that the course of the narrative follows closely the course of events in Northern Italy during the rising, and that Meredith gives a detailed insight into the various contending groups on the Italian side. The minimal truth contained in this view hardly affects the matter. It does seem to me to be true that where Meredith is making general remarks about the political and military situation he is convincing. But the fictional enactment is another matter altogether, and the experience we get from that is of the Italian struggle reduced and guyed as a series of family feuds and points of honour. The concern with chivalric conduct, good manners, the containment of enmity within the equivalence of class, is at the forefront. At several points in the novel both 'sides' are present and subject to the rules of the drawing-room.

The episode of the shirt in Chapter XXIX is in this respect instructive and representative. Wilfred and Rinaldo Guidascarpi are both imprisoned in Barto Rizzi's 'underground'. Although on opposite sides, they find themselves united against the sinister leader of the people. What connects them in gentlemanly values is so much more obvious than what makes them official foes. This sense is increased by the stress on their peculiar individual fates to which the struggle is really only a kind of backdrop. There is just one moment I want to note. The possibility of escape has arisen because Barto's wife is in love with Rinaldo (there is an obsessive repetition of the traitorous woman motif throughout the book):

The woman tended them in the same unswerving silence, and at whiles that adorable maternity of aspect. Wilfred was touched by commiseration

for her. He was too bitterly fretful on account of clean linen and the liberty which fluttered the prospect of it, to think much upon what her fate might be: perhaps a beating, perhaps the knife. But the vileness of wearing one shirt two months and more had hardened his heart . . .
(p. 385)

There is irony here but hardly enough. That concern for clean linen seems too typical of the central values of the book.

Nevertheless the possibilities of an irony, a detachment and judgment of these values is there. Conveyed almost in spite of the frantic heroics and posturing is the sense that we are watching the death-throes of a class. The fatalism of Rinaldo has a touch of this earlier in the same scene: 'We Italians of this period are children of thunder and live the life of a flash. The worms may creep on: the men must die. Out of us springs a better world' (p. 377).

At times the ironies emerge more strongly. I take this to be the case in the following, where again several of the well-born principals from both sides have met and with some strain the proprieties are being kept up, while the street battles of Milan are raging:

> Wilfred saw the lighted passage into the great house, and thither, throwing out his arms, he bore the affrighted group of ladies, as a careful shepherd might do. Returning to Count Lenkenstein's side, 'Where are they?' the count said, in mortal dread. 'Safe', Wilfred replied. The count frowned at him inquisitively. 'Cut your way through, and on!' he cried to three or four who hung near him; and these went to the slaughter. (Chap. xxx, p. 394)

This has a laconic pointedness, although it is an unworkable extra dimension that at this point in the story Wilfred has been reduced to the ranks.

At other times the privileged romantic-heroic view of the struggle is explicitly exposed. Emilia and Laura witness the battle of Past-rengo, 'They had come to see the Song of Deborah performed before their eyes, and they witnessed only a battle' (Chap. xxxii, p. 419). It is Laura again, admittedly in the crude context of pretending to abandon oneself to an Austrian, who says to Emilia, 'You have done nothing – worse than nothing . . . you have some vile Romance of

Chivalry in your head; a modern sculptor's figure, "MEDITA-TION" . . .' However this particular moment is an absurd crisis for Emilia. 'Now that it was demanded of her to play coquette and trick her womanhood with false allurements, she knew the sentiment of utter ruin; she was ashamed. No word is more lightly spoken than shame . . .' (Chap. XXVII, p. 344). This is the Emilia who exploits her beauty and presence in *Emilia in England*.

The few ironies then emerge reluctantly. What could have been a tactic, a dialectical impersonation and transformation to match the creation of Emilia's voice in the first novel, remains an indulgence. The revolt which begins in the Opera House remains there. It is only potentially significant that in order to vindicate her honour Emilia goes ahead with the insurrectionary aria in spite of the collapse of the revolt. This sense of a substitute engagement in the struggle continues throughout the novel – Carlo's final choice, against Emilia's advice, is for Brescia and not Rome. It is potentially significant only that Emilia has contact with all elements on the Italian side, including the King of Sardinia. In fact this is merely part of the spectacle of different groups, and even that is qualified by the abhorrence with which Barto Rizzi is presented.

But there are a few moments where something better seems realized, where at least one can say the prose recovers itself. An interesting if subdued tendency in the novel is towards an absurdist view of the spectacle and antics of the struggle. This gets directed mainly through the increasingly ambiguous figure of Wilfred, as the ungentlemanly spy with his large white umbrella, who wanders between the lines: 'Wilfred was fast growing to be an eccentric by profession. To appear cool and careless was the great effort of his mind' (Chap. XXX, p. 397). Of course this kind of inpersonality is motivated mainly by his forlorn, 'sentimental', love for Emilia. But it does gather some of the force of a consciousness shuffled among the parties. And this kind of impersonality is relevant to one of the finest passages in the book, the delirium of Captain Weipress when he has been badly wounded in the duel with Angelo Guidascarpi:

> A vision of leaping tumbrils, and long marching columns about to deploy, passed before his eyelids: he thought he had fallen on the battle-field, and heard a drum beat furiously in the back of his head; and

on streamed the cavalry, wonderfully caught away to such a distince that the figures were all diminutive, and the regimental colours swam in smoke, and the enemy danced a plume here and there out of the sea, while his mother and a forgotten Ciennese girl gazed at him with exactly the same unfamiliar countenance, and refused to hear that they were unintelligible in the roaring of guns and floods and hurrahs, and the thumping of the tremendous big drum behind his head – 'somewhere in the middle of the earth': he tried to explain the locality of that terrible drumming noise to them, and Vittoria conceived him to be delirious; but he knew that he was sensible; he knew her and Angelo and the mountain-pass, and that he had a cigar-case in his pocket, worked in embroidery of crimson, blue, and gold, by the hand of Countess Anna. He said distinctly that he desired the cigar-case to be delivered to Countess Anna at the Castle of Sonnenberg, and rejoiced on being assured that his wish was comprehended and should be fulfilled; but the marvel was, that his mother should still refuse to give him wine, and suppose him to be a boy: and when he was so thirsty and dry-lipped that though Mina was bending over him, just fresh from Mariazell, he had not the heart to kiss her or lift an arm to her! – His horse was off with him – whither? – He was going down with a company of infantry in the Gulf of Venice: cards were in his hands, visible, though he could not feel them, and as the vessel settled for the black plunge, the cards flushed all honours, and his mother shook her head at him: he sank, and heard Mina sighing all the length of water to the bottom, which grated and gave him two horrid shocks of pain: and he cried for a doctor, and admitted that his horse had managed to throw him; but wine was the cure, brandy was the cure, or water, water! (Chap. XXVI, p. 318)

Meredith has a particular gift for representing a delirious condition, and this is a fine example of it. The sense of shifting, coalescing experience is very precisely caught – 'the cards flushed all honours' – as is the sense of distance and commotion, and the rhythm of the accelerating desperation behind the images of it. The fluidity of the passage is very striking, and seems to me to invite comparison with the fluidity, and a similar quality of assimilation, in Emilia's letter in *Emilia in England*. In one sense of course the impersonality involved here, the impersonality of apparently approaching death, is the opposite of the life-enhancing motion that Emilia exhibits, her impersonal exhilaration. It is part of a general movement in the book towards war-weariness, peace, and death.

But as I have already indicated the novel is full, often in a grotesque manner, of life coming through death, agonizing rebirth and re-animation, the corpse coming alive, 'In such mothers Italy lives' etc. I have also pointed to the level of more explicit statement where this generation of Italians is dying for the next; and to the concealed possibility that this class of Italians (and Austrians) is killing itself off, the heroic and chivalrous antics almost literally being death-throes.

It is on this deeper level – which I have argued is hardly ever present in the second novel – that we have to read a passage like the delirium of Weipress, a level which is only fully significant in connection with the Emilia possibility of the first novel. It is only on this level that the being-fair-to-both-sides attitude which Meredith adopts escapes from facile spectacle to achieve a suggestion of a dying order incubating a new possibility, comes near to an equivalence and expansion of the dialectic of parasiticism in *Emilia in England*. And this level once again finds an adequate symbol and an adequate prose, in the pregnant Emilia facing the possibility of the death of her husband. That melodramatic 'mother of Italy' does at last find a transforming expression:

Not to hope blindly, in the exceeding anxiousness of her passionate love, nor blindly to fear; not to let her soul fly out among the twisting chances; not to sap her great maternal duty by affecting false stoical serenity; – to nurse her soul's strength, and suckle her womanly weakness with the tears which are poison when repressed; to be at peace with a disastrous world for the sake of the dependent life unborn; by such pure efforts she clung to God. Soft dreams of sacred nuptial tenderness, tragic images, wild pity, were like phantoms encircling her, plucking at her as she went, but they were beneath her feet, and she kept them from lodging between her breasts. The thought that her husband, though he should have perished, was not a life lost if their child lived, sustained her powerfully. It seemed to whisper at times almost as it were Carlo's ghost breathing in her ears: 'On thee!' On her the further duty devolved; and she trod down hope, lest it should build her up and bring a shock to surprise her fortitude: she put back alarm. (Chap. XLVI, p. 618)

2. *Beauchamp's Career*

Meredith was trying to transform a fiction of delicacy and 'morbidity' into a fiction of purpose and action, and in so doing providing a model of political and social awareness, of the possibilities of a developing consciousness in the England of the 1860s. This attempt had turned gross in the postures and heroics of *Emilia in Italy*, and, I should note in passing, become trivialized in the attempted 'plain' novel of the people *Rhoda Fleming* (1865).[4] But before committing himself fully, although momentarily, to comic detachment (the *Essay on Comedy* (1877), *The Egoist* (1879)), before writing those works, together with *Modern Love*, which still give him currency, he wrote his finest political novel, *Beauchamp's Career*.[5]

I am not going to give a full account of the novel. I think it is a finer work than *The Egoist*, as brilliant and assured as the latter, with a greater fullness and resonance, certainly a greater ambition. I am also going to neglect its more obvious political content – its reflection of the confused political scene of the 1860s, its impersonation of the available rhetorics of reaction and reform, its dissection of the uneasy alliances of Whig and Tory, Liberal and Radical, and its notation of the realities of canvas and election.

In one sense the political reality is never there, or never there nakedly. It is a novel of talk about politics, of conversation which includes politics. This may be merely to say that the novel never forgets it is a novel, never forgets to justify within its fictional world (often very adroitly) the appearance of political statement and judge-ment. To take the obvious example, Dr Shrapnel's 'revolutionary' letter to Beauchamp, for which he deserves 'hanging' and partly on account of which he gets a whipping, never comes to us straight. It is always introduced or performed by a particular character in a particular dramatic context – Cecil Baskelett, Beauchamp himself, Seymour Austen. It never speaks for itself, and in itself is remote from the realities it describes.

But then, one might say, that is the whole point of a political novel. If it is minor it sugars its politics with the trappings of fiction, if it is substantial it makes political 'realities' inevitably part of a larger reality, makes them naturally part of a dramatic context. But this leads too easily away from the connection that has to be made between this sense of an indirect mediation of politics and Meredith's characteristic fictional method. It is true of Meredith's fiction generally, as it is of *Beauchamp's Career*, that we aren't often there: we get versions of the event rather than the event itself. And this question of direct presentation is itself a version of the choice between 'delicate' and 'epical' fiction I began the essay with. And as well as typical examples of this evasion of action – the duel in France, the whipping of Shrapnel – *Beauchamp's Career* contains direct comment on the avoidance of satisfyingly simple and dramatic event. For Meredith it is part of the enterprise of resisting romantic possibilities, 'I must try to paint for you what is, not that which I imagine' (p. 6). When Renée comes to London to offer herself to Beauchamp, Meredith ruefully comments on the two heroic possibilities for Beauchamp he can't take up: 'off with his love like the rover' or 'Conscious rectitude . . . after the pattern of the well-behaved Aeneas quitting the fair bosom of Carthage in obedience to the Gods' (p. 406). And the most interesting passage of this kind comes near the end of the novel:

> We will make no mystery about it. I would I could. Those happy tales of mystery are as much my envy as the popular narratives of the deeds of bread and cheese people, for they both create a tideway in the attentive mind; the mysterious pricking our credulous flesh to creep, the familiar urging our obese imagination to constitutional exercise. And oh, the refreshment there is in dealing with characters either contemptibly beneath us or supernaturally above! My way is like a Rhone island in the summer drought, stony, unattractive and difficult between the two forceful streams of the unreal and the over-real, which delight mankind – honour to the conjurers! My people conquer nothing, win none; they are actual, yet uncommon. It is the clockwork of the brain that they are directed to set in motion, and – poor troop of actors to vacant benches! – the conscience residing in thoughtfulness which they would appeal to; and if you are there impervious to them, we are lost: back I go to my wilderness, where, as you perceive, I have contracted the habit of listening to my own voice more than is good . . . (p. 479)

This could be taken for a rather contorted statement of an unexceptional realism comparable say to George Eliot's in *Adam Bede*. But, as with George Eliot, there are difficulties and ambiguities in the statement. The impact of the passage is less that of the difficulty of some middle way (curiously frozen in the image of an island) between unreal and overreal, than the pathos of a writer without an audience who becomes identified with the figures he creates; 'My people conquer nothing, win none; they are actual, yet uncommon'. This reality is the reality of failure, the reality of frustration, the reality of the impossibility of the real – 'actual, yet uncommon'. The graspable, the conquerable, can't count.

There is something wilful in this which any simple account of the narrative might confirm. The moment when Beauchamp asks Cecilia to marry him carries succinctly the repeated and elaborated note of the novel: 'I ask you to marry me!' 'It is too late' (p. 464). It is a novel of missed opportunities, or opportunities delayed too long, a novel of unappreciated moments and unappreciated people which culminates in a wasteful death. It is its energy to connect (say) Beauchamp's refusal or inability to take possession of Renée in Venice, his reluctance to propose to Cecilia, with Shrapnel's resilient acceptance of the postponement of the inevitable revolutionary dawn, to connect the proposed radical newspaper *The Dawn* with that enchanting dawn over the Alps approaching Venice with Renée, to dwell subtly on that landscape into which Beauchamp and Cecilia are manoeuvred to finalize their love – the downs 'weaving a story without beginning, crisis, or conclusion, flowerless and fruitless but with something of infinite in it sweeter to brood on than the future of her life to Cecilia' (p. 352). The political attitude of *Beauchamp's Career* enforced by the whole weight of its incident and imagery is that of the postponed moment, poised against the 'politics of impatience' and the impatience of life: 'unhesitatingness was the warrior virtue of her desire' (p. 398).

That is Renée's desire when after a life of hesitation she offers herself to Beauchamp. And it is a reminder that throughout the novel Captain Beauchamp is the lapsed warrior hero, the good sailor making a fool of himself ashore. For his own family and class he is a personification of lost opportunity who won't get another command because of his engagement in radical politics. And yet at the same time, in a way very similar to the intricate parasitical

processes of *Emilia in England* they feed on his direct energy, even
if that energy in its political expression is a perversion of some real
warrior self. He is, and will be, 'missed'. Making sport of Beauchamp
is the continuous game of the book. There is a constant stream of
ridicule and mimicry which depends on him, which, in figures like
the Earl of Romfrey can involve an admiration for his resolution.
This admiration is again most clearly felt in the women of his class.
Rosamund Culling goes through agonies in separating the man from
the politics. Cecilia Halkett does too, and reveals much more trans-
parently the contradiction of the attitude of his class to Beauchamp.
In a brilliant passage, after 'the ride in the wrong direction', when
instead of proposing to her Beauchamp takes her to see Shrapnel
prostrate after his whipping from Romfrey, Cecilia 'condemned
his extreme wrath with his uncle, yet was attracted and enchained
by the fire of passionate attachment which aroused it . . . She was
loving him in emulation of his devotedness to another person: and
that other was a revolutionary common people's doctor! an infidel,
a traitor to his country's interests. But Nevil loved him, and it had
become impossible for her not to covet the love, or to think of the
old offender without the halo cast by Nevil's attachment being upon
him' (p. 340). This is not simply something belonging to Cecilia's
personal love agony, it is representative of a regard and fascination
for Beauchamp which finds itself having to face not only his love of
Shrapnel, and his love of other women, but eventually his love of the
people.

But of course the really telling contradictions come in Beauchamp
himself. The failure of *Vittoria* was partly owing to an inability,
except at rare moments, to achieve a sufficiently ironic presentation of
a revolutionary upper class. With Beauchamp Meredith succeeds
magnificently. As a distraction, a 'holiday', from his political commitment Renée is a key figure of course. I will come back to her, but I
would repeat the point here made of Cecilia that there is no easy way
of separating Beauchamp as lover and as politician, although I think
it might be argued that the Renée parts of the novel are somewhat
over-indulged. But what is most obviously an indication of Beauchamp's contradiction is his involvement with his family and class,
and the way that comes to focus on Shrapnel's 'insult' to Rosamund,

the whipping of Shrapnel, and the demand for an apology. The argument with his family and class comes to replace the political commitment, and although apparently involving a confrontation really is a revelation of shared values. Both sides draw on the same code of good manners and points of honour. As the novel goes on it wears increasingly the appearance of a novel of family honour where the final victory is not political at all but one of a conceded apology. At the end of Chapter LV Rosamond says to Romfrey:

> '. . . but what I feel is that he – our Nevil! – has accomplished hardly anything, if anything!'
>
> 'He hasn't marched on London with a couple of hundred thousand men: no, he hasn't done that,' the earl said glancing back in his mind through Beauchamp's career. '. . . No: we haven't had much public excitement out of him. But one thing he did do: *he got me down on my knees!*'
>
> Lord Romfrey pronounced these words with a sober emphasis that struck the humour of it sharply into Rosamund's heart, through some contrast it presented between Nevil's aim at the world and hit of a man: the immense deal thought of it by the earl, and the very little that Nevil would think of it – the great domestic achievement to be boasted of by an enthusiastic devotee of politics!

This recognition of an absurd substitution is continuously and variously present throughout the novel. It gets an added force here from Rosamund's position of unwillingly carrying the heir to the Romfrey estate who will substitute for Beauchamp, that heir who will live one hour in the Earl's arms, to be replaced either by Beauchamp's son or that 'insignificant bit of mudbank life' in the marvellously laconic ending of the book. The attention to Beauchamp's contradiction is partly conveyed through direct comment on him, such as Stukely Culbrett's, 'He speaks, but won't act, as if he were among enemies.' But again it's Meredith's great achievement to catch the contradiction in episodes as well as in sharp observation. The most striking example of this, apart from the major focus of the whipping of Shrapnel, is the plan to trick Beauchamp to ride into town with the procession supporting the second Tory candidate. The force of this episode is the suggestion that that is where Beauchamp naturally belongs, that indeed he should be the second Tory candidate, and that the procession is merely the logical extension of his being a guest at Itchincope, of 'getting to be one of them again'. The general absurdity and contradiction of that stay at Itchincope is superbly epitomized in Beauchamp's argument with his host, Grancey Lespel, the 'renegade Whig': 'You are dead . . . *Dead*, my dear Mr Lespel' (p. 192).

When Beauchamp and Shrapnel express their own political ideas directly there are similar contradictions. Typical of the period – Arnold's *Culture and Anarchy*, George Eliot's *Felix Holt* and 'Address to Working Men, by Felix Holt' (*Blackwoods Magazine*, 1868), are other versions of it – is the suggestion of a revolution to prevent the revolution. Cecilia puts it to Beauchamp in one of their many political wooing scenes ('politically he deemed that women have souls'):

> 'So you would blow up my poor Mount Laurels for a peace-offering to the lower classes?'
> 'I should hope to put it on a stronger foundation, Cecilia.'
> 'By means of some convulsion?'
> 'By forestalling one.' (p. 143)

Then the discussion shifts (the juxtaposition is calculated) to the quality of Britain's naval defences. Again, the contradiction is caught in Beauchamp's 'I say that is no aristocracy, if it does not head the people in virtue – military, political, national: I mean the qualities required by the times for leadership' (p. 269). This is potentially an argument for making the aristocracy fit to rule again (the parallels with Arnold and Carlyle are clear). The youthful Beauchamp felt sure 'the nobles might resume their natural alliance with the people' (p. 27), and that word 'head' is adroitly ambiguous, allowing the distinct possibility of 'head off'. It is not surprising that the mature Tory attitude as personified in Seymour Austen and Stukely Culbrett can accept and assimilate Beauchamp and Shrapnel to the idea of the old alliance of squire and people against the middle-class. 'Head' is again crucial in these remarks of Culbrett:

> 'Who won the great liberties for England? My book says, the nobles. And who made the great stand later? – the squires. What have the middlemen done but bid for the people they despise and fear, dishonour

us abroad and make a hash of us at home? Shrapnel sees that. Only he has got the word people in his mouth. The people of England, my dear fellow, want *heading*. Since the traders obtained power we have been a country on all fours. Of course Shrapnel sees it: I say so. But talk to him and teach him where to look for the rescue.' (p. 347)

This is partly the tactics of assimilating opposition but the 'radical' position here, by its contradictions, is ready-made for assimilation. The entrée of Beauchamp's cousin Blackburn Tuckham, the 'Manchester' of the book who does such good work in pacifying Colonel Halkett's Welsh miners, is managed quite differently of course.

It is part of this confusion of alliances (which, like confusion of mind in the novel operates to support and confirm the status quo) that Seymour Austen should be more 'radical' in his view of women than Beauchamp. He was 'a firm believer in new and higher destinies for women' (p. 262). Of course Cecilia's 'new and higher destiny' turns out to be marrying, under Austen's guidance, Blackburn Tuckham. And this does not appear a crude irony when one watches him, under Cecilia's eye, at his watercolours or turning the pages of her music: the middle class is being civilized, at least made presentable for the drawing room. Indeed it is through its attention to the role of women that the novel achieves some of its most brilliant effects, and in particular prepares for its most remarkable substitution: women for the people.

Beauchamp's attitude towards women is complex, not to say confusing. His relationships with women particularly with Renée involves him in obvious conflict of private and public ambition. But, and the same point could be made of Henry James' *Tragic Muse*, there is never a facile opposition of love and politics: the choice of one reveals the choice of the other rather than shutting it off. This is the clearest way in which Beauchamp is 'trying to be two men at once'. For the moment I would want to insist more on the connected point that Beauchamp finds himself having to accept the moral norms and conventions especially in relation to women of the society he intends to revolutionize. One doesn't need reminding that scruples about a woman's honour are at the centre of the plotting, whether concerning Renée or Rosamund. When Shrapnel says

'Rebellion against Society, and advocacy of Humanity, run counter' he is referring to sexual morality and convention. And inevitably he must state what for the book is the fullest paradox of simultaneous conservatism and radicalism: 'Society is the protection of the weaker, therefore a shield of women, who are our temple of civilization to be kept sacred.' Society must be destroyed/preserved to protect the weak.

The most relevant passage here comes after one of Beauchamp's scenes with Cecilia:

> He was dropped by the *Esperanza*'s boat near Otley ferry, to walk along the beach to Bevisham, and he kept eye on the elegant vessel as she glided swan-like to her moorings off Mount Laurels park through dusky merchant craft, colliers, and trawlers, loosely shaking her towering snow-white sails, unchallenged in her scornful supremacy; an image of a refinement of beauty, and of a beautiful servicelessness.
>
> As the yacht, so the mistress: things of wealth, owing their graces to wealth, devoting them to wealth – splendid achievements of art both! and dedicated to the gratification of the superior senses.
>
> Say that they were precious examples of an accomplished civilisation; and perhaps they did offer a visible ideal of grace for the rough world to aim at. They might in the abstract address a bit of monition to the uncultivated, and encourage the soul to strive toward perfection in beauty: and there is no contesting beauty when the soul is taken into account. But were they not in too great a profusion in proportion to their utility? That was the question for Nevil Beauchamp. The democratic spirit inhabiting him, temporarily or permanently, asked whether they were not increasing to numbers which were oppressive? And further, whether it was good for the country, the race, ay, the species, that they should be so distinctly removed from the thousands who fought the grand, and the grisly, old battle with nature for bread of life. Those grimy sails of the colliers and fishing-smacks, set them in a great sea, would have beauty for eyes and soul beyond that of elegance and refinement. And do but look on them thoughtfully, the poor are everlastingly, unrelievedly, in the abysses of the great sea . . . (p. 134)

This is discreetly yet eloquently done, the 'political' workings of Beauchamp's mind drawing with precise dramatic justification on the available images. Once more there is the note of heading off the poor – are we too many, too conspicuous? – but the crucial attempt here, and what I take to be the crucially organized failure of the book, is to connect beautiful mistress and grimy poor, to make them both 'beautiful' by the very process of thinking through images. Inevitably Beauchamp can't keep up 'a line of meditation . . . half-built on the sensations as well as the mind'. The polarity asserts itself again:

> Did Beauchamp at all desire to have those idly lovely adornments of riches, the Yacht and the Lady, swept away? Oh dear no. He admired them, he was at home with them. They were much to his taste. Standing on a point of the beach for a last look at them before he set his face to the town, he prolonged the look in a manner to indicate that the place where business called him was not in comparison at all so pleasing . . .

Beauchamp, like many of Meredith's characters, doesn't think enough, he possesses or is possessed by a hesitant, awakening consciousness. The novel indeed is full of innocents awakening and it is my proposition that they are presented as substitute images of the awakening of the people. It is Beauchamp's innocence which appeals to the women of the book. And it is the elaborate presentation of feminine consciousnesses growing aware of the world of politics and the world of men which is one of its most unifying elements. I think it is not too much to say that the novel is written for the most part through a feminine consciousness. We wait until the women hear or see. We watch with Rosamund the soundless pantomime of Romfrey, Cecil Baskelett, and Colonel Halkett on the lawn (Chap. xiv) discussing 'the leading article'. We follow the timid intrusion of Cecilia and Mrs Lespel into the men's smoking room to view the skit on Beauchamp's involvement with Renée (Chap. xx). The situation is endlessly repeated, and along with it go persistent questions about the propriety and capability of feminine consciousness, their rights of access. 'The less men and women know of one another, the happier for them,' says Mrs Lespel after the horror of the entry into the smoking room. Romfrey says, 'Telling the truth to women is an impertinence' – which is in fact the succinct account of the insult (Shrapnel babbling politics at her) to Rosamund. But the great weight of the book is on the other side, with great tact and sympathy but also an extraordinary demandingness accompanying the hesitant needs to know. It is Rosamund who eventually says, when claiming the right to know how ill Beauchamp is, with the true note of Emilia,

'Ni espoir, ni crainte, mais point de déceptions. Lumière. Ce sont les ténèbres qui tuent' (p. 499). Again, Cecilia speaks for this consciousness when undergoing one of the many male explanations of politics, this time by Seymour Austen, 'the use of imagery makes me feel that I am addressed as a primitive intelligence' (p. 261).

Now it is quite justifiable to argue that here lies the true theme of the novel, a theme which in fact did preoccupy Meredith for much of his life. If the liberation of women is this true theme, the real political possibility, then that is Beauchamp's missed chance. He is the potential champion lost to the brutal world of male politics, and hampered by an underlying assumption of women as 'beautiful servicelessness'.

But to rest there is to seriously undervalue the complexity and ambition of the novel. Cecilia is made to feel she is 'a *primitive* intelligence' and this kind of connection between unawakened woman and unawakened mass is continually made, as I have already indicated. Partly this is a question of local verbal connection. 'We are women, born to our lot. If we could rise en masse!' says Renée (p. 233). But most frequently it is the juxtapositions of women and ideas of women with the people or more commonly images or ideas of the people which sets up a kind of continuum in which the two and their terms become to a certain extent interchangeable. So that when Beauchamp says to Blackburn Tuckham, of the people, 'I mean to educate them by giving them an interest in their country' (p. 451) this could apply equally in the book to women, as could Tuckham's reply 'You don't know them.' Similarly, after Cecilia has allowed herself to become engaged to Tuckham and sinks into an 'agreeable stupor', she feels 'like one deposited on a mudbank after buffeting the waves' (p. 476) which adroitly slips her into that stream of insensate mudbank imagery which attaches to the subject of 'the people' throughout the novel. And the contempt for women, partially concealed in idealization of them, seems to find a natural expression in the savagery of the terms used in discussing the people (in such discussions women are often a mute element in the group): 'an idiot population . . . the dullest and wretchedest people in Europe . . . the various unearthly characters he had inspected in their dens . . . vermin . . . clowns . . . doltish'. Very near the end

Romfrey, when Beauchamp lies apparently dying after catching fever from a poor family he has visited, thinks 'of Nevil laying down his life for such men as these gross excessive breeders, of ill shape and wooden countenance . . . the madness of Nevil in endeavouring to lift them up and brush them up' (p. 500).

And yet, and even Romfrey recognized this in a fleeting way at that same moment, 'their love is the only love worth having' (p. 280). The language of sexual love naturally substitutes for the language of political love. And coming through the contradictions of Beauchamp's attitude to women and his political attitude finely imaged in his delirium heard by the assembled classes, is an intellectually hardened 'love' which operates as does the dawn on the Alps like 'a revelation of the kingdom in the heart of night' (p. 70). It is there in that 'capital fault of treating her as an equal' (p. 71), in 'the idea that he might reason with her (which) made her seductive to the heart and head of him' (p. 394). In his canvassing of the electors Beauchamp receives curtly a 'vote given for reasons of sentiment' (p. 171).

Of course Beauchamp dies twice. Once, symbolizing the agony of consciousness of all the classes, a second time physically restored, in a kind of throw-back to his earlier heroic sailor self, to the simplest image of his revolutionary love, rescuing an 'insignificant bit of mudbank life'. 'And do but look on them thoughtfully, the poor are everlastingly, unrelievedly, in the abysses of the great sea . . .', an earlier image had it. But this final scene is brilliantly minimal, teasing the reader with the confidence of a securely unread author into bringing the whole novel to bear, in order to make that triumphant transfer of worth from Beauchamp to the boy, 'This is what we have in exchange for Beauchamp!'

But I would suggest one earlier point of reference, where Cecilia completes – too late of course – that relinquishment of a false image of Beauchamp which – 'Incubus on incubus' (one of Beauchamp's descriptions of England) – had dominated her:

> . . . she discerned the retributive vain longings, in the guise of high individual superiority and distinction, that had thwarted her with Nevil Beauchamp, never permitting her to love single-mindedly or whole-heartedly, but always in reclaiming her rights and sighing for the loss of her ideal.

George Meredith: 'Delicate' and 'Epical' Fiction

This is the career of the book, and it is too the shape of Meredith's ambition, the promise of his Emilia possibility: to go from a condition of 'no clear central feeling' (Beauchamp concerning Renée) toward a 'strong sincerity dwelling amid multiform complexities'.

And it is the great triumph of *Beauchamp's Career* to make its people, particularly its women, in their uneasy present and in their glimpsed potentiality, almost represent the people: 'My people conquer nothing, win none; they are actual, yet uncommon.'

NOTES

1. All page and chapter references are to the standard edition of the *Works of George Meredith*, London, 1914. References are given in parentheses after the quotations.
2. *The Letters of George Meredith*, ed. C. L. Cline, 3 vols., London, 1970, vol. 1, pp. 319 and 322.
3. *The Poems of Clough*, London, 1951, p. 189. The quotation comes from CANTO II, Letter IV. of *Amours de Voyage*.
4. But see my discussion of this novel in a forthcoming book *Meredith Now* edited by Ian Fletcher.
5. First published in serial form in the *Fortnightly Review*, from August 1874 to December 1875. It seems likely that Meredith was working on the novel from the time of his involvement in his friend Captain Maxse's standing as radical candidate for Southampton in the election of 1867. My references are to the World's Classics Text. It is incorrectly stated there that the serial was a condensed version of the book form. In his letters Meredith writes of omitting scenes for the serial publication, but these scenes have never appeared in any edition of the novel. The serial form except for very trivial changes is the same as all later editions.

VII

CONSERVATISM AND REVOLUTION IN THE 1880s

JOHN LUCAS

'Oh, life would be all right if we could only be rid of these infernal fools who come to poor people's doors presenting their "demands for the ideal".' Dr. Relling in *The Wild Duck*.

In his *Memoirs of Life and Literature*, W. H. Mallock recalls his early days as a Conservative apologist and the reasons which at the beginning of the 1880s had stung him into activity on his party's behalf. He knew that the doctrines of Karl Marx 'had long been fermenting in the minds of certain English malcontents,' he had become aware of Henry George and his desire for the confiscation 'not of private capital, but simply and solely of privately-owned land,' and he realized that Ruskin was trying to rewrite economic science 'in terms of sentiment which sometimes, but only on rare occasions, struck fire by chance contact with the facts of life.' Accordingly, Mallock began to devote his time 'to the task of reducing this chaos of revolutionary thought to order.'[1] One result of this new committedness was that he joined the Liberty and Property Defence League, which began in 1883, and became its 'most vigorous pamphleteer.'[2] But more important, he produced two treatises, *Social Equality*, 1882, and *Property and Progress*, 1884, and a novel, *The Old Order Changes*, 1886, all of which set out to defend Conservatism and Conservative interests against the 'chaos of revolutionary thought'.

I make no apology for placing Mallock at the centre of a study of the conflicting forces of Conservatism and revolution in the 1880s. It is not only that he is, in Raymond Williams's words, 'the ablest

Conservative thinker of the last eighty years,'[3] but that quite simply he was the most persistent and articulate spokesman for an ideology that found itself increasingly under pressure as the decade wore on. And because he defended that ideology in both polemical work and novel he becomes a necessary starting-point for any consideration of how political ideas affected the life of fiction during the 1880s. There will be a great deal more to say about the fiction but the first if tedious step is to provide the essential context in which Mallock's work took place.

I

For several reasons, the Conservatives found the first half of the 1880s a time of reorganization. There was, for example, the problem they found themselves facing as a result of the widening of the franchise.

> In the sixties a new era opened in British political life. The electorate was much enlarged in 1867 and again in 1885. In consequence party organization became more important, much more attention was paid to political propaganda and there was a rapid rise in the oratorical productivity of politicians . . .
> Politics were also analysed and argued over in the magazines. The quarterlies, old-fashioned, solid and sedate periodicals, whose approach was full and deliberate, being supplemented by a new type of periodical, represented by the *Fortnightly* (1865), the *Nineteenth Century* (1887), and the *National Review* (1863), in which articles tended to be short, lucid and provocative.[4]

Initially, at least, the Liberals adapted themselves better to this changed political context. They had the best of the new periodicals (the *Fortnightly* and the *Nineteenth Century*), and their victory in the 1880 elections was crushing enough to trouble the most complacent of Conservatives. And whereas most of the Conservative leaders were too old to be willing to change, the Liberals could look to men like Chamberlain and Morley, both keen to redefine Liberal policy. Chamberlain's biographer J. L. Garvin is perhaps a little too insistent on his subject's central position, but in the main he is right when he says that

The epoch of middle-class Liberalism had passed; the signposts pointed to democracy . . . Many [Radicals] were declaring with Labouchere that when Mr. Gladstone withdrew from public life, 'his mantle will descend upon Mr. Chamberlain, who must be our next Premier.' This was the sentiment of the working-class rank and file.[5]

Disraeli's death in 1881 seemed to symbolize the passing of Conservative power. And yet in fact it marked the beginning of the movement to revivify the party. The great wave of sentiment that swept over the nation left a determination among the tories that they should prove themselves worthy of their great leader. Conservatives, rather than Liberals, should properly represent the nation. Becoming a national party meant, however, taking account of the opinions and desires of the new electorate, and it was here that Conservatives found both opportunity and threat. Opportunity, because they saw that if they roused themselves they might win over an enormous number of votes that the Liberals then commanded; threat, because the new voters – roughly speaking, the working-class – represented interests traditionally inimical to Conservatism. How could a party which stood for property and inequality appeal to voters who basically wanted the nationalization of private property and social equality? Yet an answer had to be found to the dilemma, for at stake was not merely the survival of the party but the fate of the nation, or so Conservatives argued. And it is the latter fear which gives such urgency to Conservative ideas during the early 1880s: fear of the loss of voters blends into fear of social anarchy.

Here, indeed, we come upon our true subject. For the fear of social anarchy was not restricted merely to Conservatives, it was widely shared. Of course, in 1880 there was practically no chance of organized revolution in England, and from this point of time the near-panic of politicians and social observers may seem absurd. But what we need to note is that the fears were capable of exaggeration because of a sudden recognition that all touch had once more been lost with the working-class and whatever forces were committed to its interests. Emblematic of this panic and ignorance is the lumping together of names like anarchist, radical, democrat and socialist, as though they all mean the same thing. Even more emblematic is a letter of *Fors Clavigera* which Ruskin wrote in 1880 and in which he made a great point of insisting that this was the first time he had ever spoken to the Trade Unions as a body. The letter begins, 'I have never before acknowledged the division . . . between you, and the mass of society to which you look for employment. But I recognize the distinction today . . .'[6] Yet Ruskin recognizes very little else, as he admits. He speaks of the unions as 'a separate class', and he gives three reasons for never having addressed them before. First, he hadn't thought of them as being separate, second, when he began to acknowledge their separateness he discovered that he had no idea who in fact they were, and third, as a university teacher he found it impossible to talk about

> certain things which I knew positively must be soon openly debated – and what is more, determined – in a manner astonishing to some people, in the national issue of the transference of power out of the hands of the upper classes, so called, into yours, – transference which has been compelled by the crimes of those upper classes, and accomplished by their follies . . .

But now:

> I turn to you, understanding you to be associations of labouring men who have recognized the necessity of binding yourselves by some common law of action, and who are taking earnest counsel as to the condition of your lives here in England . . . And I understand you to be, in these associations, disregardant, if not actually defiant, of the persons on whose capital you have been hitherto passively dependent for occu- pation, and who have always told you, by the mouths of their appointed Economists, that they and their capital were an eternal part of the Providential arrangements made for this world by its Creator.
> In which self-assertion, nevertheless, and attitude of enquiry into the grounds of this statement of theirs, you are unquestionably right.

Even so, Ruskin adds later:

> Now I write to you, observe, without knowing, except in the vaguest way, who you *are*! . . .[7]

The admission is timely, for in fact the trade unions in 1880 were decidedly reactionary, and not at all 'disregardant, if not actually defiant', in the way Ruskin suggests. Of course, there were dissident voices within various unions, but these were not yet able to make themselves heard to any effect, and essentially union officials hoped for betterment by working *with*, rather than *against*, parliament. Lynd remarks that in the early 1880s:

the policy of the old-line trade-union leaders [was] still in control, a policy which looked to employers and to politicians as allies, and which feared anything which might disturb that alliance whether the disturbance came from external causes or from other groups of workers.[8]

And Dona Torr's fine study of *Tom Mann and his Times* bears ample testimony to the truth of this. She points out that at a meeting between Mann and Sam Mainwaring late in 1879, Mainwaring

was now drawing Tom back to thoughts of working-class organization and giving him his first ideas of 'industrial action' as opposed to 'parliamentary action'.

She then quotes Mann's own *Memoirs* in which he recalls that Mainwaring was the first, 'as far as my knowledge goes to appreciate industrial action as opposed to parliamentary action.'[9]

Mainwaring may not have been the first, but he was certainly not typical of the union movement in 1880, and the fact that this should be so underlines how little Ruskin recognized what was actually going on. Fear is in excess of fact, but ignorance of fact increases fear. In Henry James's formulation (he is speaking of the *Princess Casamassima*),

the value I wished most to render and the effect I wished most to produce were precisely those of our not knowing, of society's not knowing, but only guessing and suspecting and trying to ignore, what 'goes on' irreconcilably, subversively, beneath the vast smug surface.[10]

All the same, things were going on, as James's words hint, and it would be silly to pretend that there was no cause for fear in the early 1880s. The fear has its comical aspects, as in the Duke of Pembroke's address to the Liberty and Property Defence League, in which he maintained that 'Radicalism necessarily ventures upon ground of doubtful morality, and inevitably attracts to its ranks the unprincipled, the rebellious, and the predatory elements of society,'[11] but still those words suggest that the Duke had sighted something rising towards the vast smug surface. Even above surface matters were stirring. There were, for example, a number of individuals within the unions whose more extreme voices were beginning to be heard, there were the examples of militant European socialism which inevitably suggested analogies with England, there was the formation in 1881 of H. M. Hyndman's Democratic Federation, and there was the general economic situation, which the *Times* characterized at the beginning of 1880 as combining 'more circumstances of misfortune and depression than any within general experience.'

For the Conservatives all this meant that once again they should become the national party. To defeat the Liberals would be proof of their uniting the variety of elements whose separateness threatened revolution. Old-style toryism must go. Of course, elements died hard. The *Saturday Review* criticized Mallock for even bothering to argue with socialists. Concluding a review of *Property and Progress*, the writer said:

> The most discouraging sign of the times is the apparent disinclination of the upper and middle classes to face the fact that the whole matter comes to a willingness to fight in case of need, or the absence of such a willingness. If order does not directly rest on the executioner . . . it certainly rests on the potentialities of a whiff of grapeshot . . . Talk as much as you like, appeal as much as you like to the Deity, or to the late Karl Marx, to the laws of nature, or to the laws of Martha's Vineyard, but directly you try to put your ideas in practise up you go to the nearest and most convenient gallows, unless it happens to be more convenient to shoot you. That is the right way of treating Mr. George, and Mr. Hyndman, and Mr. Wallace, and Mr. Davitt, and all the rest of the motley and mutually contradictory apostles of plunder.[12]

Wisely enough, the newer Conservatives saw little hope for their cause in grapeshot and gallows: not might but argument must win the day. And though they accepted Carlyle's law of nature, 'The Noble in the high place, the Ignoble in the low',[13] they also chose to stress the need for a common resolve. The problem was to find such a resolve. The answer lay with Disraeli.

In the year of the great man's death, the commemorative Hughendon edition of his works appeared, including an important preface to *Lothair* in which Disraeli spoke of his trilogy, *Coningsby*, *Sybil* and *Tancred*, and the ideas which had inspired them. Of the political situation in the 1830s and early 40s, he remarked that 'no party was

national: one was exclusive and odious, the other liberal and cosmopolitan.' Accordingly, the task of a reconstructed Conservative party
would be:

> To change back the oligarchy into a generous aristocracy round the
> throne; to infuse life and vigour into the Church, as the trainer of the
> nation . . . to elevate the physical as well as the moral condition of the
> people, by establishing that labour required regulation as much as
> property; and all this rather by the use of ancient forms and the restora-
> tion of the past than by political revolutions founded on abstract ideas . . .

And speaking in detail of his trilogy, Disraeli says that:

> They recognized imagination in the government of nations as a quality
> not less important than reason. They trusted much to a popular senti-
> ment, which rested on an heroic tradition and was sustained by the high
> spirit of a free aristocracy . . . In asserting the doctrine of race, they
> were entirely opposed to the equality of man, and similar abstract
> dogmas, which have destroyed ancient society without creating a
> satisfactory substitute. Resting on popular sympathies and popular
> privileges, they held that no society could be durable unless it was
> built upon the principles of loyalty and religious reverence.[14]

Without doubt, these words and the ideas they recall – centred
round the Young England movement – do much to explain the form
the Conservative revival took in the 1880s. In 1883, for example, a
periodical called *Merry England* came into existence. Wordsworth's
sonnet was printed on the title-page, and facing it was a drawing of
Disraeli addressing the House in 1853 with the caption underneath,
'I am myself a gentleman of the press.' The implication is clear:
Merry England is to transmit Conservative ideas – the ideas of Merry
England – to the nation. And there is a substantial clue to what
these involve in the first article, 'The Young England Movement',
by George Saintsbury.

Saintsbury writes about the Movement with some objectivity. He
sees its failings, and says that one of them was its being too various
in its attitudes ever to become properly coherent. Yet, he repeatedly
hints at the *relevance* of the Movement in the 1880s. He characterizes
the members as opposed to orthodox whigs and tories, and as:

> generous, intelligent, conscious of the past, hopeful of the future,
> awake to the changed circumstances of modern life, and ready, each in

his self-willed and confused way, with a plan of living to meet these circumstances.

No Conservative reading that in 1883 would be likely to miss the point that what was required for the present hour was a rejuvenated and more coherent Young England Movement. The point becomes clearer as the article proceeds

> . . . on the whole, the influence actually exerted was no doubt more social than political . . . It was of the very nature of the movement to blend social and political matters, and so in the long run the social influence, transformed in the process, became a political one. But directly in the fusion of classes, or rather in the interesting of one class in another while retaining their division, and still more indirectly in its religious, artistic developments, Young England promoted a quiet social revolution. The historian of the future, if not of the present, will hardly hesitate about his answer to the question, which have done the most for social progress, the Radical doctrinaires with their *reductio ad absurdum* in the Charter, or the advocates of cricket and wash-houses, of libraries and reasonable hours of work, of friendly communication between classes . . .[15]

Saintsbury sums up the social purpose of the movement by saying:

> Young England aimed at dissolving the rigid barriers between the different classes of the population by the influence of mutual good offices, by the humanizing effects of art and letters, by a common enjoyment of enjoyable religious functions, by popularising the idea of national tradition and historical continuity, and by restoring the merriment of life, by protesting against the exchange of money and receipt for money as a sufficient summary of the relations of man and man.[16]

The article thus suggests a role for the Conservative party; once more it must work for the 'fusion of classes, or rather the interesting of one class in another.' I imagine that the relevance of the Young England movement to the 1880s is obvious enough: it provides the manner in which Conservatives may recognize and quell the sensed revolutionary forces at work beneath the vast smug surface; and it will turn the Conservative party into a national one.

Merry England is not the only sign of rejuvenated Conservatism. In 1883 the *National Review* began its long run under the initial editorship of Alfred Austin, and the *Review* was an offshoot of the newly formed Primrose League, perhaps the true centre of the Conservative revival. One of the prime movers in the founding of the League was Lady Dorothy Nevill, who noted that the idea behind it was to mould 'into a compact body the more active and energetic partisans of the newer and more democratic school of Conservatism.' In addition, the League was to go to the 'defence of religion. Embracing all religious denominations, it was in no way to favour any particular form of faith to the detriment of any other.'[17] This smacks of Young England's efforts to use the Church as a social stabilizer, but it hints more powerfully at the newer idea that atheism and anarchy go together, as Disraeli had insisted.

> It cannot be denied that the aspect of the world and this country, to those who have faith in the spiritual nature of man, is at this time dark and distressful. They listen to doubts, and even denials, of an active Providence; what is styled as Materialism is in the ascendant. To those who believe that an atheistical society, though it may be polished and amiable, involves the seeds of anarchy, the prospect is full of gloom.[18]

Many in the nineteenth century saw Darwin as the father of atheism. It was left to Conservatives to see him as the father of social revolution.

In his account of the League, Algernon Borthwick also stresses its connections with Young England (Lord John Manners, it may be pointed out, was one of the League's founding members), and its efforts to rejuvenate Conservatism. 'The old Tory', he says, 'had become too fossilized to march with the age,'[19] so that new means had to be found of attracting votes to the Conservative party.

> The principles of Lord Beaconsfield and of the constitutional cause were pre-eminently those opposed to the spread of atheism and irreligious teaching, to the revolutionary and republican tendencies of Radicalism, and to the narrow and insular mode of thought which despised our colonies and found utterance in the words 'Perish India'. The creed of the League, therefore, was set forth as 'the maintenance of religion, of the Constitution, of the realm, and of the Imperial ascendancy of Great Britain', or, in shorter form, 'Religion, Constitution, and Empire.'[20]

Hardly the sort of thing, one would have thought, to set working-class pulses racing. Yet the effort to revive the idealism of Young England was clearly aimed at creating a government based 'on the choice and devotion of the people', which could occupy the middle ground between fossilized toryism and radical Liberalism. Young England's motto had been 'Restoration rather than Revolution', and that, together with its aim to use 'the venerable influences of religion and tradition' in order to embody true toryism by coming somewhere between '"the Party of Progress" and the Party of Resistance',[21] might well be taken as characterizing the efforts of the new Conservatives in the 1880s. And no matter how those efforts might have been spurred on by the indignity of being out of office, what gave them real urgency was fear of 'the people' and what they might do to England. It is in this context that Mallock's work of the period must be seen.

II

Social Equality and *Property and Progress* were undertaken in order to point out to the nation the imminent dangers of not recognizing and taking steps to placate the fearful armies of the night. But in common with most others, Mallock has a good deal of trouble in accurately identifying the enemy. Less honest than Ruskin, he will not admit his ignorance; but it is unmistakable, and especially in *Social Equality*, as the *Athenæum* was happy to observe.

> ... his whole line of argument is rendered feeble by the absence of any reference to a definite set of opponents. Mr. Bright and Mr. Herbert Spencer, Lassalle and Proudhon, are jumbled up in a most confusing way. It is, of course, very convenient to play off the weaknesses of one set of opponents against the weaknesses of another set; but while convenience may lead to plausibility it cannot conduce to conviction ...[22]

It is an accurate enough criticism. Mallock does occasionally go for a name, but he is happier when he can speak merely of the 'modern democrat' whom he blames for trying to make his hearers (Mallock doesn't say who they are, either, but he must mean the working-class) 'indignant with other people's riches; and the virtual question that he always addresses them is not, Why should you have so little? but, Why should others have so much?'[23]

Property and Progress comes nearer to sighting the enemy. Mallock sees, for example, that Henry George 'almost equals a Czar or an English Tory in his hatred and horror of our modern proletarian anarchists . . .'[24] It is certainly true that George was no socialist, but then Mallock appears to think that a socialist is a proletarian anarchist, and that will hardly do. The *Westminster Review* pointed out that

> He lets the cat out of the bag when he tells us that our 'modern English Radicalism, in so far as it appeals to the people, is nothing more than an unavowed and undigested socialism.' It is in fact Mr. Morley and Mr. Chamberlain he fears far more than Mr. George and Mr. Hyndman.[25]

As a Conservative trying to get his party back into office, Mallock is quite right in fearing Chamberlain and Morley since it is they who represent the opposition at election time. But to link Radical and socialist is a bad mistake (though it is one the *Westminster Review* doesn't escape from. Hyndman and George were on cordial terms, but they had little politically in common and Hyndman knew Marx's judgement on George, 'Theoretically the man is utterly backward'[26]).

Still, whatever mistakes Mallock may make over identifying the enemy, he is in no doubt as to the threat it represents. Appalled by the prospect of that 'transference of power' which Ruskin had foreseen, he insists that 'any social changes that tend to abolish inequalities, will tend also to destroy or diminish our civilization' (Mallock tends to speak of 'civilization' with a proprietary air, it is not something that all have a share in). The poor must exist for civilization's greater good, since 'Until the world relapses again into barbarism their own distance from the rich can never be appreciably diminished; and further . . . in such a relapse they would not rise towards riches, but the rich would sink towards poverty . . .'[27]

In *Property and Progress* Mallock warns his readers that 'action in modern politics so largely depends on the people, the wildest errors are grave, if they are only sufficiently popular,' and he goes on to make *Progress and Poverty* into another *Rights of Man*:

> [George's] London publishers have lately re-issued his book in an ultra-popular form. It is at this moment selling by thousands in the

alleys and back streets of England, and is being audibly welcomed there as a glorious gospel of justice.[28]

Civilization is, indeed, in a state of siege.

> When we consider the intellectual condition of a large section of the English working-classes; the spread amongst them of what is popularly called education; the consequent ferment in their minds of thoughts, hopes, and ideas, that have been schooled into activity, but have not been schooled into order; the respect for scientific authority, without the ability to test it . . . when we consider all this, it is impossible not to see that any successful attempt to propagate in this country those explicit theories of revolution, which have already had such fatal effect upon the Continent, might be fraught with effects hardly less fatal here, or might at all events bring us face to face with very serious social dangers.

And as a final spine-chilling revelation he tells his readers that there is a Democratic Federation whose 'numbers are so numerous as to be counted by tens of thousands.'[29] Actually, Hyndman's organization never had a membership of more than a few hundred and not all of those were active and paying members. In his study of Hyndman, C. Tsuzuki says that 'the Federation, existing as it did in a hostile world, had to assume certain conspiratorial features, but there is little doubt that its secretiveness was partly due to reluctance to disclose its real size for fear of embarrassment.'[30] But Mallock's point is, of course, that the Conservatives had better awaken to the threat before it is too late. What is needed are new arguments to win the people away from 'those theories which, in countries like France and Germany, have already been recognized by statesmen as a source of such serious danger, [and which] have at length begun to make appreciable way amongst ourselves.'[31] Mallock has three such arguments, though I cannot see that any would appeal to the audience he is trying to reach.

One is to say that things in fact aren't too bad. If you look at the statistics, he says, you will come to understand

> the nefarious process to which the public opinion of the country is at this moment being subjected, and to the dexterous way in which its hopes and passions are being played upon . . . and the horror and indig-

nation at the increase of a poverty which is in reality fast rising into competence.

for good measure he adds that

under this very Constitution wealth has been diffusing itself in a way unparalleled in any other country . . . whilst both rich and poor have gained, the poor have gained the most . . .[32]

But not even Mallock denies that there is some misery; it is merely that he sees it in its true proportion, or so he claims. He also claims that to account for poverty requires a science normally omitted from social and political discussions. *Social Equality* is concerned with the science of human nature; once we have understood that aright, Mallock says, we shall see just how inevitable poverty is.

Men's capacities are practically unequal, simply because they develop their own potential inequalities; they only develop their potential inequalities because they desire to place themselves in unequal circum- stances; and this desire to place themselves in unequal circumstances has its effect upon them only because the condition of society is such that the unequal circumstances are attainable.[33]

In short, those with money deserve to have it, those who don't have it don't want it and would be unhappy if they did have it. The poor are not only necessary to 'our' civilization, they are proof of the science of human nature. But then why are they discontented? Envy, Mallock says, brought into existence and aggravated by malcontents and vague theoreticians. Speaking of Radical attacks on the aristocracy, he insists that

Nearly always the first point dwelt on with regard to this class is not the evil that its existence does the community, but the exceptional position that it itself occupies. It is decried because it is enviable rather than because it is injurious'.[34]

Mallock's third argument against socialism is that far from labour being the source of wealth it is at best a contributory factor. Take the building of a house. The façade is

composed of certain materials, which have been put together by the labour of masons and bricklayers. But the labour of these men is not the cause of it as a façade; it is the cause of it only as a brick structure of some sort. *As a façade*, its immediate cause is the architect. So, too, with the rest of the house, in so far as it is luxurious, the architect is the cause of its luxury.[35]

Well, it perhaps falls some way short of meeting Marx's case, but then what Mallock is really interested in is the connection of wealth and culture: the façade of that house and its architectured luxury are really testaments to the cultural wealth of the aristocracy – not to put too fine a point on it. Mallock's belief in the integral relationship of culture and aristocracy is repeatedly stated in *Social Equality*, it exerts the most radical control over *Property and Progress*, and it is made a central theme of *The Old Order Changes*. Nor is it a new belief, though it has a certain shrill intensity in Mallock's writing which is peculiar to him.[36] As here, for example, where he considers the consequence of democratization.

> Certainly all that hitherto has been connected with high breeding, or with personal culture, would at once be out of the question. The type of character that is born of leisure and study, of freedom from common cares, of wise commerce with men, of the possession of works of art, and of memories of many lands – for this the democrat would be able to find no place.[37]

Labour may build a great house but it lacks the inner wealth of culture to make it truly great.

> Thus if the wealthy classes never gave balls or dinner parties, there would be in our house no great reception rooms. If they were not pleased with fine ceilings, fine gilding, and harmoniously coloured walls, there would be in our house none of these things either. But it is precisely these forms of magnificence that Mr. Bright, and thinkers of his order, always, when addressing the masses, take for types of wealth in general . . . if they really mean by wealth the existing luxuries and the existing splendour of the wealthy, then labour, so far from being by itself the cause of it, actually gives it none of its essential characteristics. Wealth, in this sense, is like a bronze statue, whose sole beauty is due to the mould it is cast in. The mould consists of the tastes and habits of the wealthy; labour does nothing but melt and pour in the metal.[38]

It is a crucial point and Mallock is far from alone in holding it. For this defence of the aristocracy really bears testimony to a feeling that many people in the nineteenth century had to entertain and cope with: the feeling that possession of so much that is beautiful and savours of a rich heritage – great houses, paintings, libraries – must have or have had its justification. The feeling can yield that myth of the aristocracy which is so strongly present in the work of Carlyle and Ruskin, of a golden age when the existence of such a class was fully justifiable; or it may produce the more desperate expediency that we find in Mallock's work, of the present justification for the class. But always justification is felt to be necessary just because of the discrepancies that exist or are said to exist between the fineness of what is possessed and the anomolous position of the possessors. Mallock's attitudes are best brought out if I compare his novel, *The Old Order Changes*, with two other novels which appeared in 1886, George Gissing's *Demos* and Henry James's *The Princess Casamassima*. As we shall see, both James and Gissing share Mallock's feeling that much of the passion for democratic revolution is based on envy of the rich, and they also try out the integral identification of aristocracy and culture. And though James comes closest to Yeats's troubled sense that 'maybe the great-grandson of that house/For all its bronze and marble 's but a mouse,' the insight is not what principally takes his attention. For all three writers the world of *Demos* threatens to rise to the vast smug surface and loose mere anarchy upon the world.

III

The Old Order Changes opens in a deliberately escapist manner, in the châteaux-dominated country of the South of France. Here we find the novel's hero, Carew, living in 'a genuine castle, with ramparts, tower, and scutcheons, and Heaven knows what else', which has been 'lent him for the winter by his relation, the Comte de Courbon-Loubet'.[39] The castle and its environs compose a genuinely feudal society. Carew tells the friends he has invited to stay with him that

> The old village still clings to the shelter of the feudal ramparts. In the valley below you look down on the lord's mill, whose black wheel still turns in the blue-green snow water. The villagers will touch their hats to you and seem proud of your presence. (Vol. 1, p. 40)

Ironically, this is as near as the *Old Order Changes* can come to Mallock's ideal of England, for in England itself the ideal has ceased to exist. At the very beginning of the novel Carew says that 'if our old landed aristocracy ever come to an end, *my* England will have to come to an end, also', but much later he admits that he belongs to a world 'that is dead or dying'. The central concern of the novel is to explore the reasons for the slow death of Carew's England and to see whether it can be averted.

The simplest reason is lack of money. In the *Old Order Changes* we are given repeated descriptions of aristocratic homes in various stages of decay. Carew's own home, Otterton, for example.

> The house had in former days been the largest in the West of England and had once consisted of an irregular pile of buildings, towers and cloisters, and long barn-like outhouses, ranged together round an enormous oblong court. But of this one side had little left but the foundations; and two of the others, though still stately, were ruinous. (Vol. 3, pp. 60–61)[40]

One of Carew's melancholy walks round Otterton brings him to a gate which is

> A grandiose entrance between two Georgian lodges, with the coat-of-arms crumbling from the friable stone. Within, there stretched away a long avenue of elms, some of whose boughs lay broken and untouched on the ground, whilst grass and weeds were invading the stony roadway. (Vol. 3, p. 94)

It is worth noting that Gissing's *Demos* also has a stately home similarly threatened.

> A large house, which stands aloof from the village, and a little above it, is Wanley Manor . . . The house is half-timbered; from the height above it looks old and peaceful amid its immemorial trees . . . But an Eldon who came into possession when William IV was King brought the fortunes of his house to a low ebb, and his son, seeking to improve matters by abandoning his prejudices and entering upon commercial speculation, in the end left a widow and two boys with little more to live upon than the income which arose from Mrs. Eldon's settlements.[41]

And the self-styled radical, Alfred Waltham, tells his sister that 'Our aristocrats begin to see that they can't get on without money nowadays; they can't live on family records, and they find that people won't toady to them in the old way just on account of their name.'[42]

But though both novelists see the old order as threatened by lack of money, they are more interested in the threat from without. In the *Old Order Changes* radicalism is represented by Mr Snapper, who never appears in person although he is often mentioned and is clearly based on Joseph Chamberlain. We are told that he is 'an opulent member of Parliament, who at that time was pushing himself fast into notice, and struggling to be recognized as a leader of the Radical party' (Vol. 3, p. 63). It is suggested that he may be a future Prime Minister, but one of Carew's guests indignantly rejects the possibility. 'We have sunk low enough, but we have hardly come yet to that. Fancy a man, who, in public, lives by denouncing gentlemen, and in private does nothing but vainly struggle to imitate them!' (Vol. 3, p. 83). Snapper envies the aristocracy because, not being a gentleman, he is not accepted by the gentry no matter what his wealth. The point is spelt out by another of Carew's guests who says of Snapper

> he *is* bitter – no doubt he is; and I confess I don't wonder at it. After all, he is only human . . . if you had seen him, as I have done, biting his lip at dinner, and wincing at the way in which he was – well, treated by some people as if he were one of the footmen –. (Vol. 3, p. 86)

The result is that Snapper sets poor against rich, by appealing to things 'not because they are those most distressing to the poor, but because he can manage most easily to lay them to the charge of the rich' (Vol. 3, p. 87). We should perhaps note that Mallock is writing here as an undisguised Conservative apologist against Chamberlain's 'unauthorized programme' of the land-tax; the first chapters of his novel were appearing in the *National Review* just prior to election time, 1885. But the case against Snapper is not exhausted by immediate polemic. He wants to buy Otterton – from spite and an envious desire for equality. Naturally, Mallock sees such a desire as delusive. Snapper is no gentleman, and the aristocracy will not be strengthened by admitting the Snappers of the world to its charmed circle. Studying Otterton, Carew thinks

We may be swept away, but we can never be replaced. We may have a new race of manufacturing plutocrats rising and falling like so many golden sandhills. They may eclipse us in splendour, but they never will be what we are. They never will have their roots in the historic life of the country. They never will be, like us, the aristocracy of traditional England. (Vol. 3, p. 67)

And repeatedly we are told of the uniqueness of the aristocracy. It is said to be 'made of different clay from the others', to be 'a race separate from the rest of the world', and to be 'different from the rest of the world'.⁴³ It is clear how this enunciates 'the doctrine of race' Disraeli had spoken of in the preface to *Lothair*, and it also makes clear why Snapper cannot become a gentleman.

Gissing is very close to sharing Mallock's assumptions. Wanley has been bought by an Ironmaster, called Mutimer, who marries Eldon's widow, and by means of some tortuous plotting it appears that he leaves it to his nephew, Richard Mutimer, a working-class radical with a strong egoistic streak. Indeed, it is Gissing's case that *all* political ideas of a radical nature are at bottom rationalizations of egoism. Richard Mutimer, who like Snapper is clearly based on Chamberlain though with something of Charles Bradlaugh's aggressive atheism, determines to ape the rich when he acquires Wanley, and he eventually marries Adela Waltham, the daughter of a minor family – having first broken off from his working-class sweetheart, Emma Vine. But for all his efforts to move up in the world Mutimer cannot be a gentleman. Adela says of Hubert Eldon, the widow's son with whom she's really in love, that he *is* a gentleman. '"Gentleman," uttered her brother with much scorn . . . A man's a man, I take it, and what need is there to lengthen the name? Thank the powers, we don't live in feudal ages' (p. 12). The irony of this radical statement is obvious enough – and by having Alfred say 'Thank the powers', Gissing underlines the connections of radicalism and atheism. Gissing's sympathies are equally obvious. Mutimer dines with the Walthams.

> At dinner he found himself behaving circumspectly. He knew already that cultivated taste objects to the use of a table-knife save for purposes of cutting; on the whole he saw grounds for the objection. He knew, moreover, that manducation and the absorption of fluids must be

performed without audible gusto; the knowledge cost him some self-criticism. But there were numerous minor points of convention on which he was not so clear; it had never occurred to him, for instance, that civilization demands the breaking of bread, that, in the absence of silver, a fork must suffice for the dissection of fish, that a napkin is a graceful auxiliary in the process of a meal and not rather an embarrassing superfluity of furtive application. Like a wise man, he did not talk much during dinner, devoting his mind to observation. (p. 89)

But all to no avail. He simply hasn't got it in him to be a gentleman, as Adela discovers after their marriage.

She could not avert her gaze; it seemed to her that she was really scrutinizing his face for the first time, and it was as that of a stranger. Not one detail had the stamp of familiarity: the whole repelled her. What was the meaning now first revealed to her in that countenance? The features had a massive regularity; there was nothing grotesque, nothing on the surface repulsive; yet, beholding the face as if it were that of a man unknown to her, she felt that a whole world of natural antipathies was between it and her.

It was the face of a man by birth and breeding altogether beneath her.

Never had she understood that as now; never had she conceived so forcibly the reason which made him and her husband and wife only in name. Suppose that apparent sleep of his to be the sleep of death; he would pass from her consciousness like a shadow from the field, leaving no trace behind. Their life of union was a mockery; their married intimacy was an unnatural horror. He was not of her class, not of her world; only by a violent wrenching of the laws of nature had they come together. She had spent years in trying to convince herself that there were no such distinctions, that only an unworthy prejudice parted class from class. One moment of true insight was worth more than all her theorising on abstract principles. To be her equal this man must be born again, of other parents, in other conditions of life. (p. 350)

Though *Demos* is very certain about who the gentleman is, it is less sure about distinctions between socialists and radicals (Mutimer is at different times called by both terms). But both Gissing and Mallock include more than one political figure in their novels. In the *Old Order Changes* there is a socialist called Foreman, whose likeness to J. M. Hyndman is very noticeable. He is not *quite* a gentleman.

He was a man of perhaps forty, with a broad forehead and quick but genial eyes, and though there was a coarseness in the actual shape of his features, and a certain wildness in his bushy moustache and beard, his expression was intellectual and by no means without refinement. The only immediate sign of any divergence in him from common good-breeding was a certain easiness and want of deferent distance in his manner of acknowledging his introduction to the various strangers. For the rest, there was little to distinguish him from any average man who, without many social advantages, had been brought up at a university. (Vol. I, p. 303)

Mallock is clearly puzzled about Hyndman, born to the wife of a wealthy merchant whose family went back to James I and therefore for him much more of a gentleman, yet for all that opposed in his politics to the gentry.[44] Accordingly, he tries out various possibilities to account for Hyndman's behaviour. The most desperate is to suggest that Foreman is actually as vulgar as any radical. When he appears at Courbon-Loubet to take tea with Carew and his guests, one of them offers to refill his cup and says 'and come, I must get rid of that nasty slop in your saucer for you' (Vol. I, p. 306).

But Mallock is a bit half-hearted about this and he makes more of a different possibility. Mrs Harley tells Carew:

You will . . . be amused and surprised to hear that Foreman at one time either was or thought he was a Conservative; and if he had not been snubbed by some of the understrappers of the party, he would have been prophesying the millenium in the capacity of a Conservative candidate. (Vol. I, p. 300)

There is evidence to show that before Hyndman's conversion to socialism he certainly possessed a deeply engrained Conservatism; he was an ardent believer in Empire and British might; and until his conversion in 1880 is best called, as his biographer does call him, a Tory radical. Since nobody challenges Mrs Harley's words, we must assume that Mallock believes that Hyndman's conversion was for personal reasons; certainly at no point in the novel is it suggested that it was for intellectual ones. Perhaps Mallock is right. Dona Torr says of Hyndman that 'after failing to gain a suitable position with Tories, Liberals, or Radicals, he was determined, especially after Marx's death in March, 1883, to be the chief Social Democrat and

Marxist authority in England.'[45] The problem, however, for Mallock is that in so far as Foreman is *not* based on Hyndman but is meant to embody typical socialist qualities he has to be shown as fanatically convinced of what he says. How to account for that? Mallock solves the difficulty by making Foreman mad. For example, when he leads a group of rioters, Carew, watching from the balcony window of his club, notices that 'his eyes were starting out of his head; and his whole face was flickering with the livid gleam of insanity' (Vol. 3, p. 36). There is also Mrs Harley's remark to Carew about a letter she has had from Foreman's wife.

> She fully believes that her husband will really be imprisoned, and she knows – for it is quite true about his having a touch of madness – that if he only is sentenced to solitary confinement, he will . . . have to march out of his cell into a madhouse. (Vol. 3, p. 170)

Yet in spite of this extraordinary explanation for Foreman's socialism, Mallock is kinder to him than he is to Snapper, if only because he can use him as a stick with which to beat the radical. But it is also part of his new political astuteness that he should want to distinguish between the two characters. The distinction had already been made public in the famous and widely reported debate between Charles Bradlaugh and Hyndman, where Bradlaugh stood for Radicalism versus Socialism.

> Bradlaugh was clearly a more skilful speaker than Hyndman, and it was generally agreed that after two hours' debate the champion of individualism had won the day. But Hyndman and his supporters had no reason to regret the engagement. Bradlaugh's great popularity and his willingness to discuss Socialism inevitably brought Socialist ideas to a wider public.[46]

Mallock's astuteness is, however, perhaps more apparent than real. For though Hyndman stood as the champion of Socialism, he was in fact nearer to Radical ideas than were any of his colleagues in the Democratic Federation. For one thing, he seems to have believed in the Iron Law of Wages; for another, he wanted social reform accomplished through Parliamentary rather than industrial action, and put up candidates for the 1885 election, a move which, predictably enough, turned out to be a fiasco.[47] Indeed, the dissatisfaction within the Federation came to a head at the end of 1884 when a group politically to the left of Hyndman – it included Mainwaring, the Avelings and William Morris – broke away to form the Socialist League. In using Foreman to oppose Snapper and allowing it to be clear that Foreman is based on Hyndman, Mallock therefore makes a partial mistake, since his opposition of Radical and Socialist is not as central as it should be. And I would say that in this respect Gissing is more tactful. He leaves fairly cloudy the issues and differences between Mutimer, Westlake (the dreamy idealist who owes a good deal to William Morris), and Roodhouse (the socialist rabble-rouser who has split from Westlake and who never actually appears in the novel). Gissing manages to convey something of the bewildering ferment of activity on the left-wing of politics, though he cheapens it by reducing nearly all the differences to the demands of egoism.

There is no equivalent to Westlake in the *Old Order Changes*. Foreman and Snapper are cultural philistines, as indeed they must be, for they set out to destroy culture since they do not know its worth. Culture is whatever the aristocracy possesses. Carew tells Mrs Harley in a letter:

> I am not talking of the qualities which distinguish you as an individual. I am talking of those which distinguish you as belonging to a certain class. For social purposes, individual qualities are very little more than the strings are in a violin; but that class which you belong to, with its natural position, with its memories, with its historic consciousness, is the body of the violin itself. And think what a structure this violin is! All the centuries of our country's life are embodied in it. It is as subtle a piece of work as any masterpiece of Stradivarius; and suppose it destroyed, before we could reproduce it we should have to reproduce a thousand years of history. (Vol. 1, p. 155)

In such a passage as this – and there are plenty more scattered about the novel – we can see Mallock's awareness of what is indubitably fine operating to justify what may not be. Lord Aiden, one of the most deferred-to of characters in the novel, and probably based on Lord Houghton, says that no outsider can hope to understand 'the relation that prevails, and indeed has always prevailed in England, between birth and riches, between rank, power, and talent' (Vol. 2, p. 39).

Because Snapper and Foreman are outsiders, their selfish dreams of creating a new order of society will necessarily involve the wanton destruction of the old culture.

It is the same with Mutimer. He has no conception of culture: his books show 'the incompleteness of his education and the deficiency of his instincts' (p. 42). Naturally, it is the deficiencies which matter more. Richard may have 'the best qualities his class can show' (p. 33), but he lacks the qualities that go with culture and he also lacks his uncle's percipience. The elder Mutimer had remained 'the sturdiest of Conservatives [bowing] in sincere humility to those very claims which the Radical most angrily disallows; birth, hereditary station, recognized gentility,' and as a result had demonstrated 'his own capacity for culture' (p. 28). But Richard belongs ineluctably to the working-class, which is in 'an elementary stage of civilization' (p. 149). The evolutionary image makes clear that Richard cannot be a man of culture; indeed, he cannot even 'pronounce the name of his bride elect quite as it sounds on cultured lips' (p. 183), and his drunken brother, 'Arry, provides Adela with the opportunity to reflect on 'the monstrous gulf between men of that kind and cultured human beings' (p. 282).

This is perhaps the best point at which to introduce the *Princess Casamassima* to the discussion. I realize that comparisons between James's novel and the *Old Order Changes* and *Demos* need to be handled tactfully, because *The Princess Casamassima* reveals, if intermittently, the hand of a great master. Yet the comparisons need not shame Mallock or Gissing, for their novels are interesting and informative minor works of fiction, and James comes much closer to their ideas and errors than it has been the usual practice to notice. We may as well begin with the obvious fact that all the novels have some concern with the possible social revolution that the 1880s seemed to threaten, and that all the novelists endorse the worth of inherited values which they feel will be destroyed in the portending cataclysm. More particularly than that, James sees these values as the cultural inheritance of the aristocracy, whose intrinsic fineness and separateness he seems to accept. And this is bound up with his attempt to connect causally the aristocracy of Lady Aurora Langrish with culture and inherited glory.

> She was plain and diffident and she might have been poor; but in the fine grain and sloping, shrinking slimness of her whole person, the delicacy of her curious features and a kind of cultivated quality in her sweet, vague, civil expression, there was a suggestion of race, of long transmission, of an organism that had resulted from fortunate touch after touch. (Vol. 1, p. 127)

In Hyacinth's initial vision of the Princess we have also an embodiment of the old, civilized values. The imagery of the passage connects her intimately to the aristocracy's culture, its possessions. Justification here turns her into a work of art.

> That head, where two or three diamond stars glittered in the thick, delicate hair which defined its shape, suggested to Hyacinth something antique and celebrated, something he had admired of old – the memory was vague – in a statue, in a picture, in a museum. Purity of line and form, of cheek and chin and lip and brow, a colour that seemed to live and glow, a radiance of grace and eminence and success – these things were seated in triumph in the face of the Princess . . . (Vol. 1, p. 207)

I see no point in trying to argue that the passage is ironic, that Hyacinth is too ignorant to realize that the Princess is no high-born lady but Christina Light. For James has totally altered her from the girl who had appeared in *Roderick Hudson*. Besides, if irony were intended it would be self-defeating, since we would have no way of knowing how to take Hyacinth's letter from Paris in which he announces his conversion to the cultural values which as a socialist he has been committed to destroying. In addition, any irony in the presentation of the Princess would reflect on the presentation of Lady Aurora, since it is through Hyacinth's eyes that we are given access to the 'suggestion of race'; and if James doesn't mean *that* we may as well give up trying to make any sense of his novel. So I think we must take the presentation of the Princess at face value. Yet it is undeniably vague. And masquerading behind the clichés of art-criticism – the 'purity of line and form' – is, of course, an appeal to racial purity.

James himself is worried by the vagueness of such an appeal. He plays with the notion that racial purity is causally connected with culture, but he is too scrupulous an artist not to see that this is probably a leaky refuge. Therefore he carefully qualifies the notion by suggesting it is truer of the past than of the present. In short, *The Princess Casamassima* indulges the myth of the aristocracy's golden age. Both Lady Aurora and the Princess tend to embody the fineness of the past, but they hardly confirm anything about contemporary aristocracy, which is present in the novel in the figures of the Marchants and Captain Sholto. The Marchants are quite simply stupid, unworthy of what they inherit. Their appearance is brief but memorably comic. Hyacinth talks to one of the daughters who had 'a handsome inanimate face ... a beautiful voice and the occasional command of a few short words. She asked Hyacinth with what pack he hunted and whether he went in much for tennis, and she ate three muffins' (Vol. 2, p. 29). But Sholto is of considerably more interest. James's dislike of what he represents recalls Carlyle's and Ruskin's loathing of what they saw as a degenerate, unworking, aristocracy.

> Sholto was a curious and not particularly edifying English type ... one of those odd figures produced by old societies that have run to seed, corrupt and exhausted civilizations. He was a cumberer of the earth – purely selfish for all his devoted, disinterested airs. He was nothing whatever in himself and had no character or merit save by tradition, reflexion, imitation, superstition. He had a longish pedigree – he came of some musty, mouldy 'county family', ... He had a little taste, a little cleverness, a little reading ... an immense deal of assurance and unmitigated leisure (Vol. 2, p. 82)

Since this is the Princess's description of Sholto it may be that the vigour with which he is placed owes something to her socialistic zeal. Yet this works both ways. After all, her words are meant to give us the measure of her disgust with the gentry; the Sholtos of the world have made her turn to socialistic ideas rather than those ideas being responsible for her version of Sholto. And anyway nothing we are shown of him belies the Princess's description. He is, unashamedly, one of the unworking aristocracy, a person who represents the 'race's' dwindling into selfishness; in him we see the end of the line, the playing out of the myth. It follows that the social order is ripe for change. And where both Mallock and Gissing see the inherited glory of the past as internally threatened only by lack of money, James focuses on the internal threat of 'a natural declension of the soul'; for him the aristocracy's greatness belongs to the past, whereas for Mallock and Gissing it could belong equally well to the future if only the money were there. The nearest Mallock comes to James's perception is in the figure of Lord Stonehouse who certainly has little responsible feeling for the past whose inheritance he bears. But then he is a whig. Gissing, it is true, speaks of the 'aristocratic vacuity of visage which comes of carefully induced cerebral atrophy' (p. 33), but we are never given an embodiment of this in *Demos*, so that the remark stands out as an oddly isolated piece of nose-thumbing. Certainly it is a long way from what James imagines in Sholto.

Yet in one important respect James can be identified with Mallock and Gissing. As he identifies culture with the past, so he links vulgarity to the present. The new order will destroy the old because it has no conception of the inherited worth of the past. The new lacks any 'suggestions of race'. Hyacinth's fellow-workers are said to have 'vulgar narrow inevitable faces', and Millicent Henning is vulgarity personified.

> She was none the less plucky for being at bottom a shameless philistine, ambitious of a front-garden with rock work . . . If she had a weakness it was for prawns; and she had, all winter, a plan for [Hyacinth's] taking her down to Gravesend, where this luxury was cheap and abundant, when the fine long days should arrive. (Vol. 1, pp. 164-5)

When Millicent disparages the Princess, Hyacinth thinks:

> that the girl had given rein to a fine faculty of free invention of which he had had frequent glimpses, under pressure of her half-childish, half-plebeian impulse of destruction, the instinct of pulling down what was above her, the reckless energy that would, precisely, make her so effective in revolutionary scenes. (Vol. 1, p. 321)

It must of course be said that James manages astonishingly well in making Millicent credible. Her drab beginnings, the manner in which she pulls herself up, her sloughing off the old – 'She had no theories about redeeming or uplifting the people; she simply loathed them, for being so dirty, with the outspoken violence of one who had known poverty' (Vol. 1, p. 163) – and the final achievement of becoming, possibly, Sholto's mistress: all this is a triumph of tact for James, especially since he can have known little of Millicent's type from personal experience. Moreover, his insistence on Millicent's 'frank beauty', her vitality and good nature, exhibit a generosity of spirit the more remarkable just *because* James has so acute a sense of how she threatens what he holds dear. His vision of Millicent quite transcends anything Arnold could imagine for the 'Philistine'; and needless to say it also transcends Mallock's and Gissing's powers of imagination. It is true that in *The Old Order Changes* we are shown Mallock's version of a lower-middle class person, Mr Inigo, whose aim in life is to raise himself to familiar terms with the gentry. But the presentation of the man is so vulgarly snobbish that it is only not distressing because it is so trivial. You catch Mallock at his very worst when he tries to deal with life beyond his own class interests. And the narrowness of these tell badly against him; he has none of James's effort at disinterestedness. He writes self-consciously as a proselytizer and advocate of ideas and – allowing for difference of talent – what he finds it necessary to recommend prevents him from moving towards that uninhibited observation that James could assume as the novelist's right and defend as a necessity (not that James often achieved such observation in *The Princess Casamassima*).

Mutimer's philistinism is also distressing and in a way Gissing hardly intended. I think particularly of that embarrassing scene where we are shown his drunken attempt to rape his wife.

> Without speaking, he threw himself forward and came towards her. For an instant she was powerless, paralysed with terror; but happily she found utterance for a cry, and that released her limbs. Before he could reach her, she had darted out of the room, and fled to another chamber . . . where she locked herself against him. (p. 285)

It is as though what Gissing most fears about this unholy alliance is the possibility of miscegenation. Mutimer, the working man as beast, whose envy of the gentry makes him want to defile it: that is the implicit meaning of the episode. On the other hand, Gissing manages much better with Mutimer's sister, Alice. Though she is nowhere near so fine a creation as Millicent, she is seen with some vividness and particularity. She, too, wants to raise herself and the desire is authentically presented; when the Mutimers come into money she shows how far she has learnt discretion from her brother by rejecting her working-class suitor, and she justifies herself to

Richard by saying 'at all events, Dabbs isn't a gentleman' (p. 124). What is not authentic is the contrast that Gissing points between Alice and Adela.

> Adela and Alice sat over against each other; their contrasted appearances were a chapter of social history. Mark the difference between Adela's gently closed lips, every muscle under control; and Alice's, which could never quite close without forming a saucy pout or a self-conscious primness. Contrast the foreheads; on the one hand that tenderly shadowed curve of brow, on the other the surface which always seemed to catch too much of the light, which moved irregularly with the arches above the eyes. The grave modesty of the one face, the now petulant, now abashed, now vacant expression of the other. (p. 202)

This is race with a vengeance; even Adela's 'gently closed lips' seems a pun designed to underscore her purity.

James never becomes this outrageous, though what lies behind the description of Lady Aurora is not, it must be admitted, far from the attitudes that control Gissing's description of Adela. But his effort at disinterested observation stops a long way short of Muniment. Partly this is a tactical triumph, since James can make Muniment unknowable and thus turn his own ignorance to good effect. But he compromises his ignorance by insisting that he does know *one* thing about Muniment – the man is vulgar. The initial description of him introduces the idea of his radical inscrutability; 'you couldn't tell – at least Hyacinth couldn't – if he were handsome or ugly.' But it also offers us the information that he has 'a heavy mouth and rather vulgar nose' (Vol. I, pp. 113–14). Much later, when Muniment goes to see the Princess in her rented house in Madeira Crescent, where she lives surrounded by hideous prints and knitted samplers, he tells her in apparent sincerity, 'You've got a lovely home.'

But if we find it difficult to accept the ease with which James settles for the fact of Muniment's philistinism, we are likely to be even less convinced by his manner of presenting Hyacinth, who is altogether too much the product of theory. Even the uneasy symbolism of his name – the man favoured and inadvertently killed by the God of Art – it itself indicative of how schematic and forced a character he is; the name isn't simply to be explained in terms of an ideal of 1789. James toys with the idea of Hyacinth's aristocratic father and commoner mother opening up the pathetic vanities which console Miss Pynsent and Mr Vetch, but he himself begins to take those vanities seriously. For Hyacinth's torn loyalties are, it is claimed, the result of his birth. The Princess tells him:

> You haven't a vulgar intonation, you haven't a common gesture, you never make a mistake, you do and say everything in exactly the right way. You come out of the poor cramped hole you describe to me, and yet you might have stayed in country-houses all your life. (Vol. 2, p. 60)

This is not ironical, since James uses Hyacinth as the means to register his own distress at what the social revolution will mean for the old, inherited values. Initially, Hyacinth's distress is equivocal; it is as much over what the many have missed as the few have possessed. He is struck by the fineness of the Princess's country-house.

> There was something in the way the grey walls rose from the green lawn that brought tears to his eyes; the spectacle of long duration unassociated with some sordid infirmity or poverty was new to him; he had lived with people among whom old age meant for the most part a grudged and degraded survival. In the favoured resistance of Medley was a serenity of success, an accumulation of dignity and honour. (Vol. 2, p. 7)

But later we are told that 'what was supreme in his mind today was not the idea of how the society that surrounded him should be destroyed; it was much more the sense of the wonderful, precious things it had produced, of the fabric of beauty and power it had raised' (Vol. 2, pp. 124–5). I should make clear that my objection to this is not that Hyacinth entertains such perceptions, but that they should seem to bear the weight of authorial approval since they are the consequence of Hyacinth's noble blood. The other revolutionaries do not see what Hyacinth sees; therefore they act wantonly and from envy. Hyacinth's blood is surely responsible for his long letter to the Princess from Paris in the course of which he says that

> The monuments and treasures of art, the great palaces and properties, the conquests of learning and taste, the general fabric of civilization as we knew it, based if you will upon all the despotisms, the cruelties, the exclusions, the monopolies and the rapacities of the past, but thanks

to which, all the same, the world is less of a 'bloody sell' and life more of a lark – our friend Hoffendahl seems to me to hold them too cheap and to wish to substitute for them something in which I can't somehow believe as I do in things in which the yearning and the tears of generations have been mixed. (Vol. 2, pp. 145–6)

Still, the defence of the past is strikingly uneasy in tone; that things are found to be less of a bloody sell and life more of a lark seems to me simply demeaning, and I do not for a moment believe that Hyacinth is here being distanced from his creator.

In *Demos* we find Hubert Eldon inaugurating his resumption of Wanley Manor by tearing down the factory and workers' houses that Mutimer had built in the valley. He defends his actions to Adela by saying

I see no value in human lives in a world from which grass and trees have vanished. But, in truth, I care little to make my position logically sound. The ruling motive in my life is the love of beautiful things; I fight against ugliness because it's the only work in which I can engage with all my heart. (p. 339)

Hubert's indifference to making his position 'logically sound' is the obvious counterpart of Hyacinth's oddly jocular tone and his inability somehow to believe in Hoffendahl's ideas. And actually Hyacinth, for all his background, is far nearer to Eldon than to Muniment (or Mutimer, of course). He is a book-binder by trade, and James makes use of this craft in a symbolic manner; Hyacinth is made to embody an impossible union of interests which results in his suicide. The delight he takes in his work suggests what James owes to Ruskin – and perhaps Morris. After his European holiday Hyacinth gives 'a little groan of relief when he discovered that he still liked his work' (Vol. 2, p. 155). And because of the pleasure he takes in his craftman's skills he offers to re-bind two of the Princess's books for her. The craftsman, that is, serves the aristocracy by his freely rendered work and thus helps keep alive the cultural heritage. It is of course a symbolic presentation of the feudalistic conception of the ideal society. Only the Princess doesn't want the books. She is abandoning the past; and Hyacinth ends by committing suicide.

Such thematic symbolism as this suggests that if James shares many of Gissing's and Mallock's assumptions he is at least far more of a realist in historical terms. They really hope for the survival of a feudal order, even if they are forced to recognize how severely the old order is threatened. Mrs Harley says to Carew:

> Have you ever looked into the faces of an East End mob? Have you ever realized what an appalling sight they are? The French Ambassador has several times said to me that he thinks things in England in a most critical and dangerous condition, and that the savage and sullen spirit fermenting throughout the country now is just what there was in Paris before the Great Revolution. (Vol. 1, pp. 112–13)

Gissing avoids this hysterical note but he is sensitive to the contagious illness of Radicalism which the vicar, Mr Wyvern, tells Mrs Waltham is 'in the air' and which even Adela's brother catches. And we should note that Hubert tells his mother that Mutimer stands for 'Demos grasping the sceptre' (p. 77).

Much of the *Old Order Changes* is given over to exploring the 'critical and dangerous condition' about which, as I have already suggested, fear is increased by ignorance. And by pretending to dispel ignorance Mallock makes his worst tactical blunder. He pins a great deal of the cause of fear on to the figure of Foreman, but because he wants his readers to know that he is actually talking about Hyndman he loses sight of any representativeness Foreman might have had. Besides, some of the details about Foreman/Hyndman are simply wrong. In other words, he gets the worst of both worlds.

In the first place, Foreman is outwitted in debate by a Catholic priest, who uses the statistical arguments of *Property and Progress* and adds that he is busy translating *Das Kapital*, a piece of information which bowls Foreman over. And well it might, since Hyndman was busy on his own translation, though Aveling beat him to it (in *Demos* the journalist, Keene, is also said to be translating *Das Kapital*. Everyone, it seems, wanted to get into the act). It isn't perhaps an important mistake but it indicates Mallock's essential error. For he really does feel that he has begun to dispel the fear of revolution as soon as he has arranged for a revolutionary leader to be outargued. Yet he also wants to show Foreman as advocate of violent revolutionary tactics: 'What can he know,' Foreman is made to say, 'of that coming social earthquake which will send his houses toppling like a house of cards' (Vol. 2, p. 47). To the extent that Mallock's audience was to recognize Hyndman in Foreman this is a mistake since, as I have shown, Hyndman was a gradualist. The difficulty of using *roman à clef* elements in a novel of the sort Mallock writes is that you have to be very sure you have chosen representative figures. Precisely because Hyndman isn't such a figure, Mallock has to treat Foreman inconsistently, and this becomes an even more crucial matter when we are told that Foreman is putting up members of his Federation for election to Parliament. As we know, Hyndman did persuade several of his colleagues to stand – it was part of his gradualist programme – and of course they were badly defeated. Mallock draws great consolation from the fact. Mrs Harley tells Carew in a letter:

> Eighteen out of twenty of our friend Foreman's elections have come off already. Eighteen of his Socialist candidates, who were to rally round them, in all its terrible strength, the voting force of educated and of organized labour – Foreman thought that the result would make all England tremble, probably all Europe – well, of these eighteen gentlemen, the one who polled the most votes polled – how many should you think? Out of eight thousand votes, and in a constituency supposed to be the most revolutionary in the kingdom, this terrible candidate polled a hundred and ninety-five; and none of the other eighteen polled as many as thirty. (Vol. 2, p. 160)

Though Mallock has exaggerated the number of S.D.F. candidates who stood he has not seriously distorted the results.[48] But the inferences he draws from them are a different matter. Mrs Harley's news has a great effect on Carew.

> The vast forces of change which were supposed to be undermining society, and which seemed to menace with their wide-spread and subterranean rumblings the imminent ruin of the existing fabric – these forces had put their strength to the test: and with what result? The terrible Titan, so it seemed to Carew, had shrunk to the proportions of a squalid malignant dwarf. He felt like a man relieved suddenly from a nightmare. (Vol. 2, p. 163)

It won't at all do. Mallock simply doesn't know enough and his ignorance decisively damages the case he wants to make. For during the election campaign, the Socialist League had been urging working-class voters to give no support to Hyndman's candidates and indeed not to vote at all. The League's Manifesto began 'Working men! keep away from the poll altogether! DO NOT VOTE!'[49] and although there is no way of knowing what effect the manifesto had, it is fairly safe to assume that the S.D.F. candidates' results did not fairly show the 'strength' of the 'vast forces of change'. But there is a more considerable objection against Mallock's handling of the elections. For once he has trapped himself in this matter of particular detail he is powerless to explain *why* England is in 'a most critical and dangerous condition'. According to the results and Carew's reasoning it is in nothing of the sort. But this makes nonsense of the greater part of the novel, which is given over to saying that the condition exists and that something must be done about it.

Mutimer also runs for parliament and is badly defeated. But Gissing is far more tactful than Mallock since he does not pretend that Mutimer's defeat exposes the hollowness of the threats of the new political movements. For one thing, Mutimer is defeated by an old-style Radical; for another, Westlake and Roodhouse steer clear of the elections. The trials of strength which they plan have nothing to do with playing the gradualist game.

Gissing does, however, come closer to Mallock over the Pall Mall riots which occurred on 'Black Monday', 8 February 1886, and which are introduced into both novels. Mallock is good on the actual eruption of violence, though the imagery occasionally betrays his assumed neutral stance: he speaks of the hordes of workers as 'some great volume of semi-liquid sewage' and of 'this hoarse and horrible inundation' (Vol. 3, p. 32). But again he has Carew draw the wrong inferences from what he sees. Mallock is quite right when he says that the march of the unemployed was encouraged by the S.D.F. and especially by Hyndman and Burns; but he wrongly accuses the S.D.F. of setting out to cause trouble. Carew reads in a newspaper of the winter's events (he has himself just returned from France).

There he learnt that during the last two days there had been demon-strations of working men in various parts of London, their object being to call public attention to the extent and depth of the distress then prevalent, and to the number of those who were absolutely without any employment. These demonstrations in the first instance had been orderly, both in their programme and in their conduct . . . But in each case, or nearly so, these meetings had been broken up, and turned, as far as possible, into a savage and menacing riot by organized gangs under the direction of the League of Social Democrats . . . Carew gathered further that an immense mass meeting had been convened that very day in Trafalgar Square; and at it resolutions of a more or less Conservative character were to have been put to the unemployed by certain of their most competent leaders. He gathered also that in this case, as in the others, the Social Democrats were known to contemplate interference, and that some disturbance was accordingly thought possible. (Vol. 3, pp. 41–3)

As a semi-factual account this needs a good deal of sorting out. First, it is quite improper to say that the S.D.F. broke up meetings; it organized them and had indeed been organizing them all winter.[50] On the other hand, Mallock rightly suggests that the mass meeting in Trafalgar Square was to put forward 'resolutions of a more or less Conservative character,' and there is no doubt that the S.D.F. wanted to divert the meeting to its own – peaceful – ends. But the 'competent leaders' Mallock refers to were nothing of the sort; they were 'Fair Traders' who were being paid for by Conservative money and who most certainly were not working men.[51] Once again, Mallock has misunderstood the facts of the situation and has also drawn the wrong conclusions for his novel, since the suggestion that working-class men are decently conservative except when led astray undermines the idea of the 'social earthquake' *The Old Order Changes* is supposed to be investigating.

Gissing, like Mallock, seems to feel that the working man is wrongly incited to action. Wyvern, who carries much authority in *Demos*, says that 'A being of superior intelligence regarding humanity with an eye of perfect understanding would discover that life was enjoyed every bit as much in a slum as in a palace' (p. 384). Yet *Demos* itself shows that this is not so. Gissing knows too much about the actualities of slum life not to reveal how hideous the sufferings of its dwellers are and therefore Wyvern's words inevitably seem stupid or disgracefully complacent. But the discrepancy is not intended; it occurs simply because what Gissing renders in the lives of Emma

Vine and Mrs Clay, for example, can hardly be brought into line with the political and social prejudices that *Demos* is meant to celebrate.

For this reason, he is happier when he can abandon the scrutiny of individuals for descriptions of the mob. And as soon as he starts looking at the working class *en masse* he makes use of evolutionary imagery to suggest a positivist explanation for the working man's inferiority and therefore its contentedness with slums. He describes Mrs Mutimer as 'a weak animal cruelly assailed' and we are told that 'Arry Mutimer belongs to a distinct class, 'comprising the sons of the mechanics who are ruined morally by being taught to consider themselves above manual labour.' (pp. 405 and 409). People like 'Arry create the monster Demos; Adela feels that the cheers and groans of the mob are 'like the bellow of a pursuing monster' (p. 445). When the riot starts, 'Demos was roused, was tired of listening to mere articulate speech; it was time for a good wild-beast roar, for a taste of bloodshed.' In the street is a multitude which makes 'but one ravening monster' (pp. 453 and 456). Demos simply hasn't progressed towards a state of civilization.

But however inadequately Gissing accounts for the dangerous state he sees England as being in, he does not undersell the potential of vast change, whereas Mallock's attempt to explore the critical situation constantly comes to a denial of the situation's existence. No matter how correct he may be to see that Hyndman represents no serious threat, he cannot use the insight to his novel's advantage, since the dismissal of Foreman's significance means the dismissal of the external threat to the old order. The penalties of particularization are great.

It hardly needs saying that James avoids Mallock's error. But he commits the opposite error of so *refusing* to particularize that his fear of what goes on 'under the vast smug surface' tends largely to evaporate. Nothing in the novel embodies a justification for the fear, because in the last analysis it is quite impossible to know who the real revolutionaries are supposed to be. Vetch and the Poupins are too comically treated to represent a serious threat. Hyacinth is Muniment's dupe. For much of the time he merely mouths the clichés of socialism – 'Don't you believe in human equality? Don't you want to do anything for the groaning, toiling millions?' he asks Rose Muniment; and his evenings at the 'Sun and Moon' don't at all lead him, as he hopes they will, to the heart of socialism. What goes on at the pub is a cover, and when Muniment whisks it away all that Hyacinth gains is a commission to kill someone – a commission given by Hoffendahl, an anarchist we never meet.

Perhaps Muniment should be the real centre of the threat. But then, as I have already remarked, he is unknowable. True, he and the Princess seem to be plotting together in the East End, but by then Hyacinth is no longer in their confidence and cannot therefore discover what they are really up to. Besides, at the very end of the novel it appears that Muniment himself isn't trusted, isn't at the centre of activities. James is sufficiently tactful to realize that his novel must deal with representative figures who need to have the feel of an ascribable social context about them. But although he manages quite superbly to suggest such a context, what we actually have is a superb bluff. Lionel Trilling says that the novel is 'a brilliant-ly precise representation of social actuality',[52] but quite apart from the fact that James's assumptions about aristocracy and race have nothing to do with social actuality, at the very point where we need precision we meet a baffling vagueness. The ignorance of the characters too often suggests the ignorance of their creator, as when Hyacinth thinks he has suggested to the Princess more about his 'radical' affiliations than he ought: 'he had spoken as if the movement was vast and mature, whereas in fact, so far at least as he was yet concerned with it and could answer for it from personal knowledge, it was circumscribed by the hideously-papered walls of the little club-room at the "Sun and Moon"' (Vol. 1, p. 296). As John Goode has rightly said, Hyacinth is often made ignorant of his own back-ground.[53]

Irving Howe seems to me to put his finger on the novel's weakness when he remarks that 'there are times when *The Princess Casamassima* seems almost designed to evade its own theme. Everything is pre-pared for but little is revealed, doors open upon doors, curtains on to curtains.'[54] But neither Howe nor Trilling make what is surely the most crucial of all points, that to the extent James does commit him-self he falls into error. To identify anarchism with the central threat

to established order – no matter how hesitantly you do it – is to
misunderstand the nature of the threat. For as a revolutionary
movement, anarchism was comparatively unimportant in England;
and though the scattered bomb activities of the 1880s *may* be connected with each other, there is nothing of any genuine significance
to these sporadic and mostly comic attempts at violence. Oddly
enough, Stevenson's *The Dynamiter*, which appeared in 1885, is
nearer the truth of the situation. In the title-story of that volume
anarchism is treated as a clumsy joke. This is not to say that anarchism
lacked all significance in the 1880s. By 1886 at least two anarchist
journals were being published in London, *The Anarchist* and
Freedom, and self-proclaimed anarchists, both exiles and the home-
grown variety, were prominent in Morris's Socialist League.[55] But
in no sense can anarchism be thought of as a central force of radicalism
during the decade, and James is quite wrong to assume or pretend
that it was. I shall follow up the reason for his error, but first I want
to say more about Mallock.

The failure of *The Old Order Changes* does not spring only from
Mallock's improper particularization. We must also take into account
the consequences of his wanting to speak out on behalf of a rejuvenated Conservatism, the result of which is, as all the reviewers noticed,
that he falls into didacticism. He wants to recommend a course of
action. Yet the recommendation is curiously elusive. As in the
treatises, so in the novel Mallock insists that he, or anyway Carew,
cares passionately about the poor. But except for the episode of the
riots, *The Old Order Changes* never allows working men into its
pages. They are simply somewhere 'out there,' and this gives an oddly
theoretic note to the novel, especially when it is compared with the
density of presentation of working class life in both *Demos* and *The
Princess Casamassima*. For instance, Carew shows Miss Consuelo
Burton his large library of books on political economy and asks her,
'And do you think that I care nothing about the people now?' (Vol. 2,
p. 134). Later, having witnessed the riots, he writes a letter to a newspaper in which he says that the rioters are easily stirred up because
they 'suddenly fall from comparative prosperity into privation'.

Carew, when he had written this . . . was conscious, as he said to himself,
of feeling somehow a man again. 'Blame the people!' he repeated as he

put his letter into the box. 'Poor devils! why, as I watched the crowd just now, I was far more inclined to cry over the sight than to be angry at it.' (Vol. 3, p. 49)

But even Mallock sees that this is hardly an adequate response. Still later, therefore, Carew feels

> He could no longer live on emotion, or even on thought. His whole **moral** being craved to be fed with action. His emotion had turned into a hunger for something beyond itself. It no longer sufficed him to reason about the poor and about the people; about the conditions of their employment, the rates of their wages and the cost and quality of their lodging. He longed to feel that there were a certain number of families whose daily lives he could help to order happily; that there was actual distress he might do something to cure; and that he was doing his best to set a real example of that devotion to all whom his power could benefit, which alone, in his estimation, gave power either permanence or dignity. (Vol. 3, p. 102)

The passage recalls Ruskin's definition of the true gentleman as one who works for others. It also and more importantly suggests Mallock's belief that the old order can be saved if it adopts a social purposiveness and reinvigorates the ideal of the feudal system.

Carew's desire for action is, however, complicated by the fact that he is torn between two women, Violet Capel, an American girl, and Miss Burton, a gentle-born English Catholic. These two represent opposed worlds. 'One was the world of love, and passion, and poetry . . . The other was a world of ever-widening duties, where love was not absent, but by itself never could satisfy.' (Vol. 1, p. 147). Mallock arranges that the situation between Carew, Miss Burton and Miss Capel shall come to a crisis by having Carew's uncle die and leave him the decaying Otterton and a fortune provided only that he marries an English girl. But he seems to owe prior allegiance to Miss Capel. However, it then turns out that she is secretly married to a French Count, so Carew marries Miss Burton and saves Otterton. The oddity of this is that Mallock clearly feels the marriage symbolizes Carew's new effort towards public-mindedness and that the restoration of Otterton will underline the new vitality of his dream of a feudal society. But you can hardly hope to keep the old order alive and well on the odd chance of a private fortune coming your way.

Yet although all this is silly, there is something to be said for the presentation of Miss Burton. If Miss Capel owes something to Daisy Miller, Miss Burton takes after Dorothea Brooke, at least to the extent that she reminds Stanley of Saint Theresa. As with Stella Westlake and Adela in *Demos*, she combines religious and social altruism. Adela 'saves' Hubert by her belated marriage to him (under Mutimer's guidance she has read some socialist books), just as Miss Burton saves Carew for a life of public action. And Adela gets her own strength from Stella Westlake:

> Listening to Stella's voice she could lay firm hold on the truth that there is a work in the cause of humanity other than that which goes on so clamorously in lecture-halls and street corners . . . [Stella] was of those elect whose part it is to inspire faith and hope, of those highest but for whom the world would fall into apathy or lose itself among subordinate motives. (p. 470)

How nearly this echoes the closing paragraphs of *Middlemarch* does not need emphasizing. Marriage to Miss Burton gives point to Carew's notion that the greatest of modern questions is not 'how to reconcile the People with their present lot, but how to make their lot one with which they shall be willing to be reconciled' (Vol. 1, p. 164). She inspires faith and hope in him. Mallock undeniably touches here on a matter of absorbing interest, that of the role of the gentlewoman in political and social questions in the last decades of the nineteenth century. So does Gissing, but the trouble is that neither novelist can afford to treat his heroine at all ironically; the proposals of Miss Burton and Adela cannot be seen as some vague utopia that they dream, and the novelists therefore cannot entertain the marvellously comic vision that controls James's presentation of Lady Aurora Langrish.

Lady Aurora is one of the finest things in *The Princess Casamassima*, for James sees with absolute sureness the pathetic and comic futility of her desire for service. Personally, it may offer her some salvation, but in so far as she represents the past's efforts to come to terms with the present she is irrelevant. Carew, we are told, 'longed to feel that there were a certain number of families whose daily lives he could help to order happily', and we are left to assume that under Adela's guidance Hubert Eldon will also come to recognize his public responsibilities. For both novelists the hero's change of heart emerges as a general recommendation. But James sees straight through such convenient piety. Lady Aurora acts out the longing for service, yet Rose Muniment says 'They'll trample on her just the same as on the others, and they'll say she has got to pay for her title and her grand relations and her fine appearance.' And Paul Muniment adds,

> Rosey's right, my lady. It's no use trying to buy yourself off. You can't do enough; your sacrifices don't count. You spoil your fun now and you don't get it made up to you later. To all you people nothing will ever be made up. Eat your pudding while you have it; you mayn't have it long. (Vol. 1, pp. 134–5)

And how intelligent James is in perceiving the way Hyacinth will feel about Lady Aurora's talk of the poor: 'evidently the only fault she had to find with [the Muniments] was that they were not poor enough – not sufficiently exposed to dangers and privations against which she could step in.' With the best will in the world, Lady Aurora is forced to see the poor as a cause. Hyacinth reflects that

> the rich couldn't consider poverty in the light of experience. Their mistakes and illusions, their thinking they had got hold of the sensations of want and dirt when they hadn't at all, would always be more or less irritating. (Vol. 1, pp. 315–16)

This is exactly the sort of perception Mallock dare not risk, since the idea to which Miss Burton gives practical shape is for him the way forward. Needless to say Miss Burton's plan of action is hopelessly escapist and interestingly enough Mallock himself came to recognize that this was so. In his *Memoirs* he notes that

> the vision of the Old Order as capable of being born anew by a sudden reillumination of faith and new acquisitions of Knowledge – represents, it has subsequently seemed to me, a mood analogous to that which possessed Lord Beaconsfield when he wrote *Sybil*, or when he seemed to insinuate that all social strife might be ended by doles to the poor, distributed week by week through the almoners of manorial lords.[56]

The reference to Disraeli is pertinent because the plan Miss Burton outlines to Carew smacks strongly of the rejuvenated Young England of the 1880s. She proposes that certain great land and factory owners should agree to work without profits and that money should be abolished from their lives. In this way

the monastic vow of poverty might be applied to our modern factory system. Her notion, in fact, of a monastery or convent is a modern factory where the hands should be monks or nuns; where the spire should rise side by side with the chimney; and the quiet cloister should refresh the mind after the rattle of wheels, and looms, and belts.

The effect will be that

by the stern simplicity and yet perfect content of their lives, by the decency of their habits despite their utter poverty, they will form a moral leaven amongst the labouring classes at large, and do more than anything I ever had thought imaginable to give an ideal dignity to our modern factory-labour. (Vol. 3, pp. 225–7)

But how is this to be brought about? Mallock is decidedly coy about solving so problematic a question, but obviously the only hope is to preserve intact such patches of feudal society as can be found and building Jerusalem there – which brings us back to Otterton, and also establishes the bizarre escapism of Mallock's fancy.

Carew's plans inevitably demand comparison with Mutimer's. Mutimer, after all, builds a factory in Wanley on Owenite principles. The plan fails, and for two reasons. One is that Mutimer does not travel beyond the cash-nexus in his relationships with his workers; his dismissal of a drunken hand is to be seen as unfeeling and brutal. But also the workers aren't really capable of the correct response, they are too selfish. When Hubert pulls the factory and their houses down they riot. 'Most of them took it as a wanton outrage that they should be driven from the homes in which they had believed themselves settled for life' (p. 376). The tone here is meant, I think, to imply that the workers have been corrupted by Mutimer because he has destroyed the proper relationship between master and men, and indeed the erection of the factory in Wanley valley, which disfigures the landscape, symbolizes the 'unnatural' grafting of industrial relations on to the older relations that exist in a rural society. But Gissing is at least aware that Eldon's restoration of the valley is escapist, whereas Mallock gives Carew's restoration of Otterton an assertion of representativeness. Wanley is living on borrowed time.

Beyond the peaceable valley Demos swells and roars, the future is on its side, and though it has been driven out of the valley it will shortly be back. The restoration of Wanley is less a gesture of hope than of despair – it is the sort of thing that can happen only in novels.

Gissing's concealed despair and Mallock's fatuous air of confidence reveal only too well the bankruptcy of Conservative ideas in the 1880s. Both *Demos* and *The Old Order Changes* reveal in their different ways that the hope for change yet preservation, preservation through change, has no solid foundation. And this is what James so finely sees. Yet neither he nor Mallock nor Gissing properly judges the weight of what opposes the old order, and what links them over this is a failure more considerable than merely a common ignorance of what goes on under the vast smug surface.

I have already pointed out that Mallock can conceive of nothing more powerful than personal animus as dictating socialistic aims. For Gissing it is nearly always mere envy. 'Socialism,' Hubert says, 'appeals to the vulgarest minds; it keeps one eye on personal safety, the other on the capitalist's strong-box' (p. 382). We are told that the socialism of Rodman, Mutimer's manager, 'cooled strangely from the day when his ends were secured' (p. 277), and that from the day Mutimer's friend Dabbs becomes a licensed victualler, 'comfortably established on a capitalist basis', he ceases 'to attend the Socialist meetings' (p. 388). And just in case we have missed Gissing's point, he tells his readers straight out that they should never 'trust the thoroughness of the man who is a revolutionist on abstract principles; personal feeling alone goes to the root of the matter' (p. 149). The only exception to this general rule are the Westlakes, misguided yet sublime, 'poetry-fed souls at issue with fate'.

Such a conception of the meaning of socialism and social revolution is absurdly inadequate. Yet James shares it. 'Everywhere, everywhere he saw the ulcer of envy – the greed of a party hanging together only that it might despoil another to its advantage '(Vol. 2, p. 158). That particular insight is Hyacinth's but there is no reason to dissociate James from it, for in *The Princess Casamassima* all revolutionary motives are finally tracked down to personal ones. The Poupins suffer from the ulcer of envy, so do those who meet at the 'Sun and Moon' and so does Hyacinth himself, before his conversion

– 'He wanted to ride on every horse, to feel on his arm the hand of every pretty woman in the place' (Vol. 1, p. 170). Even old Anastasius Vetch admits to envy.

And where it isn't envy, then some other selfish motive prompts the revolutionary. It is true that James half-sees his way to allowing that the Princess may be acting from disinterested motives. But the insight is heavily qualified, and James's sense of the comic improperly intrudes when he is dealing with her; when Hyacinth asks her what she would do with one particular landlady of a pub after the new social order is established she replies, 'Oh, drown her in a barrel of beer.' Anyway, she is only slumming, playing at politics; she goes to live in her hideous house to be among the revolutionaries, but she puts her furniture and possessions in store. And finally, when Muniment has taken her money and left her, she decides to go back to her husband: the ideal cannot withstand the cold touch of reality. We are left to wonder whether her passion for socialism hasn't most to do with her passion for Muniment.

Muniment is unknowable. But that serves to stress how totally selfish he is; he gives nothing of himself to others. And though James succeeds marvellously in creating the impression of a man who works ruthlessly yet irreproachably for power, in the end he succeeds too well. James, I have remarked, strives to make all his characters representative, and Muniment is clearly offered as the novelist's notion of the typical social revolutionary. Muniment and Mutimer: the names are tantalizingly close, and yet I do not see how either novelist could have known of the other's work. But both Gissing and James treat their characters cynically; if Muniment is the quintessence of inscrutable selfishness, Mutimer is more or less summed up when Wyvern says that 'The proletarian Socialists do not believe what they say, and therefore they are so violent in saying it. They are not themselves of pure and exalted character; they cannot enoble others' (p. 386).

James's cynicism is not, perhaps, so resolutely inflexible as Gissing's, but it is severely reductive. It even harms his presentation of Lady Aurora. It seems to me fatally unconvincing for James to imply that her social work is linked to her feelings for Muniment, yet when Hyacinth in his own despair goes to her, she more less says that she knows about Muniment and the Princess and that she therefore plans to start amusing herself (Vol. 2, p. 355).

It is because James wants to track down revolutionary motives to selfishness that he places anarchy at the centre of the revolutionary movements of the novel. For it is easy to see Anarchism as sudden, irrational and spiteful. Its effects are swift, spectacular or merely comic; and they can be effectively divorced from any considered ideology. Indeed, by choosing to identify the threat to the old order with such romantic or squalid irrationality James is refusing to take social revolution at all seriously. And this occasions the disturbing uncertainty of tone that affects so much of *The Princess Casamassima*. For like Mallock, James comes near to denying the importance of the threat which he yet knows is significant. And the very evasiveness of the novel suggests, I think, James's uneasy recognition that the disruptive forces he senses under the surface cannot be fuelled by anything so trivial as mere personal motive. Such recognition is paralleled in the *Old Order Changes* by the madness which Mallock ascribes to Foreman and in *Demos* by the Westlakes and their poetry-fed souls. All three novelists, that is, allow themselves a bolt-hole from their flat 'solution' to the revolutionary impulse. And all three are panicked into the solution because they settle too swiftly for a notion of change as catastrophe. Wyvern, you feel, speaks for all of them when, replying to Hubert's question 'what is before us?', he says:

> Evil; of that I am but too firmly assured. Progress will have its way, and its path will be a path of bitterness ... Two voices are growing among us to dread proportions – indifference and hatred: the one will let poverty languish at its door, the other will hound the vassal against his lord. (p. 386)

Again, Roodhouse is the sort of figure all three novelists are likely to invent in order to articulate their fears: madness, anarchism, assassination threats: they all notionalize the sense of change as catastrophe which Roodhouse utters when he is reported to have declared 'his adherence to the principles of assassination: he pronounced them to be the sole working principles; to deny to Socialists the right of assassination was to rob them of the very sinews of war' (p. 226).

But in James's case at least, the locating of all revolutionary motives in selfishness does not entirely destroy the integrity of his novel.

Indeed, it helps him to win a partial victory. For if *The Princess Casamassima* is not at all a great novel about social revolution, it is very nearly a great novel about betrayed loyalties. Opposed to selfishness are loyalty and friendship. James makes the point almost diagrammatically when he has Mr Vetch abandon what for him had always been the unreality of his radicalism and discover that what survives as real is the strength of his love for Miss Pynsent and Hyacinth. It is because of this love that he goes through the futile agonies of trying to save Hyacinth from his fate as a socialist, and is thwarted by the very socialists who should have been Hyacinth's friends. Loyalties in *The Princess Casamassima* are terribly betrayed or put upon: Miss Pynsent's for Hyacinth, his for the Princess, hers for Muniment, Lady Aurora's for Muniment, Hyacinth's for Muniment (as the great Chapter 35 demonstrates, Muniment is beyond friendship), Poupin's for Hyacinth; and so on.

It is when James is engaging this theme that he touches on an issue that can operate as a dilemma at the very heart of socialism: of class loyalties against personal ones; the demands of the ideal against the demands of the individual. Out of his deeply conservative allegiances James necessarily identifies the former alternatives as selfishness and sees the latter as true selflessness. But the elements of greatness in *The Princess Casamassima* spring from the terrific tensions James sees private bourgeois virtues having to sustain and perhaps collapse beneath. He comes very near to measuring this theme in all its weightiness, and it causes him at least partly to turn towards a problem which Mallock, who sees it far more dimly, shirks at the end of *The Old Order Changes* when he leaves Carew a way out of his marriage to Miss Capel, and which Gissing cynically and unfairly simplifies into a problem of egoism when he has Mutimer marry Adela rather than his long-suffering working-class sweetheart, Emma Vine. Here, too, they are escapist.

NOTES

1. W. H. Mallock, *Memoirs of Life and Literature*, London, 1920, pp. 129–131.
2. H. M. Lynd, *England in the 1880's*, London 1945, p. 75.
3. Raymond Williams, *Culture and Society*, London, 1957, p. 163. It is true that R. B. MacDowall has said that Mallock 'combined dialectical dexterity

with a lack of profundity' (*British Conservatism, 1832–1914*, London 1959, p. 133) and that Shaw remarked that 'any Socialist over the age of six could knock Mr Mallock into a cocked hat' (*Socialism and Superior Brains*, Fabian Tract no. 146, London, 1909, p. 7), but taking a broad view of Conservatism over the last eighty or so years, these judgements do not necessarily conflict with Williams's.

4. MacDowall, op. cit., pp. 92–3.
5. J. L. Garvin,*The Life of Joseph Chamberlain*, 2 vols., London, 1933,vol. 2, p. 55.
6. Ruskin, *Works*, ed. Cook and Wedderburn, London, 1903–12, vol. XXIX, p. 398.
7. Ibid., pp. 400–7.
8. *England in the 1800's*, op. cit., p. 255.
9. Dona Torr, *Tom Mann and his Times*, London, 1956, pp. 63–4.
10. Henry James, *The Princess Casamassima*, 2 vols., New York, 1962, vol. 1, p. xxii. All future references are to this edition.
11. *The National Review*, vol. 5, 1885, p. 800.
12. *The Saturday Review*, 24 May 1884, p. 687.
13. *Latter-Day Pamphlets*: vol. xx of the Centenary Edn., London, 1898, p. 22.
14. *The Novels of the Earl of Beaconsfield*, Hughendon Edition, London, 1881, *Lothair*, pp. x–xiv.
15. *Merry England*, vol. 1, May 1883, pp. 10–11.
16. Ibid., p. 13.
17. *The Reminiscences of Lady Dorothy Nevill*, London, 1906, pp. 284–7.
18. *Lothair*, op. cit., p. xv.
19. The *Nineteenth Century*, vol. XX, p. 33.
20. Ibid., p. 34.
21. from *Lord John Manners: a political and Literary Sketch*, by a Non-Elector, London, 1892, p. 73.
22. *The Athenæum*, no. 2861, 26 August, 1882, p. 261. But *Social Equality* was given the lead review, which suggests how important the topic was thought to be.
23. *Social Equality*, London, 1882, pp. 30–31.
24. *Property and Progress*, London, 1884, p. 7.
25. The *Westminster Review*, July–October 1884, vol. LXVI, n.s., p. 239.
26. See C. A. Barker, *Henry George*, New York, 1955, p. 556. As early as 1882 Hyndman had made public his disagreements with George, saying that 'Mr. Henry George . . . has . . . misapprehended the crucial problem of our industrial system.' See C. Tsuzuki, *H. M. Hyndman and British Socialism*, London, 1961, p. 45. Hereafter referred to as *Tsuzuki*.
27. *Social Equality*, pp. 250–3.
28. *Property and Progress*, p. 4.
29. Ibid., pp. 93–6.
30. *Tsuzuki*, op. cit., p. 281.
31. *Property and Progress*, p. 89.

Conservatism and Revolution in the 1880s

32. Ibid., pp. 244–8.
33. *Social Equality*, pp. 96–7.
34. Ibid., p. 31.
35. Ibid., p. 55.
36. I have tried elsewhere to show how arguments about the relationships of culture and class had a profound effect on fiction of the 1840s and 1850s. See my essay on 'Mrs Gaskell and Brotherhood' in *Tradition and Tolerance in Nineteenth Century Fiction*, London, 1966.
37. *Social Equality*, p. 5.
38. Ibid., p. 56.
39. *The Old Order Changes*, 3 vols., London, 1886, vol. 1, p. 15. All future references are to this edition.
40. Otterton is based on Dartington Hall, with which Mallock was connected through marriage.
41. George Gissing, *Demos*, London, 1892 edn. p. 2. All future references are to this edition.
42. Ibid., p. 13.
43. *The Old Order Changes*, vol. 1, pp. 128, 130, 29.
44. *Tsuzuki*, op. cit., pp. 3–5.
45. *Tom Mann and His Times*, op. cit., p. 203.
46. *Tsuzuki*, op. cit., p. 54. It may well be that the press reports helped James in the creation of 'realistic' dialogue for his working class characters in the *Princess Casamassima*. One of the men at the 'Sun and Moon' mutters 'And what the plague am I to do with seventeen bob – with seventeen bloody bob?' (vol. 1, p. 239). In the debate, Bradlaugh had argued the importance of thrift to the working-class, and at one point had been interrupted by the cry of 'Thrift on eighteen bob a week – bosh!' (Report in *Justice*, April 19 1884).
47. Ibid., pp. 55–6.
48. The S.D.F's London candidates polled 27 votes in Hampstead, and 32 in Kennington. But John Burns polled 598 votes in Nottingham. See *Tsuzuki*, p. 71. Almost certainly Mallock wrote the election episode into the novel *as a result* of the S.D.F.'s showing at the polls. The relevant passage in the novel appeared in the *National Review* for 1 April 1886 (where the *Old Order Changes* was being serialized), and when Mallock began serialization the elections were still to be held.
49. Quoted in *Tom Mann and his Times*, op. cit., p. 199.
50. See *Tsuzuki*, op. cit., p. 73.
51. See *Tom Mann and his Times*, pp. 226 and 334–5.
52. Lionel Trilling, *The Liberal Imagination*, London, 1961, p. 74.
53. See his essay on James and Besant in *Tradition and Tolerance in Nineteenth Century Fiction*, op. cit.
54. Irving Howe, *Politics and the Novel*, London, 1961, p. 146.
55. See George Woodcock, *Anarchism*, London, 1963, esp. pp. 416–420.
56. *Memoirs of Life and Literature*, op. cit., p. 166.

VIII

WILLIAM MORRIS AND THE DREAM OF REVOLUTION

JOHN GOODE

I

Morris takes the insights into industrial capitalism offered by the tradition whose major figures are Carlyle and Ruskin and gives them coherence through his theoretical understanding of Marxism and saves them from impotent hysteria by his persistent involvement in political action. E. P. Thompson definitively establishes his stature as a social critic in these terms, and Raymond Williams rightly describes his undeniable distinction when he says that Morris's socialism announced the extension of that tradition his book invokes 'into our own century'.[1]

But there is a major problem of value in Morris's work, and this too is brought to our attention in *Culture and Society*:

> For my own part, I would willingly lose *The* (sic) *Dream of John Ball* and the romantic socialist songs and even *News from Nowhere* – in all of which the weaknesses of Morris's general poetry are active and disabling – if to do so were the price of retaining and getting people to read such smaller things as *How we Live, and How we might Live*, *The Aims of Art*, *Useful Work versus Useless Toil*, and *A Factory as it Might Be*.[2]

This certainly suggests the right order in which to read Morris, but it seems also to offer itself as a critical judgement and as such it needs to be challenged. For although Williams recognizes that his discrimination would mean a change in Morris's status, he does not seem to realize how great that change would be. Since the distinctive feature of Morris's socialism is, as he argues, the fact that he sees it as a cultural 'recovery of purpose' through the granting of a proper social role to art, it is important that Morris should be able to create work which isn't merely the reflection of the marginal futility to which the arts are reduced in a capitalist society. If we reject Morris's creative writing, we must call into question the whole social criticism – it relies too much on what seems to be a bad conception of art.

I wish to make claims for the imaginative writing of the years of Morris's socialism by seeing it as a formal response to problems which are theoretically insoluble, except in terms of metaphors which are unsatisfactory and intractable in the actual historical situation. Art is obviously the creation of the human mind responding to values and insights which participate in continuity; socialism is a theory of change which perceives the determinant factors of change in forces outside immediate individual and conscious control. In his excellent chapter on the cultural theories of English Marxists, Williams shows how muddled any attempt to explain the relationship between economic forces and cultural events in terms of an 'in-frastructure' and 'superstructure' can become. The effect of the muddle, he argues, is to make many Marxist theorists revert to a discredited romanticism, and assimilate Marx's teaching to it, rather than to transform romanticism by Marxism. I don't want to argue that Morris overcame the acute difficulties inherent in Marxist attitudes to the arts in his theoretical writing, but that the imaginative works attempt, with much success, to find a mode in which the creative mind can be portrayed in its determined and determining relationship to historical actuality.

The proper context for the recognition of this is that of Morris's non-socialist contemporary writers. Thompson discusses this in some detail, but his account leaves an unresolved problem. On the one hand, he rightly criticizes Morris's aesthetic theory because it failed to take account of the importance of the work which was being created around him. 'In general', Thompson writes, 'Morris was blind towards the great achievements of bourgeois realism.'[3] On the other hand, in moral terms, he sees this as a basis for praise:

> The best and most honest of the literature at the end of the nineteenth century is marked by a profound disillusion, a searching for private reassurance, limited personal objectives, in the midst of a hostile social environment... Against this tide, Morris stood alone with full assurance,

with conscious confidence in life. The rock he stood upon was his Socialist convictions, his scientific understanding of history. The name which he gave this rock was 'Hope'.[4]

The split between aesthetic and moral judgements again reduces Morris's creative work to a marginal role. But it also makes the ideological assurance look almost complacent. The metaphor is dismaying. Socialism ought not to be a rock, but a creative current in the historical tide; it ought not to stand against the cultural life of the time it finds itself in but to transform it into a revolutionary consciousness. Yet this is the most common image of Morris – an intelligent man of heroic but blind faith. Certainly in his criticism, Morris's socialist faith seems to have blinded him to what was best in the literature of his own time. But a close analysis of his imaginative writing establishes that the difference between his commitment and the disillusionment of his contemporaries is not one of simple anti-thesis, of rock and tide, but one which signifies radically different solutions to shared tensions. Morris's formal experiments of the 1880s demonstrate a concern to create an historically possible revolutionary literature, and this involves a creative programme which goes in a different direction from those of such writers as Gissing, Hardy and James. We can only understand the validity of that programme if we see first how the tendency of their fiction is towards the contra-diction of what they were trying, in their different ways, to achieve, an art which would cut through the complacencies of bourgeois consciousness to the truth.

II

The classic statement of the central problem in fiction of the late nineteenth century is Engels's famous letter to Margaret Harkness of 1887. He is criticizing her novel, *City Girl*:

If I have any criticism to make, it is only that your story is not quite realistic enough. Realism, to my mind, implies, besides truth of detail, the truthful reproduction of typical characters under typical circum-stances. Now your characters are typical enough, to the extent that you portray them. But the same cannot be said of the circumstances surrounding them, and out of which their action arises. In *City Girl* the working class appears as a passive mass, incapable of helping itself or even trying to help itself. All attempts to raise it out of its wretched poverty come from the outside, from above . . . The revolutionary response of the members of the working class to the oppression that surrounds them, their convulsive attempts – semiconscious or conscious – to attain their rights as human beings, belong to history and may therefore lay claim to a place in the domain of realism.[5]

Engels is discussing the central problem of a realist aesthetic which is the relationship between specificity and typification particularly in the context of fiction's response to historical movement. Peter Demetz who has discussed the letter in detail wilfully misreads it in a way which precisely emphasizes the importance of this context. Demetz argues that the concept of typification derives from two traditions, the normative (which is theological in motivation and aspirational in aim) and the classificatory (which is scientific and descriptive). He applies this simple formula to Engels and decides that he is criticizing Margaret Harkness for failing to provide typification of the first kind: 'obviously Engels . . . was aiming at a dogmatic conception that would compress the raw material of reality into a form of the typical predetermined by partisan considerations'.[6] He thus ignores the fact that Engels explicitly rejects the notion of a *tendezroman*, and that, in a letter to Minna Kautsky, he criticizes her for creating a character in which 'personality is entirely dissolved in principle'.[7] Demetz assumes that Engels' view of the historical process is automatically wrong.[8] Yet what Engels is actually asking for is not the satisfying of partisan considerations, but the reflection of what is there, not just as a feature in the surface reality, but as an active force which gives that reality a historical identity, a potential for change. The letter is simply saying that Margaret Harkness does not portray completely the reality imitated by her novel, because she does not realize in the situation she describes the potential for change. Depiction of circumstances is particularized and static and thus unrealistic. What Engels means by typicality of circumstances is made clear in the letter to Minna Kautsky:

> . . . a socialist-biased novel fully achieves its purpose, in my view, if by conscientiously describing the real mutual relations, breaking down conventional illusions about them, it shatters the optimism of the bour-

geois world, instils doubt as to the eternal character of the existing order, although the author does not offer any definite solution or does not even line up openly on any particular side.[9]

The danger of 'realism' is that it can lose focus because it becomes overwhelmed by the phenomena it imitates and comes to see them as a permanent system of reality unconditioned by history. The voice of protest against the existing order of things may become the voice of despair through the intensity of its realization of that order; and despair is more comfortable than protest. Typification involves the realization of 'real mutual relations' which do not allow for pessimistic but consoling 'realities'. It is something that the late Victorian novelists could hardly achieve: overwhelmed by the complexities of the present, they come to write of it as a hell from which they cannot escape.

But this does not entitle us to a facile dismissal of the later Victorian novelists. The reality which Engels is talking about is very difficult to realize in concrete terms; to portray the inexorable is inevitably going to be like portraying the eternal. Engels himself almost undercuts his criticism at the end of his letter to Margaret Harkness: 'I must own, in your defence, that nowhere in the civilized world are the working people less actively resistant, more passively submitting to fate, more depressed than in the East End of London.'[10] To present the reality of historical change would mean, especially for the English writer, an abandonment of immediate realism.

The best illustration of these problems is in the work of Gissing. We can see in him both a remarkable effort to assimilate the social actuality with which he is confronted, and a final incapacity to face up to its implications in formal terms. The limitations declare themselves early on, in *Demos*. Gissing simply isn't able to understand socialist psychology (not in concrete terms: in explicit comment in letters, he shows himself much more understanding of, for example, the stand Morris takes). Westlake, the artist and socialist, is portrayed in terms of a simple antithesis, dreamer and philanthropist in guilty reaction to the dream, although Morris was able to reject both terms of the antithesis very clearly. It is clear that Gissing can only create characters in terms of withdrawal or absorption. Because of this, his working-class hero necessarily has to be portrayed as becoming bourgeois because engagement with society must be seen either in terms of condescension (the philanthropist) or conquest. The distinctiveness of Gissing's later fiction is that he is able to present this dichotomy as a subjective viewpoint which leads to the defeat of the protagonist. There is no actual escape from economic realities: however reluctant and intellectually apart a character is, his withdrawal is reduced to a rhetorical gesture. In *New Grub Street*, Reardon confidently asserts the distinction between his real self and his social being: 'If I had to earn my living as a clerk, would that make me a clerk in soul?'[11] But when Reardon does take a post as a clerk and his wife protests, his challenge to her to maintain the distinction brings out the inexorable reality:

> 'Amy, are you my wife, or not?'
> 'I am certainly not the wife of a clerk who is paid so much a week.'
> (p. 188)

The whole discussion from which this comes prevents us from trivializing Amy's remark with the word 'snobbery'. It is a scene in which the sexual breakdown of a marriage becomes inextricably involved with the necessities of lower middle class life and its aspirations. Amy ends in the arms of the 'strong man', the man of success: Reardon's failure in social terms is inseparable from his failure in moral and physical terms. Against this social Darwinism, an Arnoldian inner self is maintained, but it is one which has become purely nostalgic. The best self, the inner world which holds itself apart from the force of circumstance, no longer has the capacity to build a bridge which will find compatibility in the outer world: it reduces itself to a recessive desire which hangs on to fragments of a world it cannot have. When, later in the novel, one of the characters contemptuously talks of the working class reading public, he says: 'The working classes detest anything that tries to represent their daily life. It isn't because that life is too painful; no, no; it's downright snobbishness' (p. 314). This comes shortly after a pathetic discussion between Reardon and Biffen at the top of Pentonville Hill in the fog about 'a metrical effect in one of the Fragments' (p. 311). The snobbishness of the working class is not more absurd than the culture-hunger of the hero. Defeat is inevitable and total.

Gissing's understanding of the epistemology of this defeat is profound, but the price to be paid for the understanding is the stabilization of the historical process in order to create a sense of the permanently antithetical relationship between the self and society. and this means further that he is compelled to share that epistemology to accept its limits even in the portrayal of its inadequacy. We can see this in the critical scene where Reardon tells his wife that he has gone back to a clerkship:

He had foreseen a struggle, but without certainty of the form Amy's opposition would take. For himself, he meant to be gently resolute, calmly regardless of protest. But in a man to whom such self-assertion is a matter of conscious effort, tremor of the nerves will always interfere with the line of conduct he has conceived in advance. Already Reardon had spoken with far more bluntness than he proposed; involuntarily, his voice slipped from earnest determination to the note of absolutism, and, as is wont to be the case, the sound of these strange tones instigated him to further utterance of the same kind. He lost control of himself; Amy's last reply went through him like an electric shock, and for the moment he was a mere husband defied by his wife, the male stung to exertion of his brute force against the physically weaker sex.

'However you regard me, you will do what I think fit. I shall not argue with you. If I choose to take lodgings in Whitechapel, there you will come and live.'

He met Amy's full look, and was conscious of that in it which corresponded to his own brutality. She had become suddenly a much older woman; her cheeks were tightly drawn into thinness, her lips were bloodlessly hard, there was an unknown furrow along her forehead, and she glared like the animal that defends itself with tooth and claw.

'Do as *you* think fit? Indeed!'

Could Amy's voice sound like that? Great Heaven! With just such accent he had heard a wrangling woman retort upon her husband at the street corner. Is there then no essential difference between a woman of this world and one of that? Does the same nature lie beneath such unlike surfaces?

He had but to do one thing: to seize her by the arm, drag her up from the chair, dash her back again with all his force – there, the transformation would have been complete, they would stand towards each other on the natural footing. With an added curse perhaps.

Instead of that, he choked, struggled for breath, and shed tears.

Amy turned scornfully away from him. . . . (p. 189)

Reardon is not spared in this passage. The sexual reality of his marriage is torn apart by his social weakness. 'Stung' into male assertion, his dominance is almost comically confined to the verbal gesture. The physical superiority has become merely a matter of memory – in the present it is Amy who takes the psychological and sexual initiative, and her scorn at the end of this passage is completely justified. It if weren't so much felt to be the product of a continuous and relentless social pressure, Reardon's bursting into tears would be farcical; as it is, it is presented as an absurd anticlimax, the farce of nightmare. He is at a remove from his own male nature: the performance is a conscious effort to recapture something that is lost. He is in reality the feminine partner. Of course, the passage beginning 'Great Heaven' tries to rescue his dignity, but it is done entirely from his point of view, and it is totally irrational since it is he who has deliberately transformed the social struggle to a sexual one in the first instance. Unmanned by his failure, Reardon tries to hold on to the form of the marriage after its substance has changed; accidentally revealing the true substance by his stridency, he retreats from it into a kind of moral aestheticism. Later in the scene, he rationalizes his own failure by whining about Amy's lack of faith in him. She retorts, 'Instead of saying all this, you might be proving that I am wrong' (p. 192). We assent to her comment – the gap between protest and action is paralysing. On the other hand, what she means by proof is the refusal of the clerkship, the maintenance of social dignity. There is no escape for Reardon from the whirlpool of his economic being – but there is no specious pity for him either. He collapses because there is no adequate sense of identity available to cope with the outside world. The values that Reardon retreats to are openly those of an absolute sense of class – 'natural' is identical with 'brutal', and 'brutal' with the woman of the street corner. At the same time, the notion of his 'soul' is supposed to be separable from class – the true Reardon is not a clerk. The escape from class is through class snobbery. Reardon's understanding of the world around him is seen to be the product of what he most wishes to escape from.

All this is clearly there, judging Reardon, but we feel that Gissing's presentation of this process is limited because the language of presentation is inadequate. It cannot bend away from Reardon's

William Morris and the Dream of Revolution

conscious vocabulary towards one which will affirm the unconscious forces at work here (Amy *Victrix*). 'He meant to be gently resolute, calmly regardless of protest' is elegant and inert, and this more or less describes Reardon's mind. The trouble comes with the remark that 'tremor of nerves will always interfere with the line of conduct he has conceived in advance', which is obviously an authorial comment since it is accounting for the unconscious factor which 'interferes' between intention and action, but which is equally elegant and inert. 'Always' dilutes the concreteness of the situation by veering off towards aphorism, and 'interfere' is a ludicrously inadequate verb. On the other hand, it is difficult to see how Gissing could have solved this problem within the terms of the realistic novel. In order to portray a consciousness which is alienated in the way that Reardon's is, it has to accept the world-view of that consciousness. Gissing can 'place' Reardon but only in terms in which Reardon could, when he wasn't under stress, place himself. This means that the narrative has to enact in itself the confusion between the response to a genuine social issue (the unmanning of the artist by penury) and an absolute but subjective opposition of values (self and other). At the same time, since this opposition is purely vestigial (significantly it is Amy who wants Reardon to go on with his intellectual work – he is merely asserting his right to accept defeat and become 'a harmless clerk'), what mainly emerges from the novel is its inadequacy as an epistemology. The insights Gissing portrays seek a style which goes beyond that of the individual consciousness.

The formal limitations link with what is, in the end, a failure on Gissing's part to achieve a major confrontation between his protagonists and the social order from which they recoil. At his best, Gissing can dramatize this failure and bring out clearly its representativeness as a cultural phenomenon. At its worst it can become a comfortable rationalization. 'Keep apart' is a constant theme of Gissing's work, but it can blind him, as it does in his most dubious work such as *Born in Exile* and *Henry Ryecroft*, to what he is so competent to see, the impossibility of keeping apart. One of his few specifically political novels, *Denzil Quarrier*, clearly illustrates this tendency. It is a story about the election which followed Gladstone's Midlothian campaign which in itself is a significant point in the democratization of political discussion.[12] Gissing seems at first to have a real concern with connecting the psychology of his characters and the potential transformation of political life seen in the Liberal successes of that election. The hero is a man of means without any focus of interest who nevertheless registers a personal protest against middle class convention by living in a successful ménage with a married woman. Asked to speak at a Liberal stronghold, he preaches a moderate feminism and is immediately adopted as a radical candidate. The novel becomes then a study of the conflict between the political career and the private life. But the actual emergence of this conflict becomes lost in a much less explicable struggle between the warring egoists who try to control Quarrier's life. The quality of his radicalism in any case forestalls any real link being made between progressive political attitudes and sexual affirmation:

> So long as nature doles out the gift of brains in different proportions, there must exist social subordination. The true Radical is the man who wishes so to order things that no one will be urged by misery to try and get out of the class he is born in.[13]

Politics become reduced to specious accommodation while the real struggle is pushed to the margin of social life despite the emphasized social origin. Even in this one novel where Gissing sets out to confront a changing social world as one in which the protagonists play an active role, the protest becomes a social rationalization and, by qualifying the term 'radical' out of existence, and creating a dramatic structure in which the effective characters are almost motiveless mystifications, Gissing at once dehumanizes the impinging reality and absolves his characters from being anything other than victims of circumstance. The pessimism comforts the beneficiaries of the *status quo*.

Gissing is obviously a minor novelist, but his work illustrates clearly the dilemma confronted by greater contemporaries. James, for example, does transcend the determinism of realist 'antithesis' but he does so by the creation of a special language which creates its own rules and terms of triumph not unconscious of the economic realities which underwrite the subjective awareness of the protagonist, but taking possession of those realities and making of them moral dramas. Thus Milly Theale overcomes Kate Croy through the triumph of her moral perfection, but the agency of this perfection is her money. The real terms of the antithesis remain – Milly is rich and can control reality, Kate is poor and must struggle to dominate it before it dominates her. It is simply that the destruction of the individual consciousness by the impinging world is averted by turning the whole world into an image of consciousness.

The basis for the transformation of realism by the rediscovery of the integrated self is not in either of these writers but in Hardy. Hardy stands not, like Gissing, at the opposite extreme from Morris, as one whose very pessimism gives comfort to bourgeois optimism, but as one who affirms an aggressive role for human personality in the social world from which it is isolated – though, unlike Morris, Hardy is not supported by a coherent political theory. The subversive nature of his fiction is clear from the earliest novels, and it is clear that their subversiveness rests on a very clear sense of what can be affirmed. *Far from the Madding Crowd* is a drama of the quest for modes of expression which take account of the unaccommodated self. What Bathsheba and Gabriel find is physical contact on the hayrick in the storm – a discovery of work not as duty, the mode of accommodation to social law which is celebrated in *Adam Bede*, but as a physical rhythm, the fundamental expression of man's relation to the world around him. They are able to affirm this against the social status of Boldwood and the social duplicity of Troy because of what Joseph Poorgrass calls 'the gospel of the body'. The renewed community, purged of its overlord and its romantic hero, gains a new integrity of body and mind.

But it is a community which is far from the madding crowd. At the other end of his career, Hardy is compelled to confront the disintegration of human individuality in a society which does not belong to the past. For Jude there is no community to underwrite the integrity of body and soul. He stands in his field unaware of the past. The gospel of the body is caught in a meaningless confrontation with a dehumanized society and indifferent nature. There will only be a place for Jude if he denies either his intellectual aspirations or his capacity for love. To survive in this world is to be inhuman. But this is not a collapse into determinism. Jude is a very affirmative hero because he refuses to give up the search for integrity, and he only lies down in

death. When he speaks to the crowd at Christminster, we are conscious
of his triumph: 'But I don't admit that my failure proved my view
to be a wrong one.' Success is not rightness, and Jude speaks with what
Scott Fitzgerald was to call 'the authority of failure'. It is an authority
which has revolutionary potential, yet it cannot be brought to the
surface inside the novel itself. The halo round Christminster is
Jude's individual delusion, and it is also a response to a collective
experience of deprivation, but it cannot be realized as a collective
experience. For that to happen would mean moving out of the world
of the present and into the world of vision. Hardy was right to send
his novels to Morris, and Morris should have recognized their real
possibilities. But his inability to do so is understandable – for he has
to move away, not from the personal delusion to the magnificent
failure, but into the delusion so deeply that its basis in collective
experience becomes clear. As he puts it at the end of *News from
Nowhere*, 'And if others can see it as I have seen it, then it may be
called a vision rather than a dream.'¹⁴

III

If Morris was blind to the achievements of nineteenth-century
realism, he was nevertheless shrewdly aware of its problems. In
News from Nowhere, Clara says:

> As for your books, they were well enough for times when intelligent
> people had but little else in which they could take pleasure, and when
> they must needs supplement the sordid miseries of their own lives
> with imaginations of the lives of other people. But I say flatly that in
> spite of all their cleverness and vigour, and capacity for story-telling,
> there is something loathsome about them. Some of them, indeed, do
> here and there show some feeling for those whom the history-books
> call 'poor', and of the misery of whose lives we have some inkling; but
> presently they give it up, and towards the end of the story we must be
> contented to see the hero and heroine living happily in an island of bliss
> on other people's troubles; and that after a long series of sham troubles
> (or mostly sham) of their own making, illustrated by dreary intro-
> spective nonsense about their feelings and aspirations, and all the rest
> of it; while the world must even then have gone on its way, and dug and
> sewed and baked and built and carpentered round about these useless
> animals. (XVI. 151)

Although this is, in many ways, philistine, it also points to a central problem in nineteenth century fiction – the ambiguity of the relationship between the generalized social picture and the particularity of the protagonists who are chosen to embody its features. Gissing is only able to cope with the discrepancy through a reduction to blind determinism on the one hand and a factitious coherence of language on the other. And although Hardy is acutely conscious of the discrepancy, and is able to discover new orders of consciousness which take account of this tendency to isolate the particular and bring it into relation to the life in which it grows, he is unable to discover a social medium in which such orders can survive except one which is not available in time. One of the few novels of the period which is specifically concerned with the portrayal of historical popular movements, *The Revolution in Tanners Lane*, becomes the register of the diminishing scale of the radical mind as it transfers itself from the great historical moment to the life which continues after it. We move from the genuinely revolutionary sensibility which met the government at Peterloo to a quite starkly disconnected story in which the hypocrisy of the new generation of dissenters is exposed by a *theoretical* revolution with the result that the 'respectable' minister is replaced by an academic one. Not only do we see dissent itself becoming conservative and conformist, but the surviving radical spirit manifesting itself in an almost entirely private way, gaining a moral victory and a highly doubtful improvement of personnel. The Tanners Lane revolution is a farcical shadow of the forces displayed in the first half of the novel, and it does not change the course of history at all. The radical protagonists of the first part are recalled in the closing words of the novel only to remind us that what they stood for has really been driven underground: 'What became of Zachariah and Pauline? At present I do not know.'[15] Rutherford certainly affirms the reality of the revolutionary mind but he is hopelessly sceptical about its possible field of action.

Morris's whole literary effort in the eighties is to affirm the reality of the revolutionary mind and to see it in possible fields of action. 'It is the province of art', he wrote towards the end of his life, 'to set the true ideal of a full and reasonable life before him (i.e. the working man)' (XXIII. 281). What underwrites the possibility of this is the consciousness of historical change: 'Until recently,' he wrote in collaboration with Belfort Bax, 'amongst cultivated people, enjoying whatever advantages may be derived from civilization, there has been an almost universal belief, not yet much broken into, that modern or bourgeois civilization, is the final form of human society. Were this the case, we should be pessimists indeed . . .'[16] It is this sense which differentiates him from Gissing, Hardy and Rutherford, but we need to define carefully its distinctive nature, because it participates in their pessimism before separating out from it. In a lecture of 1884, 'Misery and the Way Out', Morris said:

> Friends, this earthly hell is not the ordinance of nature but the manu-facture of man; made I will believe not by their malice but their stupidity; and it is your business to destroy it: to destroy it, I say, not each man to try to climb up out of it, as your thrift-teachers tell you, but to make an end of it so that no one henceforth can ever fall into it.[17]

Morris here anticipates the pessimism of a novel such as *The Nether World* which sees the earthly hell as a permanent state and escape only in terms of an ironic version of self help, and even of *Jude the Obscure*. The separation is in the words 'not nature . . . but the manufacture of man' and this gives the judgement on the present, which is no different from that of Gissing and the later Hardy, temporality. The historicism is informed by two firmly grasped concepts which are the basis of all Morris's socialist writing – the class struggle and its historical consummation, revolutionary change. It was the need to cope with the sense of the first and the despair of doing so except by revolutionary theory that drove Morris to socialism initially. In a lecture of 1886, he picked up a word made current by John Bright in the reform debates of the sixties; 'there is an ugly word for a dreadful fact which I must make bold to use – the residuum: that word since the time I first saw it used, has had a terrible significance to me, and I have felt from my heart that if this residuum were a necessary part of civilization, as some people openly, and many more tacitly, assume that it is, then this civilization, carries with it the poison that shall one day destroy it' (XXII. 65). The imagery is deterministic and its sense of class is merely negative, but 'destroy' carries a definitive sense of change, and this means already that Morris is differently situated from those who imagined the present world to be indestructible. In the following year, Morris moves towards a much more active sense of change via an intensifying despair. He writes to Mrs Burne Jones, about the trial of Johann Most, 'These are the sort of things that make thinking people so sick at heart that they are driven from all interest in politics save revolutionary politics: which I must say seems like to be my case'.[18]

It is thus out of despair rather than vision that Morris moves towards the recognition of the class struggle and its necessary outcome in revolution. What Marxism gives him is an historical coherence which re-orders the relationship between visionary conceptions of man's possible existence and the despair of seeing the piecemeal progress of liberalism preventing those conceptions from becoming less and less likely. To move from the vague and emotive remarks that I have just quoted to the discussion of class in *How We Live and How We Might Live* (1885), which leans heavily on Chapter XXII of *Capital*, is to move into realms of coherence that would be quite alien to the dualistic mind of Gissing. Morris now sees the class struggle not as something which is merely dangerous and deplorable but as something which is necessary, and he sees change, therefore, not as a matter of improving the moral and material standards of a helpless residuum, but as one of that proletariat recognizing its own essence, combination:

> The working-classes or proletariat cannot even exist as a class without combination of some sort. The necessity which forced the profit-grinders to collect their men first into workshops working by the division of labour, and next into great factories worked by machinery . . . gave birth to a distinct working-class or proletariat: and this it was which gave them their *mechanical* existence, so to say. (XXIII. 11)

It is precisely this coherence that gives Morris his aesthetic. The potential of historical change predates the consciousness of its agents. Despair of change is merely a false consciousness which itself tends towards revolution: 'all history shows us what a danger to society may be a class at once educated and socially degraded'

(XXIII. 79). But if this danger is to be transformed into the possibility of revolution the false consciousness must be transformed into a consciousness which recognizes the reality of social change. To set the true ideal of a full and reasonable life before the working class is not, therefore, to be idealistic. It is merely to bring into articulate consciousness progressive forces at work in history on preconscious, or 'mechanical' levels.

At the same time, Morris's use of the earthly hell metaphor suggests how sensitive he is to the social pessimism arrived at by his most intelligent contemporary writers. This is because although Marxism gives his vision an historical basis, the central concept of his socialist ideology is one which has been with him from the beginning, alienation. But he never lets go his ability to enter into the alienated consciousness of the individual aware of social injustice, and this provides the basis of all his creative writing. Taking up the antisocialist argument that the working-class is better off than savages, Morris points to its absurdity because it takes no account of social relationships, and he goes on to define his own version of alienation: 'but for us, for the most of us, civilization has bred desires which she forbids us to satisfy, and so is not merely a niggard but a torturer also' (XXIII. 105). In another essay he demonstrates that his sense of alienation has a very forceful subjective meaning: 'all civilization has cultivated our sensibility only to disappoint it, and . . . we suffer . . . from the consciousness of the mass of suffering and brutality which lies below our lucky class, ugliness all about us, the world made for naught.' Although such sympathy is a rhetorical device and is placed by an abrasive irony, 'we discontented ones of the intellectual hanger-on group', it also acknowledges the difficulty of others in attaining his belief in change. It suggests that there is a tension in his work, which is what the creative writing is concerned with, between the vision of the historical potential which he had learned from Marx and the degree to which it is manifest in the historical actuality.

This is not the place to discuss Morris's involvement with English socialist groups but it is impossible not to recognize that underlying much of his work there is a profound unease about their historical role. Activism is central to Morris's socialist thinking and it comes out almost automatically in *How I Became a Socialist*:

So there I was in for a fine pessimistic end of life, if it had not somehow dawned on me that amidst all this filth of civilization the seeds of a great chance, what we others call Social-Revolution, were beginning to germinate. The whole face of things was changed to me by that discovery, and *all I had to do then* in order to become a Socialist was to hook myself on to the practical movement . . . (XXIII. 280)

The italicized phrase is an index of how closely Morris regarded theory as wedded to practice, but, written as it was in 1894, this must be seen as a difficult statement of faith. Very early on, he saw that the SDF had no genuine historical reality; it was, he said, a 'theatrical association in a private room with no hope but that of gradually permeating cultured people with our aspirations'. 'Theatrical', 'private', 'gradually', 'cultured' – the words add up to a socialist nightmare.[19] The sense of unreality is important again in his explanation of his break with SDF: 'the revolution cannot be a mechanical one, though the last act of it may be civil war . . . why then should we swagger about violence which we know we cannot use?'[20] And yet it cannot be said that the Socialist League discovered any more valid role: it was less active in events such as the Trafalgar Square riots of 1886 and 1887, and it was indifferent to the Dock Strike.

Socialist action in the eighties does not seem to have given Morris much sense of the way things were changing. His vision of the immediate future is, in fact, very subdued:

. . . our own lives may see no end to the struggle, perhaps no obvious hope of the end. It may be that the best we can hope to see is that struggle getting sharper and bitterer day by day, until it breaks out openly at last into the slaughter of men by actual warfare instead of by the slower and crueller methods of 'peaceful' commerce. If we live to see that, we shall live to see much; for it will mean the rich classes grown conscious of their own wrong and robbery, and consciously defending them by open violence; and then the end will be drawing near. (XXIII. 119)

It is true that the date of this, 1885, may mean that the modesty of the prediction is determined by the gloom which followed the split, but it points to an important feature of Morris's writing throughout, and that is the disciplined refusal to allow the historical actuality to be flushed with the light of the historical potential. This potential is seen as offering only struggle in the foreseeable future. The realism of this is complex in its effect. On the one hand, it prevents Morris from short circuiting the revolutionary process; on the other, in the light of the spontaneous movement from commitment to activism that is registered in *How I Became a Socialist*, it makes for a tension between the need to act and the recognition of the limited possibilities of action – limited, that is, not merely quantitatively but qualitatively: English socialism doesn't offer a confrontation with reality. We shall have to come back to this, but we need to take note immediately of Morris's alertness to the predicament of the socialist intellectual. Looking back on the early days of socialism in *News from Nowhere*, Hammond gives us an exact diagnosis:

> When the hope of realizing a communal condition of life for all men arose, quite late in the nineteenth century, the power of the middle classes, the then tyrants of society, was so enormous and crushing, that to almost all men, even those who had, you may say *despite themselves, despite their reason and judgment*, conceived such hopes, it seemed a dream. So much was this the case that some of those more enlightened men who were then called Socialists, although they well knew, and even stated in public, that the only reasonable condition of Society was that of pure Communism (such as you now see around you), yet shrunk from what seemed to them the barren task of preaching the realization of a happy dream. (XVI. 104)

The paradoxes are acute. There is no suggestion that the enlightened men are anything but right: pure Communism is here. Nor is there any suggestion that their aspirations were anything but 'reasonable'. Yet they conceive such hopes *despite* themselves, *despite* their reason and their judgement. It means that the socialist vision is in some way beyond immediate consciousness although in theoretical terms it is conceivable. The believer is conditioned as much by his alienation as the pessimists who see the earthly hell as a law of nature are by theirs.

This is the starting point of Morris's socialist aesthetic. His awareness of alienation comprehends a sense of the radical dislocation of consciousness from historical reality (with its potential for change). Art has therefore to create a new consciousness which moves away from the immediate towards the possible. Realism has to be transcended: 'as for romance, what does romance mean? I have heard people miscalled for being romantic, what romance means is the capacity for a true conception of history, a power of making the past part of the present.'[21] It also becomes a power for seeing the future in the present. But its form is determined by alienation. Art is ineluctably the creation of the individual – socialism is the recognition of collectivity. Such a recognition can only be registered through the transformation of individual epistemology, and the transformation has to take place within the individual through an entry into dream. Socialist art does not transcend alienation: it transforms it into revolutionary consciousness by the recognition of the collective possibilities of the mind's curve away from actuality. For Morris, in dreams begins responsibility.

IV

The affirmation of the responsibility of dream in a world in which consciousness has become ineradicably dislocated from the field of its existence is an assumed feature of all of Morris's socialist writing. But the most exploratory treatment of the theme predates his socialism and is the subject of *Sigurd the Volsung*. It is an acutely frustrating text because its thematic importance and narrative skill are almost obliterated by Morris's adoption of a style which is passively the product of the very alienation the story is about. The language is opaque and frequently inept – a combination of pseudo-anachronism trying to escape from the realities of modern English and an inert obedience to the demands of metre, as though all that keeps it communicating is a reflex response to a machine. The poem records the development of the extreme disaffection of the inner mind from the outward life in terms of a highly modernized myth. True, Morris writes out the worst physical brutality of the original myth, but what we have instead is a psychological drama which is more violent and inexorable – *Sigurd the Volsung* is much nearer to *Women in Love* than to the Saga, and translated into English it could have been a great Victorian degenerative myth of social alienation and the breakdown of sexual relationships.

In the story, power moves from the Volsungs to the Niblungs and finally to Atli. The first stage signifies a transference from a race in whom desire and action are unified to one in whom desire can only be fulfilled through duplicity (both that of Grimhild in doping Sigurd and that of her sons in plotting the murder). This leaves open the possibility of redemption through self-sacrifice, but the final stage, in which Atli has become the ruling power, is one in which the divorce between desire and action has become a social system in which the ruler employs retainers to sustain his power: he is, himself, physically insignificant. We have moved to the lord of the city, and only destruction of the whole society can atone for the evil nature of the ruler.

Three interconnected motifs contribute to this evolution of alienated man. The first is that the values of the Volsungs, which include heroism, community and equality 'For the man was a mighty warrior, and a beater down of kings' (XII. 19) become outlawed. By their very heroism, the Volsungs are unable to cope with the duplicity of the Goths. Sigmund scornfully rejects the offer of Siggeir to buy the sword he has drawn from the Branstock because he has no conception of trading one's actions for acquisitions. By the same token, however, the Volsungs have no conception either of conspiracy, the closed, indirect pursuit of revenge, and so fall prey to Siggeir's stratagem. The Volsungs' story is one of 'How a mighty people's leaders in the field of murder fell' (XII. 16), and murder is a mode of action that the integrity of giants, who know no dichotomy between the values they seek and the means they will employ to achieve them, cannot cope with. Sigmund survives only through the cunning his sister has learnt, and the race is perpetuated only through her secret incest with him. Sinfiotli is the progeny of a race doomed to conserve itself through secrecy and crime, and he and his father, though they are of heroic stature, are doomed to outlawry. They become for a while werewolves, and though they recover from this, it seems to declare the potential for brutality that their isolation breeds in them. And this is confirmed when Sinfiotli murders Siggeir's children: the moment is presented with a calm brutality which reduces both murderer and victim to something less than human:

> but Sinfiotli taketh them up
> And breaketh each tender body as a drunkard breaketh a cup.
> (XII. 36)

Sigmund lives to return to the land of the Volsungs, and his heroism survives in community, but his last years are without the creative vitality that we had been made to feel present at the wedding of Signy earlier. Sinfiotli has nothing to do but become a pirate, and he is in the end murdered by Sigmund's wife. Sigmund banishes her and takes a new wife who is virtuous, but in the battle he has to fight against his chief rival, as he feels himself becoming 'king of the world at last' (XII. 53). His sword is destroyed by Odin and he is killed. The Volsungs are to survive, but not as leaders of their own community. Sigurd, with whom Sigmund's new wife is pregnant, is to be brought up in a strange country. Thus an historical rhythm is established at the outset in which 'Earth grows scant of great ones, and fadeth from its best' (XII. 5), so that greatness in its social manifestation comes to seem naive and can only survive outside the social law as individual greatness.

This idea informs the second motif: we move from the saga of the heroic community to the romance hero, and thus the second book is chiefly concerned with the dynamics of individuation. The land of Elf where Sigurd is brought up is a gentile utopia – 'There no great store had the franklin, and enough the hireling had' (XII. 61) – but Sigurd, educated by Regin, the man of skill and knowledge, is given a consciousness which grows beyond accommodation in a static society:

> For this land is nought and narrow, and Kings of the carles are
>   these,
> And their earls are acre bidders, and their hearts are dull with
>   peace.   (XLL. 68)

The specific focus of the aspiration becomes, of course, the rhinegold, and this is the third motif in the degenerative myth, the development of the acquisitive mind. The story of Andvari, the original guardian of the gold, invokes the possibility of a mind being changed by the situation it finds itself in, so that the elf of the Dark, whose knowledge had been universal, becomes narrowed by its contact with the gold and is unable to concentrate on anything but the counting of the gold which it knows will not bring happiness. Fafnir, the brother of Regin, who takes all the gold for himself, turns into a dragon fully conscious of his despair. Both characters present powerfully the determination of consciousness by money, but their role is more than incidental. When Sigurd kills Fafnir (through stratagem), it is a triumph for his heroic personality – 'I, Sigurd, knew and desired, and the bright sword learned the way' (XII. 111), and thus it is an assertion of values which are not determined by circumstance. But his triumph is ambiguous, accompanied by 'sounds of a strange lamenting' (XII. 112). For although Sigurd's heroism is unquestioned, we note as the poem progresses that it is not one which creates a social world out of the triumph. His mother's prediction – 'all folk of the earth shall be praising the womb where once he lay' (XLL. 51) – only comes true insofar as he achieves personal glory. Sigurd meets what confronts him – there is no sense of specific objectives. The attainment of the gold turns him into an episodic hero. More than this, once he has tasted the heart of Fafnir and become through it aware of the conspiracy of Regin against him and taken action to forestall it, we have moved completely, with the hero, into a world in which the main task of life is a struggle for existence by the isolated individual through cunning or violence or both. From that point on, the major impetus of the poem derives from the complete dislocation of the inner and outer selves manifest above all in the distortion of sexual relationships.

Sigurd is granted a vision of transcendent love in his first meeting of Brynhild (who mediates between fate and humanity). But this is outside the realm of human life, and their resolution to recreate this vision in the world of men is thwarted first by her inaccessibility and then, as Sigurd drifts away inevitably towards where war takes him, by the drug of oblivion which Grimhild administers. What Sigurd gains is not the love of Brynhild but the complex of love and hatred which Gudrun gives him – a complex which in its destructiveness and violence looks forward to Lawrence's Gudrun. Gudrun, whose psychology is one of the most remarkable things in the poem, feels for him in terms of individual aspiration rather than any sense of mutuality underwritten by social integration: she is mainly silent in his presence, feeling both admiration and envy for his heroic deeds. This dualism is a comment on what the integrity of the Volsungs has been brought to. Sigurd's death is brought about by the same destructive ambiguity: Gudrun's brothers do not break the blood-bond they have made with Sigurd, they circumvent it, and what remains in the poem is the fullest working out of the complex interplay of law, desire and stratagem which this situation sets up. Gudrun lures her brothers to their deaths at the hands of Atli: The moment when she sits in the hall where the battle is raging, withdrawn and dressed in white, and remains passive as drops of her brother's blood stain her dress, is not Swinburnian, but one where the suppressed will takes command of the life around it by its very withdrawal. The Niblungs do achieve an heroic stature in their struggle against Atli and their sacrifice of themselves and the gold to prevent the ruler of the city from securing final power. But it is the heroism of reparation for guilt, and the guilt derives from the thrust of man's heroic energies into isolation and the withdrawal of the will into cunning. It is the mythic version of 'modern love' seen as the creation of an acquisitive society.

But it is more than this, because Morris's chief concern is the structural relationship of the dichotomy in consciousness which this theme adumbrates. Although Sigurd is made to lose his love for Brynhild, Grimhild cannot recreate him anew. His face becomes emotionless and he rides off aimlessly into the deedless dark: although the vision of transcendent love is untranslatable into the world of men, it is equally undeniable. Sigurd does make contact with Brynhild in the world of men twice, and the contact is highly ironic. Before he reaches the Niblungs, he finds her by accident in Lymdale, another earthly paradise like the Land of Elf, wearing a dress depicting the past history of the Volsungs. We have seen already that such a world is unavailable to Sigurd, and it is realized here as an echo of what has been: 'For fair they are and joyous as the first God-fashioned Kings' (XII. 141). She too is a figure who belongs to the past of the Volsungs – and soon Sigurd is to be drugged into forgetfulness, not of its aura and importance, but of its coherence. Sigurd's accommodation is not that of the historically rooted hero but that of the leader of warlike people who is also the outsider. But this first meeting is also given positive value by the second meeting which comes after Sigurd has been drugged and has married Gudrun. Grimhild sends her eldest son, Gunnar to take Brynhild as wife. Sigurd and the second son, Hogni go with him. They find that Brynhild's castle is surrounded by a wall of fire, and Gunnar's horse refuses to go through it. He takes Sigurd's horse, who also shies away in spite of a career of unalloyed fearlessness. Hogni then makes the two men hold hands and Sigurd sees Gunnar disappear and reappear again in the body of himself. He realizes that he has assumed the body of Gunnar and rides through the flames, swears a troth to Brynhild and sleeps with her laying a sword between them. Brynhild marries Gunnar but remains pale and unsatisfied as Gudrun seems 'dreamy with the love of yester-night'. When Gudrun in triumph reveals the truth of the change of identities, Brynhild begins to die of grief. Neither Gunnar, nor Sigurd who offers marriage, are able to recall her to life, and she demands Sigurd's death before she dies herself.

The significance of this is very plain. The first meeting adumbrates the lost possibilities of the vision of love in the actual world. The second depicts, mythically, its actuality. Body and mind are asunder. Sigurd can only reach love through inhabiting the body of Gunnar. Gunnar gains love (the acquisitive verb needs to be emphasized) only through employing the consciousness of Sigurd. Man must seem to lose his identity to bring love into this world. Marriage thus becomes a lie – 'And the lie is laid between them, as the sword lay while agone' (XII. 204). The realities of sexual love are distorted by the dislocation of identity and the trickery of the societal witch. Equally, however, though the realities of sexual love eventually insist on being recognized, it is not as love but as murder. The sword between Sigurd and Brynhild is as real as the lie between each of them and the Niblung they have been duped into marrying. The love has to be unconsummated – remaining a dream which can only be actualized inversely in death. Sigurd will die in Gudrun's arms.

This account doesn't pay tribute to the realization of these themes. For Morris manages to bring out through the linguistic fog the dramatic sense of what Grimhild does to Sigurd's mind by destroying its relation with the past, and, later the grimness and violence of the struggle for domination between Brynhild and Gudrun. Both features point to what is affirmative in this inexorable destructiveness of sexual distortion. The entry into man's primeval greatness of deceit and greed transforms the heroism which is the heritage of that greatness, and the love which is its vision, into the heroism of the outsider and the lie of marriage. Sigurd is successful in action but he is finally unable to hold the integrity of the Volsungs together in his mind, so that his very identity becomes the agent of other, debased forces. But Sigurd remains, even in defeat, isolated and withdrawn, unable to participate in his own wedding ceremony. And Brynhild remains apart from the world she is trapped in, holding the vision of Sigurd together separate from her marriage. Finally Gudrun, the woman of the repressed will and the withdrawn aspiration, will bring revenge on all those who are agents of 'destruction. She will draw her brothers to their death, and she will burn the court of Atli. Her alienated sexual violence will ensure that the saga does not come to rest in the lowest level of degradation. Her dramatic act affirms the ultimate freedom of mind which is postulated throughout the poem. Grimhild can divorce Sigurd from his vision of love but she cannot put it completely from his mind, and only by divorcing his mind from his body can she take possession of love for her son so that the possession is limited to the duration of the divorce. Both Sigurd's vision and Brynhild's knowledge of him ensure that finally love can only be destroyed by the acquisitive society and cannot be assimilated by it. In their dream world, and in the retreated con-ciousness of Gudrun, there remains an unviolated force which emerges in each of them in turn as a chain reaction which will come back into society to destroy it. Consciousness may be split in two, but it cannot be remade in the image of what splits it. In the recognition of the responsiveness of this division to a cleavage in the outer world, the mythic division of labour, the revolutionary mind begins its growth.

V

Sigurd the Volsung necessarily ends in destruction. The unviolated consciousness can only issue in the recoil of the individual: once Gudrun has completed the process of vengeance, she has nothing to do but to walk into the sea. The isolated mind is a sepulchre within which the lost echoes of the values of the past reverberate, and it bursts open to history only to spread death. Socialism enables Morris to envisage its withdrawal not merely as responsive but as capable of becoming a possible social experience. The inexorable historical rhythm which he creates in relation to the unassimilated consciousness in *Sigurd the Volsung* is not pervasively triumphant, but it is always hostile. A dialectical view of history grants the opposing consciousness a role in the ongoing dynamic. It means that the task of the disaffected mind is not to destroy all that is outside it, but to seek out the forces in the historical rhythm which are its objective equivalents. The relationship between subjective and objective is difficult to grasp in conceptual terms but it can be best defined vis-à-vis Engels:

> And this conflict between the productive forces and modes of production is not a conflict engendered in the mind of man, like that between original sin and divine justice. It exists, in fact, objectively, outside us, independently of the will and actions even of the men who have brought it on. Modern Socialism is nothing but the reflex, in thought, of this conflict in fact; the ideal reflection in the minds, first, of the class directly suffering under it, the working class.[22]

We shall need to emphasize later that Morris's attitude to the role of the human mind is much less deterministic than the use of a word such as 'reflex' implies, but what socialism gives him is the realization that the laws of change may only be grasped by the individual in terms of his alienation – that is, in terms of his response to the thwarting of his desires by the world of actuality. The determining role of consciousness begins in the recognition of the nature of its determination by objective contradictions. Dream, the freed consciousness, thus becomes a major, though expendable, register of the antithetical forces invisibly operating against the perceptible reality.

Thus there is nothing facile about Morris's use of dream as a convention within which to realize concretely socialist insight. Above all, it is not polemical but exploratory. Despite the intensity and commitment of Morris's social vision, and his talent for coherent argument, his fictional works are not didactic. In the first place, the lucid and confident prose of *Signs of Change* demonstrates that Morris has no need of parable to give specious support to his theory. Secondly, it is obviously absurd to expect anybody to be converted to socialism by reading *A Dream of John Ball* or *News from Nowhere*, and Morris clearly did not intend that they should be. The rightness of Socialist theory is a *donnée* of such texts, and their major concern is to explore in dramatic terms what it means to the experiencing mind to bring socialist values to an understanding of historical change. And underlying the exploration is a deep tension between the need to create a viable relationship between dream and perceptible reality, and the recognition that the fulfilment of this need is an agony as great as Jude's.

The theme of *A Dream of John Ball* allows for a highly compressed portrayal of the struggle to achieve a meaningful relationship between human aspiration and the historical process. The rebellion of 1381 had become an important event in the work of historians contemporary with Morris, particularly those whom he admired.[23] Stubbs describes it as a 'revolutionary rising' and goes on:

> The rising of the commons is one of the most portentous phenomena to be found in the whole of our history. The extent of the area over which it spread, the extraordinary rapidity with which intelligence and communication passed between the different sections of the revolt, the variety of cries and causes which combined to produce it, the mystery that pervades its organization, its sudden collapse and its indirect permanent results, give it a singular importance both constitutionally and socially.[24]

It clearly has great relevance to Morris's own situation in the eighties. Green makes a more precise point which is also important in its implications. Talking of the system of slogans and catchphrases for which the uprising is famous, he writes: 'In the rude jingle of these lines began for England the literature of political controversy: they are the first predecessors of the pamphlets of Milton and of Burke.'[25] The Kent uprising in particular reveals the possibility of a concerted political action on the part of the people which is not a protest against oppression on a narrow basis. 'Their discontent', Green writes, 'was simply political'.[26] Thorold Rogers, whose work was an obviously useful document for socialist writers, emphasizes as well that it is a revolt which shows a sophisticated organization and that it is the product of prosperity as well as oppression: 'How can men combine and organize when their one thought is for their daily bread, and that is only secure for the day?'[27] Thus it is an *articulate* uprising with real possibilities of victory. It has its literature and its ideology – its longing for justice as well as its immediate grievances (Rogers differentiates it from the peasant war in Germany and the Jacquerie on these grounds). It is a movement which expresses a definite change in the level of consciousness of the common people. Morris is therefore right to stress the real qualities of material and cultural life of the men who were in revolt. The strength of social identity is an important feature in the articulation of single grievances into political action.

But it is not merely the rebellion's formal qualities that make it relevant to the Socialist movement. 'Priests like Ball', wrote Green, 'openly preached the doctrines of communism'.[28] Rogers goes further and suggests that not only the ideas but the reaction of the people to their situation made them open to socialist thought. The Statutes of Labourers are for him important because the serfs reacted to them by forming combinations: 'in plain modern English, the serfs entered into what are now called trades unions'.[29] The poor priests who provided their ideology 'had honeycombed the minds of the upland folk with what may be called religious socialism',[30] and Tyler and the other leaders were concerned with much more than the redress of grievances; their concern was for 'the reconstruction of English society'.[31] C. Edmund Maurice, who wrote a composite biography of Tyler Ball and Oldcastle in 1875, went so far as to head a section of of his book 'The Class Struggle in Richard II's Reign'.[32] Not surprisingly, John Ball was already a major figure in socialist mythology. Hyndman, with a note of that chauvinism which was to play such a destructive role in the history of the socialist movement wrote, in *The Historical Basis of Socialism in England*: 'It is well to show that the idea of socialism is no foreign importation into England. Tyler, Cade, Ball, Kett, More, Bellers, Spence, Owen, read to me like sound English names: not a foreigner in the whole batch.'[33] Morris would hardly have subscribed to this kind of vulgarity (though he may have felt the need to redress the germanocentrism of Engels) but since he is attempting to define the basis of the historical change of consciousness it is clearly important for him to show that the aspirations of his own socialist comrades are linked with aspirations which lie deep in the inherited past.

Morris's story is thus deeply responsive to issues emerging in history in his own time. The rebellion of 1381 is a moment of great significance to the socialist movement because it is a coherent rebellion which looks forward in its aims to socialism itself. Neverthe-less, Morris could not, of course, have been satisfied with the vague labels of Stubbs, Green and Rogers. Nor could he fail to be acutely conscious of the gap between what may have been the socialist aims of the rebellion and its most important effects. All of the historians I have mentioned agree that the ultimate focus of the rebellion was the end of villenage, and that although the charters granted by Richard II to buy the rebels off were revoked, the long term results of the rebellion were to cause the end of feudalism. 'They had struck a vital blow at villenage',[34] Stubbs writes, and Green, as usual more dramatic and specific, concludes, 'serfage was henceforth a doomed and perishing thing'.[35] Predictably, the picture they give has been heavily demythologized by later historians, but if this dates Stubbs and Green, it does not affect Morris, whose concern is to evoke a dramatic concentration of a changing awareness, and not to set up a mechanical cause and effect relationship. But Morris goes beyond the historians in a more basic way. He would know from Marx that the major precondition of capitalist production is the freeing of labour. Thus whatever 'communism' Ball was preaching was dialec-tically opposed to the direction his rebellion took. The release from serfdom was part of a process which retarded 'fellowship' by dis-ruption of a sense of community. Though its ideology has socialist content, the peasants' uprising is, in its effect, part of the process by which society becomes capitalist.

This is reflected very accurately in the text. There is a marked contrast between the political consciousness of the peasants and that of Ball: the people who are actually going to create the rebellion are much more conscious of the struggle for liberty than the struggle for community. The stave of Robin Hood, for example, shows this:

> ... it was concerning the struggle against tyranny for the freedom of life, how that the wildwood and the heath, despite of wind and weather, were better for a free man than the court and the cheaping-town; of the taking from the rich to give to the poor; of the life of a man doing his own will and not the will of another man commanding him for the com-mandment's sake. (XVI. 224)

The remark about rich and poor is much more routine than the evocation of the importance of liberty, and it is, in any case, not one which suggests that the rich man has to be abolished. By contrast, Ball's sermon has a text which goes much further: 'fellowship is heaven, and lack of fellowship is hell' (XVI. 230). Even Ball's attack on feudalism is on its inequality rather than its restriction of individual liberty:

> ... ye know who is the foeman, and that is the proud man, the oppressor, who scorneth fellowship, and himself is a world to himself and needeth no helper nor helpeth any, but, heeding no law, layeth law on other men because he is rich. (XVI. 234)

Thus Morris realizes not merely the positive value of the rebellion but also its final contradictory nature. Those most directly involved in the concrete situation, the peasants and craftsmen who do the fighting, see the cause in libertarian terms. Ball, the theorist, raises the level beyond that of liberty to that of equality. But his language is revealing – his rhetoric is religious. The vision of what lies beyond the immediate objective (which comes to mean the fight to obtain a free market) demands a terminology which is not confined to the world of concrete activity: 'the change beyond the change' can only be dreamt of in terms which are bound up with 'the glory of the heavens which is worshipped from afar'. Morris's realization is close to Engels' analysis in *The Peasant War in Germany*, where Engels draws a distinction between middle class heresies which were simply anticlerical, and the insurrectionary heresies of plebeian and peasant classes, of which John Ball's is one:

> This position of the plebeians is sufficient explanation as to why the plebeian opposition of that time could not be satisfied with fighting feudalism and the privileged middle-class alone; why, in fantasy at least, it reached beyond modern borgeois society then only in its inception; why, being an absolutely propertyless faction, it questioned institutions, views, and conceptions common to every society based on division of classes. The chiliastic dream visions of ancient Christianity offered in this respect a very serviceable starting-point. On the other hand, this reaching out beyond not only the present but also the future, could not help being violently fantastic. At the first practical application, it naturally fell back into narrow limits set by prevailing conditions.[36]

Engels offers here a precise equivalent of the balance between consciousness and actuality in the peasant uprising. What is important is that his use of the words, 'fantasy', 'dream visions' and 'violently fantastic' alerts us to the title of Morris's story. What mediates the gap between aspiration and possibility is the conceivable – dream.

A Dream of John Ball contains a threefold ambiguity on which the whole tension of the story depends. In the first place, it defines the tale itself – the narrator's dream of the past (itself historically aware since the mode is a mediaeval one). But it also means John Ball's dream, which has to be interpreted in two ways. In the first place, his dream is his fantasy of fellowship. It is a romantic vision, linked with the moonlight, but which has to be set against the gloomy truth that the narrator reveals to Ball among the dead. And this revelation too is a dream – not of aspiration but of consequence. As daylight replaces the moon, a second, more objective dream replaces the fantasy: 'scarce do I know', says Ball 'whether to wish thee some dream of the days beyond thine to tell what shall be' (XVI. 286).

The drama of Ball's coming to knowledge is acted out against the coming of day. It begins in church with the moon providing the only light and the two men confronting the dead and being compelled to assert against the fact of death the only source of life's meaning, human community: 'This', said I, 'That though I die and end, yet mankind yet liveth, therefore I end not, since I am a man; and even so thou deemest, good friend . . .' (XVI. 265). Such an assertion involves coming to terms with history, and so John Ball has to confront his own death with the knowledge of what it will bring, the division of labour as the most direct consequence of the destruction of feudalism and the most important factor in the development of capitalist exploitation. As the narrator explains, the moon, image of John Ball's dream, fades. At last, his hope is merely that the population under such a grim system will diminish so that there will be fewer people to suffer. Once even this has been denied, Ball reaches despair and moves out of it again at what is the turning point of the narrative:

'I have but little heart to ask thee more questions,' said he, 'and when thou answerest, thy words are plain, but the things they tell of I may scarce understand. But tell me this: in those days will men deem that so it must be for ever, as great men even now tell us of our ills, or will they think of some remedy ?'

I looked about me. There was but a glimmer of light in the church now, but what there was, was no longer the strange light of the moon, but the first coming of the kindly day. (XVI. 276)

The glimmer of light comes because John Ball has answered his own question. Every speculation about the future reduces itself to this final one of determinism, and although there is no specific answer, by the very fact that Ball identifies in his own age the doctrine of total irrelevance of human will, taken with the fact that he is about to go out and change the course of history by the remedy he has sought, he discounts the validity of any future determinism. Determinism is a recurrent response in any age. Morris shows in this how firmly he grasped the socialist vision of man in shaping his own future. In the *Theses on Feuerbach*, Marx had written:

> The materialist doctrine that men are products of circumstances and upbringing, and that, therefore, changed men are products of other circumstances and changed upbringing, forgets that it is men that change circumstances and that the educator himself needs educating.[37]

Although the tale makes rigorous distinctions between fantasy and possibility, it affirms also the creative role of the revolutionary consciousness in a way seemingly excluded by Engels' word 'reflex'.

Nevertheless, we have passed from the light of the moon to the glimmer of the dawn, and thus got beyond the fantasy. Moon, linked with the antithetical and subjective dream world of John Ball's personal vision, gives way to the sunlight which is primary, objective and social – the community's vision which is to make possible the next phase of history. So that what follows John Ball's moment of self-discovery and self-evident affirmation is not the reassertion of his vision but a dry and bitter account of the mechanical forces of progress, ending with the most stark manifestation of alienation when the proletariat denies its very identity: 'their eyes shall be blinded to the robbing of themselves by others, because they shall hope in their souls that they may each live to rob others: and this shall be the very safeguard of all rule and law in those days' (XVI. 283/4). At this point, in order to be able to face the reality of the daylight, Ball has to seek a new vision which will not be confined to the assertion of the active role of man's consciousness, but needs to see the grounds on which it can be asserted. It is no longer enough that a remedy should be sought because the possibility of total alienation has been confronted; it is now necessary that Ball should know the kind of remedy: 'Canst thou yet tell me, brother, what that remedy shall be, lest the sun rise upon me made hopeless by thy tale of what is to be?' (XVI. 284).

The terms on which Ball may be given hope are rigorously controlled by his historical situation. Morris very carefully organizes the narrative in order to demonstrate the relationship between necessary insight and inevitable ignorance by creating a dramatic moment of developing distance between Ball and the narrator. The latter sees the dawn 'widening', and the poppy which he had plucked at the house of his fourteenth-century host is withering: he is being gathered back into his own reality as John Ball moves from the private dream world of the moonlit church to the public world of the battle. So he talks 'loud and hurriedly' as though he can only assert and not demonstrate: the affirmation is to be a different, more emotive rhetoric than the closely argued disillusioning of Ball. What he affirms is, simply, that the 'Fellowship of Men shall endure' so that he returns to Ball's visionary ideology, and he tries to explain the relationship between that affirmation and the prolonged negations of the preceding dialogue by an explicit and developed use of the moon and sun imagery:

Look you, a while ago was the light bright about us: but it was because of the moon, and the night was deep notwithstanding, and when the moonlight waned and died and there was but a little glimmer in place of the bright light, yet was the world glad because all things knew that the glimmer was of day and not of night. Lo you, an image of the times to betide the hope of the Fellowship of Men. Yet forsooth, it may well be that this bright day of summer which is now dawning upon us is no image of the beginning of the day that shall be; but rather shall that day-dawn be cold and grey and surly; and yet by its light shall men see things as they verily are, and no longer enchanted by the gleam of the moon and the glamour of the dreamtide. By such grey light shall wise men and valiant souls see the remedy, and deal with it, a real thing that may be touched and handled, and no glory of the heavens to be worshipped from afar off . . . The time shall come, John Ball, when that dream of thine that this shall one day be . . . (XVI. 284/5)

The bright light of the moon only emphasizes the darkness of its surroundings; its subjectivity has to be transcended by its extinction in the daylight. Yet, though John Ball goes to his personal death in the bright sun, his mind cleared of the illusory link between freedom and fellowship, he goes illuminated by what of his vision his comrades share with him, and this, the sun, is validated by the rebellion's long term success. But sunlight too can delude. The ultimate reality is grimmer and less comforting.

On the other hand, it does not offer the possibility of distortion either. In the grey light, the remedy will be seen not as an aspect of heavenly glory but as something secular and immediate. At this point, the structure of images has turned a complete circle. The remedy perceptible in the grim daylight of the historical consequence of the rebellion is exactly the same as the remedy sought by John Ball in dream:

> And what shall it be, as I told thee before, save that men shall be deter-
> mined to be free; yea, free as thou wouldst have them, when thine
> hope rises the highest, and thou art thinking not of the king's uncles,
> and poll-groat bailiffs, and the villeinage of Essex, but of the end of all,
> when men shall have the fruits of the earth and the fruits of their toil
> thereon, without money and without price. (XVI, 285)

Thus it is precisely what, in John Ball's vision, *isn't* taken over by the rebels in explicit terms which is the truly revolutionary force in men's minds. What John Ball has to learn is not that his dream is subjective and impossible but that it can only have articulate meaning when it replaces, as a shared and immediate objective, the aspiration of his followers. But this too commits him to death in the cause of that aspiration, since his dream can only begin the process of becoming vision by entering at once into the world of action. For, if the ideology of the rebels is what makes for the opposite of John Ball's dream, the spirit of solidarity which he inspires among them is a recognition in action of the change beyond the change. 'The philosophers have only *interpreted* the world, in various ways; the point, however, is to *change* it.'[38]

Going out to create this change, Ball says to the narrator 'thou hast been a dream to me as I to thee' (XVI. 286). It gives us the proper perspective in which to see all this, for the primary purpose of the narrative is the education of the present through its dialogue with the past, an education which reveals the role of mind in the historical process and which therefore demands the creation of an equilibrium between knowledge of the inevitability of the past and hope for the future. The encounter with Ball finally validates that hope in the context of historical inevitability, but it can only do this through insight and symbol and not through discourse. The value of the symbolism is that it reveals the education of the educator – the narrator's grasp, in the face of historical inevitability and on the basis of historical insight, of the essential rightness of vision, and of its assertion in the real world through revolutionary action. It is a grasp given force by its emergence from a coherent drama of consciousness.

The drama is latent above all in the intensity of narrative. It completely misses the point of the story to say glibly, as G. D. H. Cole does, that it is a story of a past that never was because it is merely a fable.[39] For what is most striking about the narrative is its careful attention to visual detail and its attempt to relate the particular event to a concretely realized sense of the everyday life of the community which experiences the event. The story has no point at all if it does not convey with great exactness the vision of the narrator. However, it is necessary to distinguish between the visual detail and the dramatization of the social world, because they operate on two different and contending planes of the narrator's experience. Most of the visual description comes at the beginning when the narrator wakes up to find himself in a strange world. As soon as he begins to experience the social rhythms of that world, the strangeness drops away. As soon as he is challenged to account for himself, the narrator instinctively becomes a fourteenth-century man, not one of the Kentish rebels, but an accommodated visitor confirming by his presence and acceptance the national solidarity of the movement. From this point onwards, the dramatic immediacy of the vision is much more apparent than the visual detail. Although there is a cinematic vividness about the battle-scene, it is presented not as something strange but as the activity of men whose world we are inhabiting. The involvement is disrupted by John Ball's invitation to talk privately. Again we are primarily aware of visual detail, and, with it, the recognition of distance:

So we turned away together into the little street. But while John Ball had been speaking to me I felt strangely, as though I had more things to say than the words I knew could make clear: as if I wanted to get from other people a new set of words. Moreover, as we passed up the street again I was once again smitten with the great beauty of the scene; the houses, the church with its new chancel and tower, snow-white in the moonbeams now; the dresses and arms of the people, men and women (for the latter were now mixed up with the men); their grave sononous language, and the quaint and measured forms of speech, were again become a wonder to me and affected me almost to tears. (XVI. 257)

The withdrawal is an important structural feature. The narrator has just been asked to play a more definite, active role by the leader of those who are to change the world, and immediately his consciousness reverts to the spectatorial estrangement of the beginning of the story; the key terms in this passage are 'strangely', 'become a wonder' and '*smitten* with the great beauty', and they push the narrator back into the nineteenth century. It is precisely with this distance reinvoked that the narrator has to play his role in the tale. He cannot escape his historical knowledge, which means that he cannot become part of this world (partly because what is most valuable about the world is what is making it disappear).

Only when we are aware of the complexities of the fictional structure are we free to discuss the relationship of the tale to historical actuality. Obviously the presentation of fourteenth century society is highly idealized, not because of escapism, however, but because of Morris's alert responsibility to the socialist vision of history. The genre itself demands the purification of phenomena so that the potentialities of a situation emerge from the actualities. If Morris is to show the emergence of the revolutionary consciousness at a given historical moment, then he has to concentrate on what, in the life of the community at the time of its formation, makes it possible. And, as Thorold Rogers asserted, it is just the sense of a prospering communal culture which does make its formation possible. We have to see, not what this society was (naturalism is capable of making its object exotic), but what it was capable of becoming if we are to see it participating in the historical process. Morris, in fact, takes care of the realities of mediaeval life much more effectively by placing this prosperity in a process of change than he could have done had he concentrated on naturalistic detail. The battle itself shows exactly how the relationship between picture and movement defines the relationship between value and historical reality. We are, of course, conscious of its historic significance – battles are moments in which the processes of change are accelerated. At the same time the realization of the battle scene is very much a matter of the realization of a moment of creative and undivided labour, the community working together in its own defence and each individual occupying a complete role. The conduct of the battle pays tribute to the society it is demolishing. The idealization brings out the values which underwrite the historical moment as an agent in a dialectical process: such values define the basis of the consciousness which brings nearer the immediate future of free and divided labour and at the same time looks beyond that future to socialism.

The dream vision structure is thus not only historically apt (since it is essentially a mediaeval genre) but the right register for the awareness of these potentialities and their role in history, because it makes for a purification of phenomena. But it is used dialectically both as affirmation and negation, and careful discriminations have to be made. We are conscious first of all of the psychological pressures which make for dream; it is the refuge of the alienated man: 'Sometimes I am rewarded for fretting myself so much about present matters by a quite unasked-for pleasant dream' (XVI. 215). The dream world which is described to exemplify this opening sentence is one of architectural beauty and it relates to the present merely as the juxtaposition of statically realized abstract values. The concept of dream as relief and antithesis is, however, radically revalued already by the end of the first paragraph; 'All this I have seen in the dreams of the night clearer than I can force myself to do in dreams of the day' (XVI. 216). 'Force' suggests that dream, though an alienated activity, is one which is open to discipline, and 'clearer' implies that the relief which is sought still has a responsibility to truth. Dream is given a positive intellectual role. More importantly, however, the sentence makes an important distinction between the involuntary dream of night and the willed 'dream of the day': not only do dreams have specific responsibilities but these responsibilities are fulfilled better by the proper assessment of the involuntary invasion of consciousness than by the conscious effort to bring these values into the mind. The fullest possibility of vision is available only to the dream which is beyond the individual will.

These discriminations reassert themselves at the end of the story with, of course, our understanding of the role of dream for the creative revolutionary mind giving them a new urgency. Like John Ball, the narrator has come to a dream of truth, and he too has to carry that dream into the actual world, not as antithesis, moon-vision, but as dialectically engaged consciousness. John Ball has, however, a battle to go to, a moment of revolution in which to transform his interpretation of the world into an agent of change. For the narrator, there is only the continuing present and so the daybreak involves a more complex process of coming to terms with vision:

I got up presently, and going to the window looked out on the winter morning; the river was before me broad between outer bank and bank, but it was nearly dead ebb, and there was a wide space of mud on each side of the hurrying stream, driven on the faster as it seemed by the push of the south-west wind. On the other side of the water the few willow-trees left us by the Thames Conservancy looked doubtfully alive against the bleak sky and the row of wretched-looking blue-slated houses . . . the road in front of the house was sooty and muddy at once, and in the air was that sense of dirty discomfort which one is never quit of in London. The morning was harsh too, and though the wind was from the south-west it was as cold as a north wind; and yet amidst it all, I thought of the corner of the next bight of the river which I could not quite see from where I was, but over which one can see clear of houses and into Richmond Park, looking like the open country; and dirty as the river was, and harsh as was the January wind, they seemed to woo me toward the country-side, where away from the miseries of the 'Great Wen' I might of my own will carry on a day-dream of the friends I had made in the dream of the night and against my will.

But as I turned away shivering and downhearted, on a sudden came the frightful noise of the 'hooters', one after the other, that call the workmen to the factories, this one the after-breakfast one, more by token. So I grinned surlily, and dressed and got ready for my day's 'work' as I call it, but which many a man besides John Ruskin (though not many in his position) would call 'play'. (XVI. 287/8)

He has been cut off from the dream by 'a white light, empty of all sights', and what we have here initially is the defeated landscape of the dawn of actuality after the triumphant dawn of the day of rebellion in the dream. The vestigial life, however, creates a rhythm of return and the first of these paragraphs carefully plots the most obvious relationship of the dream to actuality – that of cherished antithesis. The residual affirmations of the river and the wind are enough to involve the perceptual mind in a retreat not from reality but into a world beyond perception, a world whose existence is testified to but only as imagination. Within such a world, the values of the dream can be wilfully kept alive in day-dream, away from the city and the inexorable process of urbanization and exploitation. The rejection of this relationship is prepared for by the ironic separation of the imagination from the eye which begins its operation: he moves from the part of the river he can see to the bight he cannot but which he can think of as offering, beyond houses, a view of Richmond Park which in turn offers an illusion of the country. Already, by the time we get to day-dream, we are conscious not only of the illusory nature of the withdrawal but of its remoteness from his own range of experience. The only possibility is to turn back to the city, and turn towards his own and others' misery. Equally, because the dream is not the product of the individual will, it can only be kept alive at all by a return to the conditions which gave rise to it – the fretting over modern life. Only by turning back into his own alienation, the source of the dream, can the narrator make his dialogue with the past meaningful. What happens in the last paragraph is that the values for which John Ball and the men of Kent stood, are kept alive by the negation of the present not in withdrawal but in irony. 'Grinned surlily' is a gesture of acceptance of the actuality which does not acquiesce in it. What dominates the final paragraph of course is the sense of the division of labour which is in direct antithesis to the whole presentation of the fourteenth century community. And yet, as we have noticed, it is also what the rebellion most immediately achieved. So that at the end we are made both to measure the distance between human possibilities and the actual world, and to acknowledge the necessity for those possibilities to be worked out in the historical process. We know that the dream of John Ball is not a nostalgic dream of the past, held apart from the

Great Wen, but John Ball's dream, that which made him participate in the history that created the Great Wen and which brought him, in fantasy, to a conception of the change beyond the change, the revolutionary future which the surly grin does not resign to the depressing present.

The tale thus pays full tribute to the determinants of history, but it refuses to collapse into a defeated pessimism, and it equally avoids the dangers of 'economism'. But we need to emphasize how limited the claims which are made are. For John Ball there is a dream both of the possible and the actual, and he is able to relate the two in the action by which he goes out to his death united with the community which is changing the course of history. For the narrator the gap is not to be bridged through action. Nothing fills the white light between dream and actuality. All that we can claim is that the dream, becoming through the careful interplay of its psychological possibilities a formal literary genre, offers a vision of the mind and its values which creates man's destiny. What remains is the problem of recognizing the precise basis of the transformation of that mind in action.

VI

In an essay which sets out to explore the relationship between theory and practice in Marxist thought, Antonio Gramsci identifies mechanical determinism as the 'aroma' of a particular phase of the socialist struggle, and in explaining it he states very clearly the problem that Morris was faced with in his life and which his creative writing coherently portrays:

> When one does not have the initiative in the struggle and the struggle itself is ultimately identified with a series of defeats, mechanical determinism becomes a formidable power of moral resistance, of patient and obstinate perseverance. 'I am defeated for the moment but the nature of things is on my side over a long period', etc. Real will is disguised as an act of faith, a sure rationality of history, a primitive and empirical form of impassioned finalism which appears as a substitute for the predestination, providence, etc., of the confessional religions.[40]

Morris doesn't, of course, entirely escape the charge of 'impassioned finalism', and *A Dream of John Ball* ends ambiguously, rejecting the concept of dream as retreat but not offering the means by which it participates in the socialist narrator's programme of action. The revolutionary consciousness cannot be passive and withdrawn, but neither can it impose itself mechanically on events when it does not have the initiative.

And whereas, after his dream acknowledging the historical limits of his achievement, Ball goes forward to a changed situation and a change-creating act, the narrator *returns* to the daily routine, strengthened in his mind but without the prospect of choosing action. The contrast is too marked not to be deliberate. And this recognition of his own limitation of consciousness to the disjunction of thought and action in the present informs the choice of mode in the stories which follow *A Dream of John Ball*, the German Romances. The role of Morris's art seems increasingly to be one which combats the tendency to collapse into a determinist act of faith by presenting the potentialities of human growth in a situation in which it is enabled and compelled to take the initiative. The German Romances base themselves on an epoch in which the choice between involvement and retreat is a real one between two ways of defining personal identity rather than between self-isolation and self abnegation in an act of faith. Dream becomes both an agent of change and a doorway of withdrawal; it offers itself as the stasis of atrophy or as the starting point of the transformation of consciousness into revolutionary and collective action.

Morris's choice of a society which resembles that of the early teutonic tribes demonstrates, as does *A Dream of John Ball*, a fine awareness of contemporary historiography. Maine, Freeman, Morgan and Engels himself had all given a good deal of attention to this epoch since it seemed to offer a point in time when the needs of the individual for private freedom were balanced with maximum equilibrium against the coherence of the community. There is a frequent contrast with Rome, most fully worked out by Freeman in *Comparative Politics*, in which he argues that the Roman and the German concepts of society represented respectively 'two great ideas of the State, the conception of the State as city and the conception of the State as a nation'.[41] The essence of the Germanic state for Freeman, as for Morris, was that it made for the maximum distribution of power: 'For the whole history of our land and our race will be read backwards', he wrote, 'if we fail always to bear in mind that the lower unit is not a division of the greater, but that the greater is an aggregate of the smaller.'[42]

Freeman's concern is primarily with the external structure of society. Morris goes much deeper than this and portrays the consciousness of the people who create such a constitution. Above all, the Germanic nation is built on the free acknowledgement of kindred as against the legalistic acquiescence in the realm of the Roman *res publica*. Morris, in fact, closely resembles Marx whose *Pre-Capitalist Economic Formations* is concerned to distinguish between three attitudes to the individual's consciousness of his social existence, the Asiatic, the Greco-Roman (both defined in the following passage in the first paragraph) and the Germanic:

> Community is neither the substance, of which the individual appears merely as the accident, nor is it the general, which *exists and has being* as such in men's minds, and in the reality of the city and its urban requirements, distinct from the separate economic being of its members.
>
> It is rather on the one hand, the common element in language, blood, etc., which is the premise of the individual proprietor; but on the other hand it has real being only in its *actual assembly* for communal purposes; and, in so far as it has a separate economic existence, in the communally used hunting-grounds, pastures, etc., it is used thus by every individual proprietor as such, and not in his capacity as the representative of the state.[43]

It is thus the moment in society when the individual is least divorced from the conditions of his existence and most closely linked with other men in the struggle against nature and hostile forces. The salient feature is dramatically presented in *The House of the Wulfings* when, on the eve of battle, Thiodulf goes into the woods to meditate and becomes spontaneously caught in his own affirmativeness, building a small dam as a token of his creative link with his own world:

> As he sat, he strove to think about the Roman host and how he should deal with it; but despite himself, his thoughts wandered, and made for him pictures of his life that should be when this time of battle was over; so that he saw nothing of the troubles that were upon his hands that night, but rather saw himself partaking in the deeds of the life of man. (XIV. 105)

There is no tension here between personal aspiration and a sense of belonging to the community: even reverie returns him to its acknowledgement. And yet this can be precisely because this personal life is neither possessed nor divided by society but accepted by it as of a contributing individual. The whole story is pervaded by this sense of integrity, and when it emerges explicitly at the end, we acknowledge its validity:

> For to the Goths it was but a little thing to fall in hot blood in that hour of love of the kindred, and longing for the days to be. And for the Romans, they had had no mercy, and now looked for none: and they remembered their dealings with the Goths, and saw before them, as it were, once more, yea, as in a picture, their slayings and quellings, and lashings, and cold mockings which they had dealt out to the conquered foemen without mercy, and now they longed sore for the quiet of the dark, when their hard lives should be over, and all these deeds forgotten, and they and their bitter foes should be at rest for ever.
>
> Most valiantly they fought; but the fury of their despair could not deal with the fearless hope of the Goths. (XIV. 189)

For the Goths, the battle is a campaign for their own individual being as well as for the community's integrity. For the Romans it is their tribute to the 'separate economic being' of the city, against whose claims they can only advance those of pessimistic resignation.

But if the Romances respond to features of contemporary historiography, they do not, of course, make any attempt to portray an actual historical situation – not even in the mediated way *A Dream of John Ball* does. They couldn't, since the documentary portrayals of such a period have to be extremely vague and lacking in decisive 'event'. The historians themselves approach the period in a highly conceptualizing way, presenting the structures of different societies rather like archetypes of social structure. The starting point of Morris's work is an idea of what men can conceive society to be rather than what they have achieved. And this too relates to an essential feature of the historiography, for the Germanic *gens* is used ideologically as an example of what is good or might be good in a social structure. Freeman uses the concept of state as nation rather than as city in order to explain why England is 'more just and free than the other'.[44] Morgan argues that this kind of *gens* is what will be the model of the future, and, not surprisingly, Engels concluded *The Origin of the Family* by quoting this passage:

> Since the advent of civilization, the outgrowth of property has been so immense, its forms so diversified, its uses so expanding and its management so intelligent in the interests of its owners, that it has become, on the part of the people, an unmanageable power. The human mind stands bewildered in the presence of its own creation. The time will come, nevertheless, when human intelligence will rise to the mastery over property, and define the relations of the state to the property it protects, as well as the obligations and the limits of the rights of its owners. . . . The dissolution of society bids fair to become the termination of a career of which property is the end and aim; because such a career contains the elements of self-destruction. Democracy in government, brotherhood in society, equality in rights and privileges, and universal education, foreshadow the next higher plane of society to which experience, intelligence and knowledge are steadily tending. It will be a revival, in a higher form, of the liberty, equality and fraternity of the ancient *gentes*.[45]

Morgan's judgement offers the exact terms of the rationale of Morris's Romances. In *A Dream of John Ball*, we see man's desire for change as a potent but almost imperceptible thread in an historical process which he cannot foresee. Only through irony does the tale prevent itself from becoming a mechanical antithesis of dream and necessity, and the irony secures itself against complete immersion in the actual through the creation of a chinese box of dreams: if my faith is a dream based on the past, it is also a dream of that past's dream which is validated partly by what it achieved, my actuality, and partly by its ability to communicate with my dream, which is a negation of my actuality. In order to escape this eternal reflection, Morris has to dramatize the revolutionary mind in a world in which it has not lost the initiative, has not become bewildered by its own creation so that its beginning must be in negation. The individual consciousness has to be seen in the situation in which it has mastery over the society which mediates its relationship with others. Only such a mind can be a determinant in direct forms of action. The world of the Germanic tribes represents the closest model for that situation, but it is impossible to pretend that the revolutionary mind can be realized through a simple historic recreation, because that realization would have to contain the seeds of degenerative change. The real significance of the *gentes* is that they look forward, as Morgan suggests, to the future, to the next 'plane' of society. So that we are confronted with a *projection* of the Germanic nation, a concrete realization of what it portends. And this is not an escape from the exigencies of the present, but from the possible comfort to be gained from a too passive awareness of those exigencies. The Germanic Romances, especially *The House of the Wulfings*, give us the moral ordeal of the revolutionary mind unprotected by determinist rationalization.

This particular tale can achieve as much, because a great deal of it is successfully devoted to establishing a social world in which freedom means integration. The people are united with the objective conditions of their existence: 'and they worshipped the kind acres which they themselves and their fathers had made fruitful, wedding them to the seasons of seed-time and harvest' (XIV. 29/30). We are reminded of the description of the Brangwens at the beginning of *The Rainbow*, and the rhythms of Morris's prose, when they are not crippled by the oddity of his notion of a fit language, anticipate Lawrence. But whereas in *The Rainbow* there is an inevitable aspiration away from the gentile culture, in Morris's Romance the process of achieving individuality is not seen as antithetical but as realizable within the social structure. Hence one of the major episodes in the story is the election of Thiodulf as war leader. It both acknowledges the individual capacity for choice in each of the members of the community, thus endorsing Marx's point that community takes its existence from assembly, and it grants a social identity to the exceptional man without placing in his hands the social existence of the individual members. The sense of the world beyond which, in *The Rainbow*, destroys community, in this tale, as we shall see, endorses it.

All the tensions of the tale, nevertheless, stem from the recognition that the individual consciousness takes its existence from outside the community as well as within it. But the resulting conflict between individual and social selves is seen not in terms of social determination, but purely in terms of psychological growth. Thiodulf, leader of the Wulfings, has a child by a semi-divine creature of the woods, Wood-sun. Within the house, the child, Hall-sun, is passed off as

265

his foster child. Wood-sun tries to isolate Thiodulf from the community by a series of temptations, which offer not so much moral conflict as psychological strain. First she tells him that he is not by birth a Wulfing, but a stranger; later, she persuades him to wear a hauberk which will protect him in battle, but which dissolves his attention to the fight. Her hold over him is specifically linked with dream. Wearing the hauberk, he swoons and dreams of his childhood and his old mentor. It is a dream of joy until first the mentor turns to stone and then he feels himself to be turning to stone. He stirs himself from the dream and finds 'a white light empty of all vision' (XIV. 150). He can return to life and the battle because his friends have taken off the hauberk to look at his wounds – 'and the joy of waking life came back to him, the joy which but erewhile he had given to a mere dream' (XIV. 150). He returns to the fight, but he is again given the hauberk, and this time withdraws into a dream world in which Wood-sun seems to be by his side and the battle becomes a resented distraction. He remains withdrawn at the next council and a spokesman has to speak for him. Later, he explains this withdrawal to Wood-sun:

> But now must I tell thee a hard and evil thing; that I loved them not, and was not of them, and outside myself there was nothing: within me was the world and nought without me, Nay, as for thee, I was sundered from thee, but thou wert a part of me; whereas for the others, yea, even for our daughter, thine and mine, they were but images and shows of men, and I longed to depart from them, and to see thy body and to feel thine heart beating. And by then so evil was I grown that my very shame had fallen from me, and my will to die: nay, I longed to live, thou and I, and death seemed hateful to me, and the deeds before death vain and foolish. (XIV. 169)

There is a withdrawal into the self of the same kind that we have seen in *Sigurd the Volsung*, but here it is not the social conditions which determine it, but love itself, which in turn is characterized as man's meeting with the divine (again, a repetition of the Brynhild motif). The hauberk is clearly a symbol of personal relationships which isolate the self from the community. It creates a dream world, but one in which the self becomes involved in the past and in which, in turn, the past begins to petrify, having no organic relationship to the present. As in *A Dream of John Ball*, the return from dream is bridged by an empty light, but here, in the actual world, there is a possibility of joy asserting itself outside dream. It is not that the past has to be made meaningful by the creation of a fictive participation, a leap of the imagination, but that it has to be accepted as growth rather than as fixity. Earlier, Thiodulf has said that whenever he tries to recall his childhood, he always finds his mind moving to-wards a larger sense of the past, 'the tale of the Wulfings', and to see himself, not as a single life but as a participant in the ongoing life of the race: 'and I amidst it ever reborn and yet reborn' (XIV. 109). The petrifaction image is an exact reversal of the image of stone and stream in *Easter 1916*: for Yeats, the stone is the image of the committed self, 'hearts with one purpose alone', enchanted by the external political world, troubling the living stream of the personal life. For Morris, on the contrary, the personal life becomes a petrifaction, a refusal to accept growth and a fixated dream of childhood, unless it participates in the world 'outside myself', that is, both community, the free acknowledgement of the social relation, and the future, 'the kindred and the days to be' (XIV. 145).

But if this is, in ideological terms, an opposite affirmation from that of Yeats, it is not a factitious escape into 'duty'. The tale has to create a relationship with 'outside myself' which does not deny selfhood. Wood-sun singles out Thiodulf because she is divine; her divinity disables her from understanding the communal reality of human nature: 'such is the wont of the God-kin, because they know not the hearts of men' (XIV. 171). In positive terms, this means that Thiodulf's encounter with the world beyond, that which Wood-sun represents, is an encounter with that which recognizes his own *excellence*, the excellence which, within the community, makes him leader. The basis of his social relationship is thus in his belonging to what is outside the society. The story of the hauberk is an attempt to resolve this paradox through total individuation. The account of its origin offers the projection of one potential of selfhood, that which isolates itself from the community. The hauberk is the creation of a Dwarf who desired a Goddess who loved a mortal. The Dwarf offered her the hauberk which would save her beloved in battle in return for her body. She agreed but at the moment when he was about to take his pleasure, she paralysed him, and in revenge he put a curse on the hauberk so that although its power of protection remained, its wearer, saving his life in battle, would have also the battle's shame.

The allegory is a highly compressed account of the development of the individualistic consciousness. The Goddess seeks to isolate the excellenceof the mortal by granting him immortality: she is prepared to *bargain* in order to achieve this, so that there is a concept of *price*, and hence the beginning of the division of labour. The price she is prepared to offer to satisfy her love for another man is the gift of her body to the dwarf, so that love becomes dualistic – body and soul are potentially separable. And finally she withdraws from her bargain, keeping her body intact, so that the concept of sexual exploitation is also involved: sex becomes a commodity, but it finally becomes an intangible commodity. The real price that is paid is the severance of the mortal from the life which surrounds him. Reduced to romantic love and religious aspiration (towards immortality), man's encounter with the divine, with what singles out his individuality, comes to be estrangement from the community, and, finally, therefore from the conditions of his existence. Furthermore, it denies the possibility of growth (because death is the inevitable effect of growth), and joy turns inward to a dream world. We have reversed the situation in which we find ourselves in *A Dream of John Ball*: dream vision and the prose of actuality have changed places. Morris establishes a society in which the severed self is glimpsed as a *potential* but not *inevitable* manifestation. He affirms the necessity of a new order of consciousness, but he realizes its possibility in the context of the alternative realized in capitalist society, that context convincingly rendered as nightmare.

This is possible and unsentimental because there is no simple antithesis. The psychological process which lures Thiodulf into the dream world of severed individuality is precisely that which grants him an ineluctable relationship with the community. The child of the divine encounter, Hall-sun, is also a dreamer, but her dream is prophesy: the child of loneliness brings knowledge greater than her consciousness can retain for the community: 'Also she perceived that she had been weeping, therefore she knew that she had uttered words of wisdom. For so it fared with her at whiles, that she knew not her own words of foretelling, but spoke them out as if in a dream' (XIV. 41). She is the result of man's solitary encounter with divine love, but in the world of the kindred, which contains the possibility of the perfect cohesion between the individual mind and the social field of action, there is accommodation of that experience. Hall-sun, in her prophetic role, acknowledges a double recognition. On the one hand, the divine aspirations of the individual only make for truth within the community (so that dream is vision and not day-dream). On the other hand, what knits the community together is not its blood ties (the undynamic dictatorship of the past over the present), but the continuous homage paid to man's outsider reality. In her dramatic role, Hall-sun realizes the possibility of a much greaert integration than this. Recognizing what is wrong with Thiodulf, she goes to Wood-sun and argues that the way in which she is trying to save Thiodulf is a form of possession which will destroy his identity: Wood-sun cannot save the real Thiodulf, only a thrall who is his shadow. Only in heroic death, committed to the cyclic rhythms of the kindred, can Thiodulf be himself. The totally individuated individual loses his individuality. Selfhood, in such a world, is the recognition of the collectivization of experience and commitment to the kindred and its future. Thiodulf is not a Wulfing, but only through the continually renewed process of becoming a Wulfing through action is he truly Thiodulf. It is this that makes the story a *revolutionary* Romance rather than a reactionary one. We are given the forces which made for the destruction of the gentile community in a transformed relationship – on the one hand as reduced to the world of nightmare, and on the other transformed from their destructiveness into precisely what makes for its defence.

VII

I have been trying to show that Morris's literary work cannot be seen as a mere relief from or appendage to his directly active work as a Socialist in the eighties. It constitutes a formal response to the realities of his own situation which can be validated in terms of the historical consciousness with which he came into contact (both Marxist and non-Marxist). Specifically, he invents new worlds or reinvokes dream versions of old worlds, not in order to escape the exigencies of the depressing actuality but in order to insist on a whole structure of values and perspectives which must emerge in the conscious mind in order to assert the inner truth of that actuality, and give man the knowledge of his own participation in the historical process which dissolves that actuality. We have seen that this insistence needs to take full account of the particular moment and that this demands a remarkable sensitivity to the responsiveness of form. The moment is one in which, for whatever complex of reasons, the individual is seen more and more to be totally circumscribed in his actions by an apparently self-acting social law. Confronted with such hopelessness, the socialist is likely to be forced back on an elaborate determinism in which the forces of progress inevitably assert themselves irrespective of the action of individuals, so that the socialist mind becomes merely reflexive (some of Engels' comments on the English scene seem to me to show a marked defeatism which resembles this). This is contradictory because it must take as its starting point the divorce of man as a conscious being with a subjective sense of his own reality from the conditions of his existence in which he finds his objective reality; and it must take as its end the moment at which this divorce is repaired through the reconciliation of the mode of production with the forces of production: in other words, the moment in which man takes hold of his own life. Yet this has to be achieved by forces outside himself: man's alienation will be brought to an end by alien forces.

The very act of creating fictions which will take account of the historical movement of forces in society, however, implies resistance to this contradiction. Fiction can only depict people – it cannot depict forces of production: it is committed therefore to the portrayal of the operation of the historical processes by which it is informed in the minds of its protagonists. It is this very confinement of the fictional mode to the concrete and perceptible which leads us to say of a work born in an era when the possibilities of change are extremely distant that its acceptance of the inexorability of the social law makes it more 'realistic' than a work which strives to bring to the fore those possibilities. The most obvious way of escaping this is to present the accomplished change as a utopia existing in antithesis to the present.

Looking Backward is this kind of novel and despite its specious evolutionism, it has no sense of the change as a process. And, of course, it is as equally deterministic as a Gissing novel because its characters are *products* of the resolved society as Gissing's are of a contradictory one. Morris's work, on the contrary, attempts to recognize in concrete terms that the reconciliation of man with the conditions of his existence will be a process in which both man and the conditions change in their relationship to one another and in which man can be seen as a determining as well as determined force. Inevitably this places on the creative writer the obligation to create forms in which the forces of change are portrayed as they appear in the conscious minds of the characters he creates, and it means also that the created world of his characters must have a relationship – carefully defined within the generic significance of the work – to the 'unchanged' instant which does not escape irresponsibly from its epistemology. It means creating forms which neither accept as eternal man's alienation, nor retreat into worlds in which it has no relevance, but which provide for both its recognition and its assessment by realizing it as a subjective response to an objective condition which is not only valid as subjectivity in recoiling from the objective world, but which is also capable of returning to that world as a subversive force. It means the recognition of the estranged mind of man not merely as an escape, but also as a revolutionary agent. The dreamer of dreams has to recognize that he is born in his due time. This includes recognizing, as in *The House of the Wulfings*, a time when dreams will have to be turned away, but it does not mean that dream can be transcended in the present.

Estrangement is subversive in Hardy too, but only by reference to defeated social values. Morris's Romances are attempts to give concrete expression to values which are best seen in possibilities offered by defeated social orders, but also to recreate those orders so that they speak to the dreams of the estranged man not merely as something gone but as something containing values that must be striven after, and can be attained only by the transformation of dream into vision. This transformation is portrayed in *The House of the Wulfings* as the entry of the individual, recognizing the true nature of his self in the community, into action for the community – Thiodulf's storm. Beyond that, however, and extremely important in forging a relationship between the realized revolutionary mind and socialist practice, is the discovery of the potential for transformation of vision into collective action. It is a discovery enacted in *The Roots of the Mountains.*

Here too we are concerned primarily to make discriminations about the historic role of dream. The hero is caught in a dream world by his very satisfaction with the gentile community until the dream leads him to the broken community which lies beyond the Burgstead, and from this to a direct confrontation with the Romans, so that the values of the kindred become affirmed by its ability to face what are, in fact, bourgeois structures of society. Although the tale is therefore one of education, leading the protagonist to discover in his personal aspiration a dynamic role within his society, it becomes finally a romance about revolutionary strategy. The key episode of the last section is the war council in which Face-God and Folk-might (man's personal divinity and his power of association linked in revolutionary war) plan their assault on the territories beyond the vale which are already occupied by the Romans. They plan on a basis of combining permeation with invasion so that we are alerted to the need for the revolutionary act of the leaders to be taken up by the participation of the masses. Collectivity means not only the integration of personal intelligence and the sense of community but also a new collectivity of mind. The relevance to the present moment is clear. In a world where man's alienation seems to be complete, only my dreams are my own, and so it is through my dreams, and my attention to them, that I shall take hold of my life again. Yet, insofar as my dreams *are* my own, they are in danger of enclosing themselves in a sea of blankness and isolation, becoming perpetual islands whose refuge enables me to make my peace with the alien world. Only insofar as my dreams push outward into action, only insofar as they claim the understanding of other people through my commitment, can they become creative and revolutionary.

The Romances enact the events which dramatize in an actualized world this need and this possibility, but Morris needs to go further than this. The Romance looks back to potentialities vested in the past but unrealized in the present: ultimately, the socialist writer needs to push forward the consciousness of his readers directly towards the responsibility of creating community. Romance also celebrates the hero and his revolutionary consciousness. Although *The Roots of the Mountains* dramatizes the encounter of this consciousness with the oppressed masses, it does not portray that mass consciousness, because, of course, as soon as it is portrayed, as soon as it becomes explicit in the minds of the people, we have reached a totally changed world. The only form which portrays the revolutionary consciousness of the people is one which looks forward and invents a new society – Utopia.

News from Nowhere has received a good deal of intelligent attention from A. L. Morton and E. P. Thompson, and so I shall deal with it very briefly, giving what is really only a reemphasis of their points to make the text relevant to the main concern of this essay. They stress the importance of seeing *News from Nowhere* in its generic tradition: it is itself conscious of the limitations of the dream vision. What it sets out to portray is not what the future will be like, but how a nineteenth-century socialist might conceive of it in order to communicate the rationale of his faith in his socialist activity. We have seen already that dream plays a definite but limited role in the formation of the revolutionary consciousness. In these terms, *News from Nowhere* has the same structure as *A Dream of John Ball* except that the narrator is now in the same position as John Ball, looking to the change beyond the change. And like John Ball, it is partly an affirmation of the particular intelligence of the perceiving consciousness. So that at the centre of the tale is the socialist commitment to the role of historical necessity which makes no attempt to by-pass the class struggle, and, at the end, the narrator is thrust back into the nineteenth century to take up his role in history, by bringing the values of the new world into the minds of those who are to fight to bring it about.

However, if this were all, then *News from Nowhere* would be a much simplified account of the historical role of the revolutionary consciousness compared with *A Dream of John Ball*. For, in the earlier tale, we are concerned with the dream of John Ball's dream, so that we have the sense of the dynamic role of knowledge as well as aspiration: the narrator's imaginative leap into the past's possible imagination of the narrator's present and the assessment against the actual present bring the revolutionary mind into focus with the historical process. The past can inform the present to make its conception of the future more clear. In *News from Nowhere*, on the other hand, the narrator is dramatically powerless. He can comfort only himself, and he can change nothing in the future with which he holds a dialogue, so that we can only be aware of that future as antithesis, as a static world different from ours – at best, the historical account can only be a bridge which links present and future but which in itself remains a separate entity belonging to neither.

What prevents *News from Nowhere* from becoming gratuitous and dehumanized like, for example, *Looking Backward* in which the new world which inspires Bellamy's sickly optimism is significantly like that which now feeds the witty despair of J. K. Galbraith, is that it never tries to become objective by creating a social system of a totality of institutions. Utopia is the collectivization of dream, as opposed to Romance which is the transformation of individuality through dream into leadership. We are presented with, above all, the shared dream: the personal aspiration is actualized as a whole society. All the figures in the land of perfection are aspects of the dreamer himself: all must voice his attitudes and responses. This is true even when there are disagreements, since the major psychological affirmation of Morris's utopia is that the world can contain a fully free individualism. In terms of the narrator's own consciousness, the discussions are simply the free play of temperamental inconsistencies, so that although the characters have their basic differences they are all sympathetic. Thus Dick's historical philistinism isn't challenged by Hammond's scholarship but lives in peaceful coexistence with it, and even the acerbity of Ellen's grandfather can exist in balance against the sometimes priggish sanity of Ellen herself. We are in a world where human flexibility does not become involved in destructive conflict: the essence of collectivity is freedom, and by the same token, the peak of individuality is the open community in which individuality has ceased to be aggressive. This emphasis is, I think, a right one. Although the discursive bent of the novel brings out the inextricability of the unalienated mind with the conditions which can allow it to grow, the dramatic emphasis is always on the attitudes rather than the conditions. We don't have, as we do in Bellamy, a sense that human beings have become superfluous particles in a perfect system, and although we don't, and couldn't get involved in the story any more than we can get involved in Adam's labour in the Garden of Eden, we do get a very real sense of what human values might be liberated in a communist society.

But if the pressure of the dreamer's personality on the shape of the 'future' makes the novel more open about its subjectivity and therefore more accessible to the readers' participation than *Looking Backward* which manifests so distinctly aggressive a complacency that in the end Bellamy can't even bring himself to admit that the narrator was dreaming, it also must radically limit its scope. What is remarkable about its achievement is its articulateness about these limitations. We have an heroic effort to present imaginatively those values which the socialist mind is working towards as part of a social experience. But questioning that presentation is a concrete realization of the psychological pressure which thrusts the narrator towards his vision of those values. And although the major aim of the utopian form is the collectivization of dream, as the closing sentence implies, what we are mainly aware of is that those pressures derive from a radical sense of isolation, of the man who is lost and can only find himself by the projection of his personality into a dream community. The opening of the story carefully establishes this. We begin, not with the oppressiveness of modern life, but with the centre of the activity which is to change it, the League. What most characterizes the League is precisely the destructive individualism which the story escapes from: 'For the rest, there were six persons present, and consequently six sections of the party were represented' (XVI. 3). The oppressiveness of modern life is there as well, in the tube train and the ugly suspension bridge. Nowhere will be set up in direct opposition to this 'civilization'. But not before the League, the agency of socialist activity in the present, has been already precluded as a valid response to the civilization which is to be rejected. The narrator dismisses his comrades as 'fools' and, although this reflects on his own intolerance as well, it does mean that there is no prospect of the communication of dream, the creation of vision, within the party. On the contrary, it is as a relief from the despair of working within the party that the narrator moves towards utopia: he needs 'an epoch of rest'.

This is all perfectly clear, but if we press it a little further, we have to challenge Morton's description, 'scientific utopia', which is based mainly on the historical section. Chapter XVII shows very clearly Morris's grasp of the meaning of Revolution. But it is still an *invented* history, and whatever the clarity of the account as a whole, the account of its beginning, that is of the present, is extremely vague: 'When the hope of realizing a communal condition of life for all men arose, quite late in the nineteenth century' (XVI. 104). The syntax is betraying. 'Arose' evades a human subject so that we are uncertain about whose hope it was – was it, for example, one fostered by the six Leaguers who do little but squabble but who are presumably more conscious of the hope than those outside the League? And that 'quite' is inexcusable: has it happened already or is it to be even later than the present? This is the phrase which establishes the link between present and future in historic terms but it is a link which does not come into focus, and it is in marked and significant contrast with the clearly delineated chain of events which follows. In this chain, the League has no part, nor does any other socialist organization which would be recognizable from the eighties. It is an invented history as much in antithesis to the present as the statically realized future. The alienation which produces the dream of Nowhere is a response to the present, both recoiling and subversive. But equally there is a recoil from what, in the present, is the most coherent and collective register of the subversiveness. 'How the Change Came' is as much a dream as Nowhere itself. It does touch on the actuality in a way which suggests continuity rather than antithesis, but it is a very special continuity: 'Looking back now, we can see that the great motive-power of the change was a longing for freedom and equality, akin if you please to the unreasonable passion of the lover; a sickness of heart that rejected with loathing the aimless solitary life of the well-to-do educated men of that time' (XVI. 104). 'The unreasonable passion of the lover' links Morris much more closely, surely, with Hardy than with any socialist movement. It makes the change related to the eruption of unconscious forces into the individual consciousness of the contemporary mind.

The Utopia itself becomes therefore primarily not so much a picture of enacted values as a reversal of the rejected values of modern life. The novel is essentially one of protest (and frequently personal protest, as the mediaevalism suggests). In such a context, the ending is extremely subdued. The narrator remains a spectator figure until the feast at the end. The feast opens up the possibility of integration, but before the narrator has participated in the communion, he becomes invisible. It is a remarkable passage because the effect is not to distance the scene from the narrator, but to withdraw the narrator from the scene: 'I turned to Ellen, and she *did* seem to recognize me for an instant; but her bright face turned sad directly, and she shook her head with a mournful look, and the next moment all consciousness of my presence had faded from her face' (XVI. 209). Confronted with the social realization of the values by which he affirms commitment, the narrator loses his own reality. The gap between the present and the future becomes a nightmare of one's own non-existence. The narrator can be no more than voyeur in his own dream; there is no way of realizing how he can speak to it through his own life as John Ball had spoken to the present. Nowhere is nowhere except as a conceptual antithesis in the mind of the exhausted activist. And although the end cannot be taken as ironic, it cannot be seen as offering much consolation for the immense sense of the distance between the dream and the actuality which made it necessary. It is all very well for Ellen to seem to be saying 'Go back', but go back to what? To the League? The only specific identification of a role for the narrator is deterministic: 'you belong so entirely to the unhappiness of the past that our happiness even would weary you' (XVI. 210). It is difficult in the end to see how this affirms values on a much more social basis than the death of Jude. The collectivity of dream is not brought into relationship with the possible collectivity of the present.

But beyond *News from Nowhere*, there is *The Story of the Glittering Plain* which suggests a revised account of the role of dream in the revolutionary consciousness. The plain itself is a timeless paradise offered the hero as consolation for the loss of his betrothed, but although old men seek it as the answer to their senility, he escapes back into a world where time and age are active to seek his beloved.

'I seek no dream', he says, 'but rather the end of dreams' (XIV. 273). We have seen that in *News from Nowhere* dream is the product of a twofold disaffection: from the society of the late nineteenth century (the revolutionary alienation) and from the community of those who meet to discuss hopes of change. For this too is rigorously circumscribed by its historical situation. I am not, of course, implying that Morris's faith in socialism was deteriorating, but that *News from Nowhere* registers acute doubts about the mode of action that socialist theory had to take. Running away from the feast, the narrator is recognizing his own imprisonment in disaffection, but he is also perhaps running away finally from dream, holding within himself the knowledge of values other than those manifest in the present. It seems to me that we have, in this novel, much less a Utopia than an account of the agony of holding the mind together, committed as it is to the conscious determinants of history and the impersonal forces of change – united only in conceptual terms. But more than that, it is the fullest recognition that dream itself insists on isolation, and that it can only become a collective experience in terms of history – a history which is not communicable in articulate terms.

This means that the difference between Morris and Hardy is not one of the former's greater affirmativeness so much as his greater insistence on the compulsion of the isolate self to seek a collectivity in the historical world. We may need to say that finally Morris fails to carry this insight into the world of action and that his writing has no way of coping with this failure in the context of the nineteenth-century experience. But this is much more a judgement on the Socialist League than it is on Morris. For what is truly important about his achievement as a creative writer is that his work attests to the need to create a revolutionary sense of community in order to reflect fully the estrangement of the disaffected mind, and that in its confrontation with this need it portrays the intensity of conflict which is inherent in the effort to relate it to the historical situation. Morris creates a revolutionary literature because he discovers forms which dramatize the tensions of the revolutionary mind. And I don't know any other writer in English who does that.

William Morris and the Dream of Revolution

NOTES

1. Raymond Williams, *Culture and Society*, London, 1958, p. 158.
2. Ibid., p. 155. It should be *A Dream*. I think it makes a difference.
3. E. P. Thompson, *William Morris: Romantic To Revolutionary*, London, 1955, p. 763.
4. Ibid., p. 779.
5. Marx and Engels, *Literature and Art*, Bombay, 1956, pp. 36–7.
6. P. Demetz, *Marx, Engels and the Poets*, London, 1956, p. 138.
7. Marx and Engels, *Literature and Art*, op. cit., p. 39.
8. It is obviously absurd for Demetz to say that what Engels means by reality is the 'realities postulated by his ideology', since this is true of anybody.
9. Marx and Engels, *Literature and Art*, pp. 39–40.
10. Ibid., p. 38.
11. George Gissing, *New Grub Street*, London, 1967, p. 163. All references are to this edition. Page numbers are given in parentheses.
12. See H. M. Lynd, *England in the Eighteen-Eighties*, London, 1968, p. 200.
13. George Gissing, *Denzil Quarrier*, London, 1892, p. 35.
14. William Morris, *The Collected Works*, New York, 1966, Vol. XVI, p. 211. All references to the works of Morris are to this edition unless otherwise stated. Quotations are followed by their locations in parentheses, the volume number in Roman numeral, followed by the page number in Arabic numeral.
15. Mark Rutherford, *The Revolution in Tanners Lane*, London, 1887, p. 388.
16. Morris and Belfort Max, *Socialism, its Growth and Outcome*, London, 1893, p. 16.
17. May Morris, *William Morris*, Oxford, 1936, vol. II, p. 162.
18. William Morris, *Letters*, London, 1950, p. 149.
19. Ibid., p. 202.
20. Ibid., pp. 228–9.
21. May Morris, *William Morris*, op. cit., vol. I, p. 148.
22. *Socialism, Utopian and Scientific*, translated by Edward Aveling, London, 1892, pp. 47–8.
23. Morris and Bax, *Socialism, Its Growth and Outcome*, op. cit., p. 76.
24. Stubbs, *The Constitutional History of England*, 3rd edn., Oxford, 1887, vol. II, p. 471.
25. Green, *History of the English People*, London, 1878, vol. II, p. 475.
26. Ibid., p. 476.
27. Rogers, *Six Centuries of Work and Labour*, London, 1949, p. 271.
28. Green, op. cit., p. 474.
29. Rogers, op. cit., p. 252.
30. Ibid., p. 254.
31. Ibid., p. 262.
32. Maurice, *Lives of the English Popular Leaders in the Middle Ages*, London, 1875, p. 128.

33. Hyndman, *The Historical Basis of Socialism in England*, London, 1883, p. 4.
34. Stubbs, *The Constitutional History of England*, op. cit., p. 485.
35. Green, *History of the English People*, op. cit., p. 486.
36. Engels, *The German Revolutions*, ed. Lionel Krieger, Chicago, 1967, p. 38.
37. Marx and Engels, *On Religion*, Moscow, 1955, p. 70.
38. Eleventh thesis on Feuerbach. Marx and Engels, *On Religion*, p. 72.
39. G. D. H. Cole, *William Morris*, London, 1948, p. xviii.
40. Gramsci, *The Modern Prince and Other Writings*, London, 1967, p. 69.
41. Freeman, *Comparative Politics*, London, 1893, p. 86.
42. Ibid., p. 76.
43. Marx, *Pre-Capitalist Economic Formations*, London, 1964, p. 80.
44. Freeman, *Comparative Politics*, op. cit., p. 81.
45. Morgan, *Ancient Society*, Cambridge, Mass., 1964, p. 467.

INDEX

Main entries for both authors and works are shown in bold type.
The index is by author, with works appearing under his/her name.

Index

Index